S0-CCJ-958

LPNT
Oct 63
to
M Dow

My Language Is Me

If you understand and appreciate my language,

you must understand and appreciate me. My language *is* me.

My Language Is Me

Psychotherapy with
a Disturbed Adolescent

BEULAH PARKER, M.D.

FOREWORD BY

THEODORE LIDZ, M.D.

BASIC BOOKS, INC. Publishers

NEW YORK

Copyright © 1962 by BASIC BOOKS PUBLISHING CO., INC.

Library of Congress Catalog Card Number 62–9373

Printed in the United States of America

Designed by Guy Fleming

Foreword

By Theodore Lidz, M.D.
Yale University School of Medicine

IN MY LANGUAGE IS ME, Beulah Parker provides a unique opportunity to follow and examine the detailed course of the analytically oriented psychotherapy of a schizophrenic or preschizophrenic youth. It is not a summary or a description of what the therapist believed took place, but the ample verbatim reconstructions of more than two-hundred hours, interspersed with chapters that discuss the therapist's theoretic guidelines, her techniques, and her understanding of what was happening, as well as her own feelings and concerns. The book was written not to report a scintillating therapeutic triumph but to recount a painstaking and determined therapeutic encounter. We are permitted to follow the steps forward and backward, the understandings and misunderstandings, the right words spoken at the right moment and the words that the therapist would gladly have swallowed a moment after uttering them. The book is, in brief, a true exposition of therapy as conducted by a psychiatrist highly skilled in the treatment of schizophrenic patients. The reader can share the knowledge and insights that Dr. Parker has acquired during many years of persistent interest in the problems of schizophrenic patients and of training herself to understand and treat them. The treatment of this patient, carried out under adverse circumstances, required a devoted therapist; only a psychiatrist dedicated to the struggle against schizophrenia could write this book, which presents frankly her difficulties, indecisions, and problems as well as her skills and insights. Few psychiatrists have been willing to reveal so fully and freely what they do and say. It is just this openness, honesty, and commitment that has enabled Dr. Parker to work so effectively with schizophrenic patients.

Every psychiatrist may find that he would have conducted the therapy differently. The technique must be suited to the therapist as well as to the patient. Those who have worked intensively with schizophrenics will appreciate most fully how Dr. Parker met the inordinate difficulties of attaining and maintaining the relationship. I believe that the author wishes to provoke thoughtful consideration of the ways useful communication and a working relationship with such a patient can be established, rather than to promote inappropriate repetitions by others of the methods she used with this specific patient. There are guiding principles that are essential for successful work with schizophrenic patients, and Dr. Parker has adhered to them and discussed them cogently.

The author's dominant interest in writing this book seems to lie in the process of reaching a patient who wishes to communicate and at the same time to conceal—who is frightened away by direct understanding or interpretation of his cryptic metaphor and yet needs to feel that he is being understood. Establishing communication is a primary task in the treatment of all schizophrenic patients. This case illustrates clearly that achieving useful communication involves much more than the therapist's understanding of primary-process thinking and translation of idiosyncratic language. It required the development of the patient's trust in the therapist, with the repeated testing to determine whether she was really "for" him and could—unbelievable as it seemed to him—be involved without using him for her purposes; testing to be certain that she would not tempt him from his protective isolation only to reject him when she knew what he was like, and that she would neither devouringly engulf nor castrate. Real communication had to await the emergence of a modicum of self-esteem and the security of ego control, lest the boy's sexual and aggressive impulses overwhelm and annihilate him or the therapist whom he needed. Dr. Parker recognized this youth's need to continue metaphorical communication for an unusually long time. It was his means of maintaining the relationship at a distance that he could tolerate without feeling overwhelmed. The maintenance of a meaningful relationship on any terms or in any language took precedence in working with this patient who was congealing into an inanimate machine or drifting off into outer space. Her probes at more direct communication and interpretation were tentatively repeated until they were finally acceptable. The means of establishing the tenuous transference, and its careful nurturance in the face of the patient's precipitous flights from involvement, make an intriguing—and moving—study.

Some of Dr. Parker's actions deviate from the usual prescriptions for the psychiatrist: telephoning the patient after missed appointments, giving the patient spending money, communicating with the parents, the handling of the fee, etc. The treatment of schizophrenic patients requires plasticity of approach. The therapist was secure and free enough to trust her judgment, but she considered each decision carefully, with self-searching analysis of the counter-transference. The patient fears commitment, but the therapist who wishes to treat such patients must be committed. The psychiatrist who cannot tolerate this commitment and the discomfort or anguish it can bring is unlikely to carry a schizophrenic patient to a successful conclusion. The reader learns as much from the ways the therapist conducts herself and analyzes her feelings as he does from reading what she hears the patient say and what she says to him. Although they are not recorded, the many hours of contemplation given to the patient, between the hours actually spent with him, clearly influenced the outcome.

As the reader will see, Dr. Parker and I disagree on the exact terminology of diagnosis. She considers her patient to be further toward the "normal" end of a continuum of disturbance in thought processes. But whatever the terminology, the method of treatment is akin to that which is useful in the treatment of schizophrenic patients.

The book moves into a vacuum in the psychiatric literature. It provides a document for teaching students at all levels of training about the conduct of treatment of schizophrenic patients and the understanding of their behavior and language. It offers guidance to beginning psychiatrists perplexed by the intricacies of establishing relationships with schizophrenic patients, and the experienced therapist will study the fascinating material and the therapeutic maneuvers. It will encourage others to persist through discouraging phases of work with such patients. Hopefully, some will be inspired to emulate Dr. Parker's example, not only in the conduct of therapy, but also in the recording and publishing of what actually transpires for others to examine.

Contents

PART II

PART III

My Language Is Me

Introduction

THE BOOK

THIS IS THE STORY of a mutual learning process taking place between a troubled boy and his therapist. Each learned valuable lessons. The boy learned, eventually, that he could allow another person into his private world to work with him on conflicts that he could not master alone. The therapist learned, slowly, to talk a new language and to share the vivid images in which a creative mind gave expression to universal problems.

The story is being written primarily as a study in the development of direct communication. By learning to "tune in" on a highly personal thought process, the therapist helped the boy to translate his code. When the code could be used for communication rather than for protection, it was gradually abandoned as a private language and converted into metaphor, by which thoughts were colorfully expressed. A long and complex technical process was necessary to establish between patient and therapist a climate in which this conversion was possible.

Certain factors of technical interest are illustrated by this case. Treatment took place under difficult practical conditions. The therapist's private office was located at a considerable distance from the patient's home. Even during periods when contact was tenuous, the boy had to assume responsibility for getting there, usually by hitch-hiking or by making complicated connections on public transportation. For various reasons it was necessary to limit interviews to one a week, with the total number of hours totaling less than the average usually considered necessary to conduct "intensive treatment." Under these conditions of time and space, the boy managed to stay in therapy for six and a half years, between the ages of sixteen and a little over twenty-two. Despite feelings of strong ambivalence at times, he was seldom late and missed very few appointments. When he did so, there was either an acceptable reality reason or there was evidence that the absence was a specific transference resistance.

Forces operating within the boy himself enabled him to make successful use of weekly out-patient treatment. David was representative of a group of people whose capacity to develop insight is determined to a large extent by strong motivation to understand their psychic processes, regardless of consequence. At one point he described his own view of his motivation. "It is frightening to think one might lose one's creativity in therapy—that after one has gotten rid of the pain, there might be no motivation beyond. However, even to get rid of the pain is worth it. Even the loss of creativity would not keep me from going on and finding out what's in my mind" (81).* He therefore allowed his therapist to experiment with various methods of establishing contact until a satisfactory working relationship could be set up. The weekly spacing of interviews also proved to be optimal for him. Late in treatment he said, "Actually, I think it's O.K. that we have a week in between times. Sometimes if I hit on something painful, it takes a long time to build myself up so that I can talk about it. The time in between isn't lost, because I need it to work at keeping down the feelings that want me to push it out of consciousness again" (179).

The interchange with David was conducted by a therapist of basically Freudian orientation within the theoretical concepts on work with autistic patients delineated and published by workers from Chestnut Lodge. As Frieda Fromm-Reichmann herself pointed out, intensity of treatment for this kind of patient is not achieved by virtue of any one specific pattern of continuity or formality in procedures. A successful therapeutic relationship depends on highly intuitive factors in both patient and therapist which enable them to "click." A discussion of case management and technical procedures will be found in another section. Problems of countertransference and reactivity, which play an important part in therapy with a boy like David, have also been described in some detail. It will be enough to say here that throughout treatment, I frequently examined and reexamined the material for evidence of interference from my own unconscious reactions.

At the time that this therapy took place, I was doing part-time research in schizophrenia at Yale University, with a limited private practice in New Haven. I was afraid that my interest in symbolic communication would distort therapy. The text shows where this happened. Once, when the boy

* Throughout this book, numbers in parentheses refer to the interview from which a quotation is taken or a significant fact abstracted.

had been talking symbolically in terms of a machine on which he was at the same time working in reality, he brought several machine parts with him to the therapeutic interview. I recognized that reality aspects of what he was discussing were also important to him. When this was interpreted, the boy's relief was striking. Anxiety was released in the first marked muscular movements he had allowed himself to make during the interviews (127).

In a case of this kind, the possibilities of activating the therapist's own unconscious are an ever-present danger. The therapist can only try to be aware of the possibilities and handle his own reactions as they become conscious. In David's fantasy material were frequent references to two forces fighting to control him. This was clearly a projection of his own conflict, but it was also necessary for me to ask myself repeatedly whether I was unconsciously exhibiting competitiveness with his mother. There seems to be occasional evidence that some competition was present, but a serious attempt was made to control expression of the feeling whenever it was conscious. Each reader may judge for himself what particular balance of conscious and unconscious interactions between therapist and patient enabled the work to progress successfully.

The material was recorded as nearly verbatim as was possible by reconstruction after each interview. It is being presented in this form for several reasons. In the first place, there has been almost no publication in the psychoanalytic literature of complete case material in therapy with this kind of patient. Such publication is advisable not only to demonstrate the language but to show the sequence and content of communications as the therapeutic relationship develops. It also shows, better than any summary could, the time and patience required for working through resistance of a particularly intractable sort. Technical procedures and problems become manifest in verbatim presentation, and many clues which may have escaped the therapist at time of treatment become available to others who examine the discussions. Secondly, this particularly intelligent and articulate boy gave a graphic description of the autistic state as it felt from within, and discussed a wide range of conflicts and confusions experienced by many. Use of his own words seems imperative to convey a true and vivid picture of the autistic boy and his development throughout the course of therapy.

Originally there was no plan to write up the case; I kept detailed notes purely to satisfy my own interest in symbolic language and to help clarify the content of the boy's communications for therapeutic purposes. Interviews were written up anywhere from an hour to several weeks after they occurred. For the most part, notes on the sequence of topics were jotted down immediately after the hour, and verbatim dialogue reconstructed as accurately as possible within a short time thereafter, while it was still fresh in my mind. Interviews reconstructed after they have occurred are, of course, subject to unconscious distortions by the memory of the therapist. However, conscious distortions have been avoided. I have had considerable experience in verbatim memorizing and have, within the limits of human fallibility, recorded all mistakes, misinterpretations, and personal involvements. The mere recording of certain material brought to light obvious meanings that were by no means obvious while the interchange was in progress. Sometimes these were picked up before subsequent interviews; often they were missed until later. Fortunately, the patient was very forgiving and persistent. When he really wanted to say something, he eventually forced me to understand him.

Quasi-verbatim material for the first three years has been presented exactly as recorded except for changes necessary to disguise identity of David and his family. Descriptions of parents and family interaction are kept vague to avoid portraying specific individuals. Protracted interchanges occurring in the second half of treatment are condensed into sentences of dialogue which contain essential elements of the discussions in approximate wording. Abridged material has been checked with the original by independent readers qualified to assure that no transactions of significance between patient and therapist have been omitted or their emphasis changed. I am particularly indebted to Dr. Lidz and to Dr. Mary Sarvis of Berkeley, California, for this aspect of the work. Participation by Dr. Sarvis in discussion of the theoretical sections has also been an invaluable aid.

A question will arise in the mind of the reader as to whether confidentiality has been violated in such a detailed exposition of therapeutic interviews. I gave considerable thought to this point before the book was ever written. Because the preservation of a patient's confidence is such an important factor in all psychotherapy, I did not seriously consider writing up the material for several years after the desire to do so first occurred. However, at a point late in the treatment, David himself first raised the possibility. In discussing the distorted ways in which movies and popular literature portray psychotherapy and analysis, he suggested that somebody should write "how it really is" (188). Maybe my interest had been unconsciously transmitted to him. In any case, I told him at that time about my notes and obtained his permission to write a book in which his therapy would be described through actual dialogue to show professional workers how communication had developed. He thought it would be "wonderful."

When the book was finished, David had been out of therapy for a long time, and everyone connected with the case was living elsewhere. Occasional letters from David showed realistic attitudes and told of successes in current situations. I wrote him, describing the book in detail and offering him an opportunity to see it before publication. I expressed the conviction that he had a right to full knowledge of what had been written, but nevertheless warned that he could not expect to read it without ambivalence.

No patient can fail to be affected by seeing his therapist's focus on technical aspects of their relationship. Hesitant words of youthful conflict and speculation, no matter how poignant and creative they may appear to adults, invariably create self-consciousness and embarrassment in the young person who uttered them unless he has achieved considerable distance from his adolescence and the painful emotions connected with it. I did not feel that he had as yet achieved such distance, and told him so. I also told him that any subsequent therapy might be complicated by his reactions to the material, even though his feelings could eventually be worked through. I was willing to accept the consequences of any decision he might make, but nevertheless made it clear that I did not consider it to his advantage to read the material until more time had passed.

David was able to make his decision without conflict. He was proud that people thought his words and ideas could contribute to a wider understanding of young people among professional workers in the field of psychology, and glad that he had been considered "book material." Although curious to see what had been said, he felt no pressure to relive his therapeutic past and only hoped that I would "put an autographed copy away" for him to look at sometime in the future. He had one question. Why had "David" been chosen for his pseudonym?

The answer was clear. "David" is the name of a young boy who, against enormous odds, willingly undertook single combat to destroy the destructive power of a giant. No other name would have seemed quite so suitable.

PART I

1

An Autistic Boy

David was just sixteen when he was brought into therapy. Theft of a carpenter's level from the school workshop climaxed a long series of minor delinquencies, mostly in the nature of pranks, which had brought him under the watchful eye of local police. Anxiety about the boy's general adjustment had mounted over the years, and there was now a fear that acts of childish rebellion were beginning to presage a pattern of confirmed delinquent acting-out.

The mother came to me at her husband's suggestion after a brief therapeutic relationship between the boy and a male therapist had ended in a burst of frustrated hostility. Some time previously, I had worked with her on a committee, and she had confided some of her problems to me. Although the contact had been brief and informal, she considered it valuable; when her husband suggested that I might be able to work successfully with David, she expressed full agreement.

From the story as she presented it, I had grave misgivings about accepting the case. I usually refer adolescent delinquent boys to a male therapist who serves as a strong figure for masculine identification. In view of my friendly feelings for the boy's mother, however, I agreed to see him, with the understanding that I would probably undertake no more than a diagnostic evaluation.

By the middle of the first interview with David, I felt reasonably sure that we could work successfully together. I am not quite sure to this day why this was so. Perhaps it was the conspiratorial look in his eye when he responded to my question as to whether he was always so compliant with the wishes of others; perhaps it was his sudden, defiant leap into symbolism upon being asked what he would like to do to make things better for himself. In any case, something had been established between David and me before the end of our first hour together. I think it was on the basis of this feeling of rapport that we were able to proceed.

In the course of two hundred and thirty hours David gave vivid expression to problems characteristic of the autistic state. Certain features of autism and thought distortion exist, in varying degrees and combinations, in normal adolescents under stress as well as in the more disorganized personalities. The degree of distortion in the communication process present in this patient at the beginning of treatment would place his condition outside the range of normal adolescent "Identity diffusion" as defined by Erikson,[1] despite relatively good ability to form an emotional relationship with the therapist. Both the degree to which he tended to think symbolically and the content of the symbolic expressions are closely related to primary process, even though he seemed for the most part to be in affective contact.

Diagnosis in a case like this is often a semantic problem. Use of the terms "schizophrenic" and "borderline" varies even among experts in the field of psychiatry. Perhaps we cannot put an exact label on David's condition. Dr. Lidz calls him "schizophrenic or preschizophrenic." Some authorities who have read the material consider him closer to the normal end of a spectrum. Different readers may put him into different categories. The author has chosen a diagnosis of "borderline condition" as described by Melitta Schmideberg.[2]

Firstly, David's behavior and environmental adjustment during the early years of treatment were in many ways similar to those of the typical borderline patient. In dress and appearance he was slovenly and often dirty, a major source of conflict with his mother. There was a facade of passivity and affectlessness. In spite of high creativity and intelligence, he maintained a marginal level of functioning in school work, and even this was achieved only under protest. Lack of motivation for concentrated effort, and underlying negativism, were represented by extreme unevenness of performance. His record was a patchwork of A's and F's, depending on momentary interests. Although physically well coordinated and mechanically gifted, he took part in athletic activities only sporadically, and refused to involve himself in any kind of sustained or remunerative work unless it had a particular personal meaning to him. He was also involved in several minor and one more major delinquent episode, which brought him up against the law periodically for a number of years.

The meanings of these behavioral manifestations will

emerge clearly in the text itself and will show characteristics of autistic thinking. A few quotations in the boy's own words may be used here to illustrate his view of the situation.

At one point he spoke of "sloppy people without intellectual interests, who live in pig pens and are 'different.' They feel insecure in any other surroundings, and are defying society for wanting to pour them into a mold. They simply can't live up to more exacting standards" (59). A little later, in speaking of a group of "primitive people," he made it clear that they "weren't really primitive; they had just voluntarily reverted to primitive ways because civilization seemed too complicated and unsatisfactory" (60).

Physical immobility and apparent lack of affect resulted from attempts to prevent the betrayal of intense feelings. David verbalized this concept frequently, in different ways. During a period of direct communication he explained, "I've taught myself to ignore bodily feelings. At the beginning, I didn't dare to move in here for fear of giving myself away" (172). And, "I guess I'm not so afraid any more. Maybe it isn't so important to keep from expressing things unconsciously through gestures and movements" (176).

The minor delinquency which precipitated his entrance into therapy was due to impulsiveness and lack of reality testing. The boy could state this himself, even at the beginning. When asked whether he had considered the consequences of taking a level from the school he answered, "No. I needed it. There was a feeling of excitement about taking it. I didn't think of anything else." After a later episode he commented sadly, "I thought about the trouble I might get into, but it didn't seem important. Being with my friends was much more important at the moment. I realize that it wasn't, but I realized too late" (136).

A relationship between the nature of his delinquent acts and the content of his fantasy life will be seen in the body of the material. Here it needs only to be stated that the delinquency was at first an integral part of his personality dis-organization, in which the symbolic value of the stolen object was of great importance. Later difficulties resulted from a restitutive effort in personality reorganization. Identification with a delinquent gang was an early step in his retreat from isolation, forming a bridge to more constructive interpersonal relationships. In his own words, "They don't realize that I might have to act in certain ways so as to be accepted by the only group that will have me" (107). Elsewhere he again made clear the ambivalence about his group identification. "Probation didn't bother me; in some ways it had face-saving aspects. It was a good excuse for not doing things that might get me in trouble, without losing status with the crowd that doesn't care if it gets in trouble or not" (95).

Secondly, *the boy's developmental history has many features which are typically found in autistic and borderline patients.* In order to preserve confidentiality, it is necessary to omit a detailed discussion of David's earliest years. The mother did, however, describe family history and interactions to the therapist in an unusually undefensive way, even at the cost of considerable personal exposure. Although the developmental history must be described in generalities, it has been corroborated by specific details from family doctor, previous therapist, and nursery school guidance personnel. Only items significantly related to the therapeutic material will be mentioned here.

David was born during a time of stress for his parents. Of necessity his father was often away for long periods, his mother lonely and depressed. The infant was vigorous and well formed, but developed severe feeding problems in the first year. At a later developmental stage he encountered difficulties in bowel training, and remained eneuretic until the age of thirteen. Birth of a brother at two and a half was experienced as a traumatic event, as was a tonsillectomy at four. In nursery school, and later in grade school, David was considered to be a "problem child" by his teachers; he spent one year at a Quaker boarding school in the Middle West. On two different occasions he had been taken to a child psychotherapist, but treatment was not recommended. Both his parents had guidance, and his mother underwent a short period of therapy herself in order to help him.

In the years between two and school age, David had periods of great loneliness, but also times in which he shared exciting companionship and gaiety with his mother. The mother was an artistically gifted person who enjoyed teaching her child songs and music in the time she spent with him, and was delighted when, at an early age, he showed artistic promise. Although she helped augment family finances by doing clerical work in a concern connected with aircraft, her recreation and major interest was figure skating, which occupied a great deal of her spare time and took her often to New York in competitions. She was pleased with early signs of advanced physical coordination in her child, and did much to encourage him in activities involving bodily movement. Thus David underwent periods of understimulation alternating with intense stimulation, a situation frequently found in the histories of autistic children.[3]

It can be seen throughout the material that David was in many ways consciously identified with his mother and interested in her activities. Fancy skating and the flying in which they both had an opportunity to participate through her connection with the aircraft industry later became recreations that he too enjoyed. It will also be obvious that he saw his mother as strong, powerful, and to some degree masculine.

In David's early childhood, his father had often assumed physical care of the children, and was seen by them as a nurturant, motherly figure. He worked in an arms manufacturing plant as a minor executive, and was also technically proficient in the use of tools and machinery, highly masculine activities. David can be seen as greatly identified with his interests as well as those of his mother.

David was confused in his sexual and role identifications with both parents. He saw his mother as more male than female, and his father as more female than male, although in neither case was the picture clear cut. He unconsciously picked up attitudes and feelings from both parents which seemed also to be unconscious in them, and made mixed identifications in his way of thinking and his behavior. Such factors cannot be discussed here.

At this point I should like to digress for a moment to address any reader who may not be specifically trained in the field of psychology. Throughout this book, he will see a discussion of the mixed feelings which David had for both his parents, and will see reference to unconscious ambivalences on the part of the parents toward David. Professional readers take such ambivalences for granted, and make a sharp distinction between unconscious impulses and overt behavior. People who are not well acquainted with psychological terminology often find it hard to make this distinction, and react as though impulses and actions were synonymous.

It must be kept firmly in mind throughout the inspection of this material that unconscious conflicts concerning sexuality and aggression are present in everyone to one degree or another, and that the existence of erotic or aggressive impulses in a child toward his parents, or vice versa, does not in any way imply unnatural *behavior* between them.

It is also necessary to remember that in any case of psychotherapy, many statements by a patient are presented as fact which are actually projections onto others of his own feelings. David's view of his family combined fact with fantasy. The reader can follow the boy's interaction with his therapist, and see how he worked out his problems, without needing to know the exact degree to which his observations were colored by his own imagination.

In therapy David was able to bring out mixed feelings about his parents and talk of the unconscious impulses he felt toward them and thought they felt toward him. The parents were willing to expose themselves freely so that the therapist could understand the realities as they saw them, and gave permission that anything in their own lives could be discussed in work with David if the therapist thought it would help him to know. Few families are able to display such courage in order to allow their son the benefits of treatment, and tribute should be paid to them here. The text will, I think, demonstrate some of the ways in which David's past experiences and relationships contributed to his problems.

Lastly, the attitudes and preoccupations expressed by David show a concept of self and others which is characteristic to one degree or another of all autistic people. He gave gross evidence of a need to withdraw from close affective contacts, and of a strong distrust of anyone who might attempt to penetrate his isolation. Negativism, a facade of passivity, and a wall of obscure communication served to ward off any encroachment on his privacy. Identification with machines indicated his fears of human relationships.

At the same time, he showed a desperate fear of his increasing isolation, of what he sensed as evidence of psychopathology, and of his talent for making himself misunderstood. The conflict between dependent wishes and distrust was acute. Closeness was equated with loss of identity—the threat of being "owned" and manipulated. Relationship threatened discovery of his hostility, vulnerability, and the intensity of his demands. Therapy was dreaded as much as it was longed for, carrying the danger of loss of control over aggressive impulses and breakdown in the grandiose concepts of powerfulness with which he compensated for deep-seated fears of inadequacy. Abandonment was even more frightening. The unknown was, to him, always hostile and destructive until proven otherwise, and to prove it otherwise required constant testing. David, at one time or another during his therapy, himself verbalized clearly his needs for these protective attitudes, his awareness of them, and the feelings that lay behind his manifest behavior.

The distrust and the need to test were expressed in various ways over a long period of time, first in symbolic language and later more directly. To cite only a few: in the second interview he commented directly, "If you stick your neck out with a lot of good ideas, you are apt to get it chopped off . . . if people get unlimited power over others, you can't be sure they won't use it for their own ends." Later, "Some English teachers say they do [want to hear what you have to say] but you can't be sure they mean it" (5). "Gases have to be tested with mice and plants to see if they are poisonous. The mouse wouldn't know if it was oxygen or carbon dioxide except by the effects; he would have to know the intention of the experimenter to be helpful or harmful" (8). And again, "It would depend on the motives of these people as to whether they were dangerous or not" (13). Even well along in therapy he was still concerned with problems of how much one can trust, making the comment that "the best way to avoid a trap is to spring it from a distance" (149).

The boy was well aware that obscure communication served a protective function. "He's like me; he has devious ways of communicating." (These might have a value.) * "Yes. They keep people from getting close to you" (91). His feeling was most graphically expressed in a comment on "Here Come the Martians" (92). "[The writer of Western

* Throughout the book, the comments of the therapist are set in parentheses.

stories] is busy writing; one of the Martians comes up behind him and says 'Hi Ho Silver!' It scares him into a catatonic state. Why? Because he talked to him in his own language. . . . When a person is threatened by another who tries to break through his isolation, it often makes him very angry at that person." At a point when David once reverted to the code after a period of direct communication, the therapist attempted to interpret his message. David reacted with annoyance. "It's a hard subject for me to talk about. I didn't *want* you to understand me" (158).

His awareness of his impassive facade was expressed early in therapy. "A bookcase door puts up a front that keeps people from knowing there's a secret room behind, where all sorts of things are going on. Like me" (8). That the facade hid aggressive impulses of various sorts he also seemed to know. At several points he identified himself with Gandhi, who "brought the whole British Empire to its knees by just doing nothing." He felt that the interest of another person could be tested by his own remaining passive. "If two people want something done, and neither of them do it, sooner or later the one who wants it most will do it." (Do you operate like that sometimes?) "Often, I think" (162). Later he expressed the idea that his impassivity served to hide impulses which might arouse me sexually (172). Early in treatment, he indicated that at least part of his negativism was conscious withholding until he could establish a feeling of trust. "It's difficult to know how a bee feels. He might not feel at all as we think we would feel if we were bees." (The only way to know would be if a bee could tell us.) "Could—or *would*" (7).

David's identification with machines and other non-animal forms appears vividly throughout the material, particularly in the early part of treatment. This tendency is frequently to be seen in those who feel themselves to be losing libidinal connection with people, and are grasping at anything that may represent a link with the objective world.

This will be discussed further in the section on symbolism.
It can be said here that when human beings are seen as
dangerous and destructive, it may be necessary to disidentify
with them. The unbearable feeling of loneliness is then com-
bated by identifying with non-living objects which are pre-
dictable, automatic, and not subject to devastating emotional reactions. This type of identification is a restitutional
symptom which attempts to create a less threatening world-
connection, independent of unreliable human beings.

   "I read of a machine that could reproduce itself if the
parts were fed into it. I'd like to invent one that would go
even further and mine the ore for its own parts." (So it could
exist completely independent of other people for its survival.) "Machines are like that because they have to be"
(102).

   Sechehaye,[4] and other writers who will be mentioned
in the later discussion of symbolism, have emphasized that in
autistic thinking there is an unclear boundary between the
symbol and the object which it represents. To David a
sports car, for instance, was simultaneously a machine
offering reality outlets for his mechanical skill and interest, a
part of his own body, and the symbolic representation of
himself as a whole. The lack of reality testing shown by his
participation in work on a machine that he knew to be stolen,
can be understood when the machine is seen as fulfilling
deeply unconscious needs for maintaining object relationships. In his own words, "They don't understand how important it is for me to stay close to a machine after I've put
time and work on it. It's almost as though it belongs to myself" (53).

   The boy was nevertheless afraid of increasing isolation, ". . . a situation just the opposite from quicksand. If
you lift one foot up, you can't get it down again, and pushing down keeps pulling you further and further up, as though
you were on a ratchet. You yourself would be operating the

lever, but couldn't stop cranking yourself up. There are three kinds of people, . . . and those that are climbing but don't want to. They are getting further and further away from people and can't stop themselves" (41).

His desire for contact with the therapist, and his feeling of tenuousness, were portrayed in one of his many mechanical images. "I want to make a switch where a needle makes contact with a certain place on the rim that crosses a connection and builds up some kind of pressure system. The problem is that as soon as the contact is made, it breaks again before the pressure can build up very much. I'd like to introduce a magnet that would hold the contact until a spring had built up enough strength to pull it away. Meanwhile, the pressure in the system would have had time to build up" (30). Even earlier, a fear of the impermanence of longed-for relationships was verbalized when the therapist was about to take a vacation. ". . . unstable compounds in chemistry. One ion can be attracted away and then the other is discarded as unusable" (14).

At the same time, the need to protect himself from being swallowed up in such a relationship was also strong. ". . . you need the outward force to keep them [planets] from bumping into the sun and being absorbed—losing their identity" (9). This conflict between dependent wishes and fear of manipulation was repeatedly enacted and verbalized between us. A close relationship meant to him the threat of being "owned." In his own words, "To feel that a person is willing to give makes the one who is given to have a sense of self-value, but it also puts him in danger of being possessed" (14). Symbolically he was frequently preoccupied with situations in which a number of forces were competing for the control of someone or something. Once he expressed openly that he was afraid of being manipulated by me through some magic that was "making him talk" (70). Throughout most of the therapeutic relationship, he found periodic need to test his independence, even after conscious trust in my good intentions was well established. He saw himself as possibly able to exist, well insulated by his withdrawn attitudes, in a narrow margin of safety between closeness and abandonment. "I wonder what it would be like to take a trip to the moon? On one side, next to the sun, it is too hot to support life; on the opposite side it is too cold. But there might be a small strip in between the two where one could live if one had on the proper kind of space suit" (26).

Fear of being controlled was enhanced by doubts as to his capacity for acting independently. In talking about a robot, he commented, "Perhaps it should run like those cars for beginning drivers that have two sets of controls. It could gradually then become independent, but only if its judgment proved to be good" (11). All through the early material he expressed concepts in which two machines work together, one standing by to supply power only if the other proves unequal to the task. He wasn't sure that the machine representing himself had adequate control mechanisms.

The greatest danger in closeness was, however, the threat of exposure. Inside himself, David felt, was ugliness and "garbage," a mass of violently explosive, destructive impulses that nobody could really accept, least of all himself. "If one digs around in the garbage, one can sometimes find things, but it gets terribly messy . . . nobody cares if I dig around in there, but I'm the one that has to be careful there are no explosives" (6). "Sometimes a motor that isn't hitched up to anything explodes of its own power" (13). ". . . some guys from the future went to teach a child new ideas about what to do with the past, but they left some stuff lying around that was dangerous. The child got into it and was blown up" (88). "Nobody would want to build a house on an island that was going to be used for an atomic bomb test" (134). "If the robot had reasoning powers like a human being, it might not be so docile; it might decide the world needed destroying" (11). In a discussion of the ferocity aroused in wild animals by the frustration of their needs, he commented warningly, "A rampant elephant, though, might be less dangerous than a person under the same circumstances, because he makes a noise. You can hear him coming" (22).

The boy also felt that if he ever allowed himself to show a need for someone, the intensity of his demands would destroy the other. "A robot was designed to make war unnecessary, but it drove its inventors crazy, because it came to a standstill. All it could say was 'Want!'" (101).

The idea of therapy mobilized this mass of intense, contradictory feelings. Fear of the therapist's ambivalence was ever-present. "A robot became attached to a certain man, but at some point it came near to making an explosion. The man got scared and influenced it to forget what he had taught it" (11). "I'm thinking of various inventions that would stop a burglar from . . . coming through the door into private quarters. . . . Better let him come partially inside and then trap him." (Why not lock the door?) "Too much trouble to keep locking and unlocking it. You could cause the person to be shocked electrically if he tried to get in . . . only enough to discourage him so he wouldn't bother to try unless he was willing to bear some discomfort" (16). David was, of course, projecting some of his own fears of losing control, becoming dangerous, and suffering punishment for his aggression. "One might be going a lot faster than one realized" (11). ". . . people who lived in a city surrounded by a dome charged with electricity. They wanted to atom bomb the world, and had to protect themselves against retaliation" (17).

He could, however, see no other way out of a seemingly hopeless situation, and felt he had to take his chances. "At present I see therapy as a narrow path between a high, sheer bank on one side, which represents the demands of society, and a sheer crevasse on the other which is insanity. The bank that is society keeps moving inward, making the path narrower all the time. There is no way over the top, and no foreseeable end to the path where it would open into a field. Originally the path was wider. In a young society, you could do more what you wanted in expressing hostile impulses. If you wanted to kill someone, there was a chance you would be overpowered, but at least you had a chance. Now society has, so to speak, taken away your knife" (90).

Therapy also threatened to take away a valuable defense weapon, the grandiose concept of personal powerfulness with which David compensated for feelings of inadequacy. "I read a story about a guy who knew a word that would destroy the world if he said it. At the end he hadn't decided whether to say it or not. The most frightening part would be to find that you *had* said it, and nothing happened. You might want to destroy the world because you felt so helpless, and then to find you couldn't would make you even more helpless" (95).

Therapy was the unknown, and no matter how much good it promised, the fear of pain was even greater. "It's like if a man is approaching a dark cave and sees two eyes staring out—he becomes wary. If, as he gets closer, the light falls in a different way, and he sees they were only two beer cans, he wonders how he could have been so scared. But the next time he's in a similar situation, he's just as scared."

Under these circumstances, David stayed with it. This fact is a great tribute to the boy's innate courage, and to the power of even a small spark of Hope in the human personality.

Contact and a *modus operandi* were established in the first five interviews, reconstructions of which follow.

REFERENCES

(1) Erikson, E., "Identity and the Life Cycle," *Psychological Issues*, Vol. 1, 1959, pp. 122 ff.

(2) Schmideberg, M., "The Borderline Patient," in Arieti, Silvano, ed., *American Handbook of Psychiatry*. N. Y., Basic Books, 1959.

(3) Sarvis, M., and Garcia, B., "Etiological Variables in Autism," *Psychiatry*, Vol. 24, 1961, pp. 307–317.

(4) Sechehaye, M., *A New Psychotherapy with Schizophrenia*. N. Y., Grune & Stratton, 1956.

2

The Contact

"It doesn't know what it wants. It's just in a state of wondering."

1. [The boy sits down stiffly and maintains a rigid position, hands folded in his lap, staring fixedly over and to the right of my left shoulder.]

(Your mother tells me you are not happy, and that this is why she wants you to come here. How do you see the situation?) I had some trouble over a level that I took from school, but it doesn't bother me, because I got caught. (Would it if you hadn't?) Don't know. (Is it true that you are not happy?) I'm happy enough, I guess. (Have you any problems that you are aware of?) I guess I must have; most people do. (Can you tell me about them?) I don't know what they are.

(Do you have any desire of your own to come here

and talk to me, or are you coming just because your family want you to?) I don't know just why I'm coming. (Are your parents putting pressure on you to come?) No. I'm coming because they think I should, but I don't know why. (Are you usually so compliant about doing what people want you to do?) [*Quick smile, immediately replaced by original blank expression.*] No.

(Do you think you might have some curiosity to know "what's cookin'" within yourself?) Maybe. (Are you willing to give a try at finding out what your problems might be?) Yes. If you'll tell me what they are, I'll cooperate. (Well, I don't know what they are either, but perhaps if we work together on it, we can find out. Tell me a little bit about yourself.) [*Shrug.*] What do you want to know? (Anything you feel like telling me.)

[*Long pause.*] (It's difficult to think of anything to start with.) Yes. [*Long pause.*] (What kinds of things are you interested in?) I like to roam around the University. I'm interested in math, chemistry, and physics. (You like to find out about things?) Yes.

[*Long pause.*] (What were you thinking just then?) I guess you are annoyed because I'm not giving you much information. (No. I'm not annoyed, although I would like to be able to find out how to help you if I can. Tell me something about your family.) They are doing all right as a family.

[*Pause.*] (Did you know that a long time ago I knew your mother?) Yes. (I wonder if that makes it difficult for you in some way?) I don't think so. (I imagine you have some feeling about it, though.) No. (Lots of boys would if they were in your position. They might think I would be bound to see things through their mother's eyes—"Women stick together," that sort of thing.) I don't think I feel like that. (It wouldn't be surprising if you did—but anyway, the way I think is that everyone in a family sees things differently. The important thing for each of them is their own feelings about what goes on.) That's right.

[Long pause.] (Is there anyone that you've felt able to talk to?) I can talk to my friends. (Tell me about them.) I haven't got many in the neighborhood. Joe is in college. I don't see him much. [Pause.] I don't see anyone much. (Can you talk at all with your family?) It's easier just to listen.

[Long pause.] (What would you like to do to make things better for yourself?) I'd like to take a crack at being President of the United States. The government may have problems, but they shouldn't make as big a mess as they are making. They spend a quarter of a million dollars a day to store up food when there are people hungry. (I see you are concerned with the problems of people in need. I agree that there should be a plan by which those who have the resources could help them without upsetting the level of economy.)

[Long pause.] (What have you been thinking?) About level. I needed a level for my experiments. (Did you think at all about what might happen if you took it?) No. I needed it. I didn't think about anything else. (I think it might not have been the level itself that was most important to you, but the taking of it.) Yes. (There was a feeling of excitement about it?) Yes. It was a good feeling. (Under what other circumstances do you get that kind of a good feeling?) When working on a problem. (Apparently the taking of something satisfies a need in you that gives you a good feeling, but also gets you in trouble. Perhaps we can understand the need, so that you can get the same good feeling in ways that won't get you into trouble.) Yes.

(O.K. I'll see you next week.)

2. [He assumes the same rigid position which becomes characteristic of his approach to every interview. On occasion he

sighs deeply but inaudibly, and appears to be keeping strict control over any manifestation of emotion. Speaks only in response to questions from me.]

(What would you like to talk about?) [*Shrug. Pause.*] (Do you want me to ask you a few questions, just till we get started?) I guess so.

(Tell me some more about the kinds of things you like to do.) I like to make things. (What do you like to make?) I had shop in junior high, but you had to make what the teacher wanted, not what you wanted. (What would you have wanted to make?) Maybe a small car. If I took shop in high school, I'd like to make a gun. (Are you interested in hunting?) No. (Shooting a gun is one way to get rid of some of the feelings inside a person.) [*Smile. No response. He stares at the curtains, and glances briefly around the room.*]

(What strikes you about the room?) [*Shrug. No response.*] (Tell me about your room at home.) It used to have a lot of junk in it, but they redecorated it when I was away at school. Now I don't care anything about it. Most of my junk is in the yard. (All your things got cleared out when you weren't there?) [*Shrug.*] I didn't care.

[*Long pause.*] (You find it difficult to talk about what you are thinking. That's natural enough—it's never easy to feel comfortable with someone you don't know.) If you stick your neck out with a lot of good ideas, you are apt to get it chopped off. (Under those circumstances, one isn't apt to stick one's neck out. There is no reason why you should have any particular trust in me at this point.) [*Smile.*] That's a good point.

(Nevertheless, I'm prepared to try to help you in any way that I can.) I'm interested in finding out about myself. I'm interested in how the mind works, and what it can do. I'm interested in telepathy. (Perhaps you wish I could read your mind and know how you feel without your having to tell me.) It would be easier. (I think so too. Unfortunately, it doesn't work that way. We can only communicate by words or other cues that are picked up in a direct relationship between us.) I know.

(You know, therapy is something like doing a jig-saw puzzle. You don't know what the picture is going to be, but you pick up a few pieces to start with, and maybe find a few others of the same color that fit together, and after a while you begin to know what to look for.) That's an interesting idea. (At this moment we have a few pieces in your puzzle. We know that you get a good feeling from taking things, and we know that you don't want to talk about things because you feel nobody would understand anyway, and you aren't sure it's safe.)

[Pause.] I don't like the idea of people getting rich, but I don't like communism either. What is bad about both is that people get unlimited power over others, and you can't be sure they won't just use it for their own ends. (Maybe we can fit in another piece or two now. You have strong feelings about people getting power over others and pushing them around. Perhaps you feel that if anyone really knew you, they would get power over you that could be used against you. The best way to protect yourself is not to let anyone get close enough to you to be able to hurt you.) [Smile.] That's true.

(Your mother called me this week to ask whether she should remind you about your appointments each week in case you forget. Are you sometimes forgetful of things that are important to you?) Sometimes. (Do you like to be reminded?) I like to be reminded only if I forget, but I realize this would be impossible. I sometimes forget things like the dentist. [Smile.] (Laugh. No wonder! It's convenient to forget things that will be painful. You may feel the same way about coming here. However, I think you can take the responsibility for getting yourself here. Naturally your parents are concerned, because if you don't keep your appointments they have to pay for them anyway, but I would like to handle the situation completely with you. If these appointments seem to you like going to the dentist, I would like to talk with you about it.) They aren't—yet.

He doesn't show up for the next appointment; I telephone and make another with him. About fifteen minutes before that one, the father calls to say that David tried to call me in the morning to find out the appointment time, but couldn't reach me. I tell him never mind, I'll see the boy next week. I then write David a note, saying I am sorry if the time was not made clear, and that I will see him at his usual hour the following week.

3. [*He arrives a few minutes late.*] I had to go to the football game. (How did you feel about that?) Do you like football? (Not particularly, but tell me about it.) Welcome aboard! [*Pause.*] (What are you thinking?) Nothing much. [*Pause.*] (What's the feeling at the moment?) [*Shrug.*] (It seemed as though you had some feeling about my not being very interested in football.) I'm not interested in it either. [*Long pause.*] (I'm in something of a quandary. I could keep on asking you questions, but I'm not sure whether that would be helpful. I'd rather hear what you have to say. All I can say is that I'll try to do whatever seems most useful.) *Sarcastic tone:* That's all you can say! (Laugh. No, I suppose I could say a great deal more. I guess that sounded to you like pretty stereotyped talk.) [*Smile.*]
[*Long pause, during which he looks anxious.*] (You look to me as though you might feel like crying at this moment. If you feel like that, it's O.K. with me.) I don't feel like that. [*Anxious laugh.*] Do you really think I look like I'm going to cry? (You did for a moment. It strikes me that you quite often look unhappy, yet you seem to be feeling that you don't dare to let anyone know how you feel because this

would expose you to having your feelings used against you.)
[Smile. No response.] (You seem to feel that letting anyone
get close to you will make you vulnerable. That may be why
it's hard for you to talk.) I don't have any feeling of not
wanting to talk. I just don't know what to say. (Does that
make you uncomfortable?) No.

(Do you think you can remember the appointment
next week? I'd like you to remind me; then I can check on
whether I remembered or not. (O.K. I'll send you a postcard,
just to see.)

4. [Long pause.] (You know, there are a number of things
you could be saying with your silence. One might be that you
are being forced to come here and are saying, "Here I am,
but that's as far as I'm willing to go." Or it could be that you
want this to be a guessing game for me, to see how close I
can come to what you are thinking and feeling, without your
having to tell me.) [Smile.] No. That isn't it.

[Pause.] (What did you anticipate about coming to
see a psychiatrist?) Just talk. (Can you think of any way I
could make it easier for you?) No. It's always hard for me to
talk unless I have something specific to say. (You have also
apparently felt that nobody would care much what you did
have to say.) [Smile.] (You have expressed a desire to find out
what goes on inside you, and the best way to do this is just
to say whatever comes to mind. Therefore, in this situation,
there is no "specific thing to say.") [Nods yes.]

[Long pause.] (What would you do if you had a million dollars?) [Looks startled.] I'd get something that would
bring me in an income. I'd want to be sure I had a house,
food, and clothes. (You want to feel secure. You must worry
about this at times.) I have no worries. (Oh? Why not?) I
just don't worry about it. (What do you mean?) I have no
money worries. [Pause.] The conversation between us is like
the funnies. Someone asks a question and the other answers

it, and then the first one says "What?" (Yes. People often aren't sure they are talking about the same thing. This is a good example, because while you thought I was still talking about money worries, I was thinking of worries about other things you might not feel secure about.) I haven't any worries.

[Long pause.] (What are your plans for the future?) I want to be a chemist or an engineer. (Do you like chem at school?) All except the problems. I don't like to have to write things down. (That's kind of like not wanting to put things into words. Lots of things can be worked out in your head, but it's more difficult to communicate them to someone else.) Yes. (I get the feeling, however, that you yourself are confused by some of the things going on in your head. I might be able to help you clarify some of your own thinking.) Yes.

[Pause.] (What are you thinking?) I was wondering why we don't build our streets underground; then we could have the surface for things like houses and things that are nicer to look at than gray, gloomy streets. (Maybe the houses would be prettier on the outside, but it isn't only the pretty things that are important in life. Most of the really significant action may go on in the busy places that may be ugly and sad. I wonder if it isn't the same with you. You wish all the active, maybe not so pretty things could be kept below the surface.) [Smile.]

[Pause.] (What now?) I wonder how one gets rid of smoke? (I would like to know too. Certainly one can't see very clearly through it, and it often makes the eyes sting.)

[Pause.] I was wondering if your phone ever rings. (Were you wondering if we would be interrupted?) That's one way of looking at it. (There might be others. That was what I thought of when you asked the question, but I'd like to know what was on your mind.) I was just curious. (When it rings during an interview, I try to cut my conversation short.) That sounds like a threat—a squelch. (Apparently you thought I meant something about you. Perhaps you fear that you will be squelched if you try to communicate.)

[Pause.] Your pillow looks as if someone had dropped a log on it.

(Our time is up. Do you want to have me keep on sending you a card about the appointment?) Yes. (All right. I'll do so until you tell me you don't need to be reminded any more.)

5. [He arrives twenty minutes late. Makes no comment.]

(I guess it's a rush to get here from school. What have you been doing?) Nothing special. [Pause.] (What are you thinking?) No special problems. [Pause.] (How are you feeling now—comfortable? Uncomfortable?) Neither. [Pause.] I'm not thinking. [Pause. Glances at a picture.] (What was your thought just then?) That picture reminds me of the pine trees. I like to be with them. (At least trees don't bother you and ask questions.) [Smile.]

[Pause.] Some teachers shouldn't be let in. The Spanish teacher—she doesn't like anyone unless they like her subject. I used to be able to speak Spanish, but they wanted everything written and now I've forgotten how to speak. (A person might want to say something, but not necessarily the way the teacher wants it said.) People might not always talk well in the same language. They might want to try different languages to get their ideas across. (Do you think there are some teachers who might want to hear what you have to say, and not care how you say it?) Some English teachers say they do, but you can't be sure they mean what they say. But if they told you to write whatever you wanted, they shouldn't be displeased with what you choose to say. If they are, it's their tough luck, and I wouldn't care. A teacher should be willing to listen and not have preconceived ideas. (That is 100 per cent true.)

[Long pause. Smile.] My brother and I had a fine time this weekend at the steam bath. (Sweating it out?) [Smile.]

[Long pause.] I'm thinking about a story I'm reading. It's about a Thinking Machine. I've just begun it. The machine is up on a hill. Everyone has gone, and it is thinking what to do next. (Is it lonely?) Not lonely, just wondering. (Does it think it can get along by itself, or would it like to find a companion?) It doesn't know what it wants. It's just in a state of wondering. (It might have to wonder for quite a while before it can make any decisions.)

[Pause.] It would be nice to be able to fly around in the air. It would relieve the sidewalk jams. (Yes. It would be nice to be above the crowd and not have to be pushed or jostled.)

[Long pause.] I'm thinking about a physics problem. If a very light weight and a very heavy weight were both pushing down on each other, and both being pulled up, which would move? (It sounds like an uneven contest as far as weight is concerned, but both seem to be pushing with approximately even strength.) It might be important to change the direction of the forces so they wouldn't be pushing against each other, but would be using the energy generated between them to produce effective work.

[Pause.] (Time is up.) He turns at the door. I'll tell you what the Thinking Machine does. (Do. I'll be interested to hear.)

———

The foregoing material illustrates a number of technical points in the establishment of a therapeutic relationship with patients in this diagnostic category and, to some extent, with all adolescents.

It is of great importance to make clear as soon as possible a distinction between the patient's own motivation for therapy and whatever the parental motivations may have been for bringing him. Progress of the whole case may depend on the degree to which an early interest can be aroused in the patient to understand for himself "what's cookin'" in his psychic processes. Emphasis in this direction from the start is particularly significant when treatment has been precipitated by delinquent acts, and when anxiety has been high in the environment about overt behavior as opposed to evidences of internalized stress.

Although David's parents had both been exposed to psychotherapy themselves, and possessed awareness and sympathy for the boy's underlying feelings, actual treatment had been initiated by them when his behavior became threatening to those around him. This is often true when adolescents are brought for treatment. To convince a young patient, therefore, that the goal of psychotherapy is to understand his feelings, is a long-term project, requiring repeated demonstration as well as explicit statement. The amount of curiosity and interest in psychic process which can be elicited at the beginning is a good prognostic indicator.

Much may also depend on the therapist's ability to accept the patient on his own terms, without demanding conformity to any preconceived procedure. Young patients are universally, and quite naturally, frightened and suspicious of relationships with strange adults whose function is to change them in some way. No matter how innately trusting they may be, they feel they must ease their way into a new situation. How much more is this true when previous experience with adults has been full of ambiguity! Most adolescents come to therapy only after many and devious attempts have been made to manipulate their behavior and attitudes. They are more apt to accept help if it is offered within a framework which they have themselves established, and at a pace which they themselves have set.

In the first interview, David immediately placed himself in a passive position. "If you will tell me what my prob-

lems are, I'll cooperate." In response to this, I suggested that
therapy could be a mutual process—"We'll work it out together"—but nevertheless proceeded to take an active role
which attempted to strike a balance between stimulating his
participation and not pushing him in any particular direction. His assumption that the passivity would be a threat to
me (as it had always been to others) was denied both explicitly and implicitly by my continuing to take the lead
while still leaving the door open for him to do so.

We went ahead by trial and error. From time to time,
I offered to relinquish leadership, and he either accepted or
rejected the offer according to his feeling of tolerance. How
this operated in the realm of the symbolic communication
will be demonstrated in the next section.

In the beginning of therapy, the issue was one of
determining how much responsibility he could take for coming to his interviews. The boy clearly stated his mixed feeling. "I like to be reminded only if I forget." To my suggestion that he could take the responsibility and *talk* about the
ambivalence, he passively protested by failing to show up the
next time. I then agreed to remind him until he himself felt
ready to remember. By the eleventh interview he could say,
"This is a part of my life now." From then on he willingly
undertook to keep the appointments, and failed only at times
of stress.

It also became evident almost immediately that David
had difficulty in starting to communicate, but would respond
to an open-ended question, a tentative interpretation, or the
offer of several alternative hypotheses from which he could
take a choice in direction. Throughout most of the therapy,
we followed a pattern in which he paused at the end of one
topic and waited for some sign from me to start him off on
the next. His feelings about the need for my assuming the
responsibility for drawing out his remarks will be discussed
later in connection with specific material in the text (212).

He apparently felt, however, no threat from prodding. When finally able to express feelings about the conduct of therapy, he spoke of difficulties with his previous therapist. "He wanted me to do all the talking, but I didn't always want to talk" (83). In the same interview, when asked whether he felt I had been pushing him, he responded, "No. There's a difference between being pushed and being helped. Anyway, I don't think I could be pushed." Somewhat later he spoke resentfully of people "who like to touch a button and have a machine start up." (I wonder if you feel that's what I do when I start you off with a question?) [Laugh.] "I can remember the times when I couldn't start at all without prodding. I wish I could remember how you put your questions —the most noncommittal way imaginable. No, I don't think so" (193).

The impact of this therapeutic method upon David is elucidated in his own words. "I think I'm using with other people some of the methods I've learned from you. In making relationships—neither to push nor to pull. Not trying to get anything in particular to come out, but just something. Like spreading icing on a cake—not pounding it on with a sledge hammer—just pushing it around gently" (188).

There are, of course, many methods of making and maintaining a therapeutic contact with boys like David. No communication can proceed, however, without a conspicuous effort on the part of the therapist to eliminate as far as possible gaps that may exist between what is openly said and what is really meant. It would seem to some that this is a truism needing no stress. There are times, however, when absolute clarity of meaning is difficult to establish. Stereotyped expressions and behavioral mannerisms are so prevalent among us that we are often unaware of subtle insincerities introduced into the therapeutic relationship. Insofar as these remain outside the area of our awareness, they may help to damage communication between therapist and the type of patient who has been sensitized throughout his lifetime to varying degrees of double-talk. Such expressions may be interpreted literally by the patient in a way that distorts the interaction unless meanings are explicitly clarified, and may, in any case, represent to him the kind of meaningless superficiality with which real communication has been warded off by people in his environment.

Many authors have emphasized the extent to which schizophrenic and borderline patients can detect attitudes which are unconscious in the therapist. Fortunately, this works both ways, and positive feelings are sensed as well as negative ones. Nevertheless, a boy like David has been exposed throughout his entire experience to vast discrepancies between what is said and what is really felt by those around him. He must, at all costs, come to recognize that the therapist is consciously *trying* to be aware of his own attitudes and to express them honestly. Until he is convinced on this point, a truly therapeutic milieu does not exist.

David made the first test when, at the beginning of the third interview, he asked me if I liked football. I did not know at the time what football meant to him, but *did* know that an insincere expression of interest, intended to draw him out, would soon be detected and raise a barrier between us. A few moments later, he brought into the open his resentment of stereotyped expressions, which, if applied literally, would indicate insincerity on the part of the therapist. When I said, "All I can say is that I'll try to do whatever seems most useful," he replied sarcastically, "That's all you can say!" It was necessary to make explicit at once that I would make a serious effort to avoid meaningless expressions and create a climate in which real feelings could be voiced. My reply, "No, I suppose I could say a good deal more. I guess that sounded like pretty stereotyped talk to you," produced an expression of evident satisfaction from him.

One of David's major problems was difficulty in the

ability to trust. This difficulty is characteristic of all patients who have had his kind of life experience. If a therapist fails, even occasionally, to be trustworthy, ground may be damagingly lost in the relationship. As the boy himself once said, "You have to be hurt only once by the dentist's drill in order to be afraid of it, no matter how many times it *hasn't* hurt" (148).

Constant vigilance is thus required on the part of the therapist to avoid any attitude which may be interpreted by the patient as an intent to deceive or placate him. No promises may be made other than an expression of willingness to try to understand. No pretenses may be made at understanding something that is not clear. It must be made explicit that trust is not expected unless it is earned by the therapist.

In the second interview, David volunteered his reasons for passivity. "If you stick your neck out . . . , you are apt to get it chopped off." When I accepted the validity of his reluctance under these circumstances, he shortly volunteered an interest in learning about psychic processes. In the fourth interview, it was necessary to accept frankly his criticism about confusion in the communication and to state explicitly that we would not always understand each other.

The patient must at all times feel free to check and recheck his perception of meanings. The therapist must constantly check and recheck his own conscious and unconscious reactions. More will be said about problems of countertransference and counter-reactivity in a future chapter.

One other technical point is important in working with this type of patient. A quality of prime necessity in the therapist is an ability to sit back and wait without getting impatient. Time has a very different impact on him than it has on the patient. Often while he wonders whether there is any motion in therapy at all, the patient feels himself to be racing along at a dangerous speed. The therapist must undertake the relationship in full knowledge that it is a long-term proposition, fraught with the possibility of many complications which must be worked out slowly and without pressure.

In David's case there were a number of factors which may have facilitated an acceptance of therapy with me. In the first place, his reality situation was deteriorating and, in spite of doubts and fears, he desperately wanted help. Secondly, although feelings about his mother were highly ambivalent, he respected her judgment and saw her as a strong and powerful figure. The knowledge that she felt her contact with me to have been helpful may have been encouraging for him. At the start, I was afraid that my previous relationship with her would be a handicap, but actually his awareness that I understood something about her problems proved an asset rather than a liability. As the material will demonstrate, he was closely identified with her in many ways. My obvious respect and liking for her was reassuring to him while he struggled with his own ambivalence.

One may speculate on the degree to which somewhat magical expectation on the part of both parents facilitated therapy. Unconscious ambivalence toward me, and toward David, was obvious throughout, but until well along in therapy they were both consciously cooperative and interested in helping us. There seemed to be a strong assumption all around that something constructive would happen.

The boy himself initiated the symbolic mode of communication. Its use was tacitly agreed upon by us practically at once. My response was both conscious and unconscious, as can be noted in the interchange around the word "level" in the first session. A vague awareness that stealing a level in some way represented a symbolic form of behavior was reflected by my use of the word in replying to his fantasy. By making an association back to the level, he confirmed my perception and indicated his own semi-awareness of it. Interviews conducted almost entirely in this mode may be followed in the succeeding chapters.

3

The Language
and Thought Process

Ⅰᴛ ʜᴀꜱ ꜰʀᴇQᴜᴇɴᴛʟʏ ʙᴇᴇɴ ꜱᴀɪᴅ ᴛʜᴀᴛ ᴛʜᴇ thought and language of autistic patients is dominated by primary process.[1, 2, 3, 4] Under pressure of intense anxiety, regression to more archaic ways of thinking has taken place, and many of the mechanisms normally operative only in dream thinking are used in the waking state. However, the degree to which primitive mechanisms influence the total thinking process of any individual person is not always clearly defined. In learning to communicate with that particular individual, it is important to estimate the extent and the way in which primary process is operating in him.

Archaic thought has certain well-known characteristics. Directed almost exclusively toward providing discharge for the affect generated by instinctual need and forbidden desire, it departs from both the mode of expression and the system of logic used in more mature forms of mental activity.[1] It is carried on largely in pictorial images constructed through the use of primitive devices. Among such devices are the condensation of many ideas into one image and the ignoring of contradictions and of distinctions between past, present, or future in the experience of time. Symbols poorly differentiated from what they represent are used extensively to depict thoughts and feelings. In forming such symbols, similarities are treated as identities; objects sharing one or more qualities, or which have existed contiguously in time or space, are represented interchangeably. Equally complete equations are made between objects and their parts, part representing the whole and vice versa. Objects are simultaneously represented as themselves and as other objects or ideas.

Lack of differentiation between symbol and what is symbolized characterizes a low level of integration in mental activity. In earliest life, concepts, images, feelings, and words overlap, while in the course of mental development, they become separate and discrete.[5, 6] If regression occurs for any reason, the ability to differentiate symbol and object decreases proportionately. A patient reacts as though the symbol were, in fact, the object it represents, and attaches the same affect to it.[3]

Words are a special class of symbols.[7] In earliest life, verbalization serves a strictly autistic, primary-process function. The individual derives instinctual pleasure purely from perception of sound and sensation. Words first enter the psychic life rooted in association to body parts, products, and needs.[5, 6, 8] They gradually become attached to concrete objects outside the self, and later represent more abstract concepts of objects. As language develops through the use of conventionalized symbols shared by others, early connections with body image and functions are repressed, and the shared associations between word symbol and the objects or ideas symbolized remain conscious. Word symbolization makes possible a large part of interpersonal communication and of conceptualization, forming the basis of secondary-process thinking.

In states of regression, primary-process thought progressively resumes domination of language through loss of consensually validated symbolization. Shared meanings for words are replaced by strictly personal meanings, frequently closely related to body image and function. Ability to form abstractions gives way to concretization in which a word denotes a very specific object and loses its broader connotation. Differentiation between word symbol and the object represented recedes until a complete equation occurs between them, and the word for an object can generate the same affect as the object itself. Words may become interchangeable substitutes for each other and for the objects symbolized. Pleasure is again obtained primarily from the sounds and sensations created in producing words and from the creation of private symbols. Ability to communicate thoughts and affects is progressively lost until, at the lowest level, verbalizations become "word salads" completely unintelligible to others.

Early psychoanalytic writers described primary and secondary process in such a way as to permit some of their followers to maintain a falsely sharp dichotomy between the two processes.[9] It is often assumed that complete domination by one or the other occurs in the mental state of an individual at any given moment of time, rather than that both may be operating simultaneously in different degrees. More recent work has made it possible to think largely in terms of gradients in psychic activity.

Symbolization was first regarded as a strictly primary-process activity, designed to allow representation of deeply unconscious, repressed ideas only, and was considered as distinct from other forms of indirect representation such as metaphor, etc.[9] More recently Kubie and Rycroft have stressed the concept that symbol formation occurs in the service of both primary and secondary processes, and that the mechanisms of condensation, concretization, etc., can be used on conscious and preconscious as well as deeply unconscious levels.[6, 7] This inclusive view of symbolism more closely approximates a general and literary usage of the term. Kubie makes clear that where such "economizing devices" occur predominantly on conscious and preconscious levels they mediate thought and language. When they occur on a deeply unconscious level, they "determine the shapes of our dreams, and in a waking state the shapes of our illnesses."[6]

Any given symbolic expression may represent at the same time a conscious, preconscious, and unconscious idea. "Every moment of thought and feeling involves simultaneously the activation of literal, allegorical and a dreamlike meaning of the symbolic concepts which are relevant to that moment of psychic activity."[6] In any individual, various streams of mental activity flow simultaneously, blending to a degree and still remaining discrete; it is difficult to measure the proportionate flow from various levels of consciousness. Although direct conscious functioning can usually be recognized fairly readily, the exact blend of preconscious and unconscious activity in an expression which is clearly "not conscious" may be impossible to estimate. Other scales for determining the "maturity" of psychological process also fluctuate within themselves and independently of each other. One of these is the degree of volition used in choosing a mode of communication, direct or symbolic; another is the degree of animateness of human forms as depicted in imagery.[10] In any one symbolic expression, voluntary blends into involuntary, and forms may not all be on the same level even in the same image.

A good index to the depth of a person's feeling of isolation is the kind of symbolic image chosen to represent himself and other human beings. Use of a symbol closely approximating the person symbolized, such as substitution of one human form for another in an analogous situation, indicates a relatively high sense of relatedness. The disguise is not great, and the communication is nearly direct. Use of a human figure in a different context, or of a completely personified machine such as a robot, gives way to substitution of subhuman animate forms (animals and then plants) as isolation increases. Images consisting purely of cosmic or microscopic phenomena, in which all signs of life have been deleted, indicate the deepest sense of dehumanization. They occur under the greatest pressure of anxiety.

The same basic problems are expressed in numerous forms from different layers of consciousness at different times, or at the same time, and with different degrees of volition. Concern with bodily matters or interpersonal relationships may be discussed consciously, preconsciously through analogic or allegorical representation, or in dreamlike symbolism depicting deeply unconscious ideas.[11] Allegorical representations may use inanimate forms, and dreamlike symbolism make use of human figures. Maturity can be high on one scale and low on another, lying at different points on the continua from voluntary to involuntary imagery, from highly developed forms to completely depersonalized forms, and from conscious to unconscious. Primary and secondary processes are operating concurrently in different ways and in different proportions. It becomes impossible to categorize definitely the psychic process taking place in any individual consistently, or influencing a single reaction of that individual in any moment of time.

David's "code" is an example of language based on a symbolic thinking process. It demonstrates many of the foregoing points and shows the gradual progress which took place along scales of "maturity" in psychic process during the course of therapy. The material illustrates clearly how difficult it is to categorize the degree of consciousness and volition in communicating or in using symbolic imagery.

It was obvious that thinking consistently took place in pictorial images, and the boy made this explicit fairly early in therapy. "I have visual pictures while I'm talking that I can't describe" (57). However, there were differences in level between separate communications and within each particular symbolic expression. An extensive range in animateness of human symbols and quality of mood was expressed. Although David presented ideas largely by analogy and allegory, he made frequent recourse to more dreamlike symbolism. His use of the symbolic mode of communicating was largely involuntary, but nevertheless gave evidence that a degree of voluntary obscurity in meaning was being maintained for protective purposes that were at least partially conscious. Shifts from consciousness to unconsciousness in use of symbolic imagery seemed to be constantly in operation. A few illustrations taken from early interviews are characteristic of communications during the first few years of therapy.

David's first symbolic statement occurred in the first interview, when he responded to a question of mine by saying he would "like to take a crack at being President of the United States" because the government was making a mess of handling things. Here the imagery was on a fairly "mature" level along the scale of form animateness, one human figure substituting for another in an analogous situation (members of the government equaling parents). Meaning of the symbol was probably at a preconscious level, although one can say surely only that it was not directly conscious at the moment of utterance. However, the level of volition was less "mature." At a later period, the boy himself made clear that his use of imagery was not voluntary in the sense of a purposeful embellishment of language, but a "devious" mode of expression over which he had no control. "I can't seem to think any other way sometimes" (62). ". . . I don't seem to have much control over the ways I think" (77). That the process lay somewhere between preconscious and unconscious seemed indicated when he explained, "Things come to me in those terms; although I'm vaguely aware that I'm talking about something else, I can't translate into more direct expression ahead of time" (120). Nevertheless, the boy was also aware at times that "a bee" might be able to talk more directly if he were *willing* to expose his feelings (7). The degree of volition was not static.

The first statement on somewhat deeper levels of symbolism occurred when David wondered "why we don't build our streets underground; then we could have the surface for things like houses and things that are nicer to look at than gray, gloomy streets" (4). Here one can sense desolateness of mood in a gloomy scene without human figures. Although on one level it seemed to be an allegorical, more or less preconscious, expression of his wish to stay on the surface in therapy and not get into deeper problems, there was also a possibility that the underground streets full of mess and confusion might be more dreamlike symbols with direct body image meanings on an unconscious level. Here one can see how related ideas from different layers of the unconscious, generating the same depressed mood, are expressed simultaneously by one concrete image.

One may note throughout the material that ideas appeared to David in symbolic forms which became more regressed and remote when intensity of feeling increased in connection with matters under discussion. Since, for instance, it was not particularly threatening to the boy's self-esteem to feel that his parents were "making a mess of things," he could communicate the thought directly, in symbols which only thinly disguised the real people. Painful ideas about himself, however, were expressed in images showing his identification with relatively dehumanized forms, progressing from subhuman animate to completely inanimate figures. The more painful the idea, the lower the degree of animateness in the self-symbol. "A dog doesn't feel like biting if anyone pays attention to him . . . if he thinks you are going to attack his house, he will . . . bite you, but if you act friendly, . . . he'll realize he doesn't need to be hostile" (14). (. . . vegetarians think about what it would feel like if they were being eaten.) "Doesn't anyone ever worry about how a plant feels?" (9). The idea of being devoured was obviously more threatening than being ignored, and here he identified with the plant rather than with the animal. When he felt need to put great distance between himself and others, David thought of himself as a machine. Sometimes a robot or thinking machine (5) approximated human form, but more often the machine was depersonalized and remote. Discussion of fears about bodily function produced marked anxiety, was indirect, and produced less "mature" symbolism. ". . . a motor. I don't know whether there is anything wrong with the mechanism, or whether there's a problem making connection with the current. I think there's something wrong with the switch . . ." (10). The most intense feeling of loneliness and despair came out in cosmic symbols. "I wonder how long the earth can go on producing people without shrinking and becoming depleted. People take more out of it than they can put back" (8). He was enormously afraid that the intensity of his demand would destroy the person upon whom he counted for supplies, and could express the concept only in highly abstract terms. Even when far along in treatment, the boy almost invariably reverted to use of "code" in expressing ideas that generated a high degree of anxiety (36, 73, 76, 152, 174).

For a long time, anxiety in the therapeutic relationship made it necessary for David to communicate indirectly.

"Young people can't talk directly about the things that really concern them" (85). He himself did not realize immediately that he also *thought* indirectly. "I only need the code to communicate; when I'm alone I can face my unhappiness more directly" (122). ". . . I can think things directly, but not talk" (158). Late in therapy, however, when he had already been able to abandon it for purposes of communication, he was able to recognize that the code was not only an interpersonal protective mechanism but a means of deflecting subjective feelings of anxiety. ". . . I never realized until recently that I was even coding for myself . . . I guess I'm actually beginning to *think* more directly" (207). Without further discussion, the reader may watch the gradual transition by which involuntary use of symbolic communication gave way to a more literary type of symbolic language.

R E F E R E N C E S

(1) Arieti, S., "Schizophrenia," in Arieti, ed., American Handbook of Psychiatry. N. Y., Basic Books, 1959.
(2) Fenichel, O., Psychoanalytic Theory of Neurosis (section on schizophrenic thinking). N. Y., W. W. Norton, 1945.
(3) Sechehaye, M., A New Psychotherapy of Schizophrenia. N. Y., Grune & Stratton, 1956.
(4) Kasanin, J., Language and Thought in Schizophrenia. Berkeley and Los Angeles, University of California Press, 1951.
(5) Kubie, L., "Body Symbolization and the Development of Language," Psychoanalytic Quarterly, Vol. 3, 1934, pp. 430–444.
(6) Kubie, L., "Distortion of the Symbolic Process in the Neuroses and Psychoses," Journal of the American Psychoanalytic Association, Vol. 1, 1953, pp. 59–86.
(7) Rycroft, C., "Symbolism and Its Relationship to Pri-

mary and Secondary Process," *International Journal of Psychoanalysis*, Vol. 37, 1956, pp. 137–146.

(8) Meetings of the New York Psychoanalytic Society, December 1950, *Psychoanalytic Quarterly*, Vol. 120, 1951, pp. 500–501.

(9) Jones, E., "Theory of Symbolism," in *Papers on Psychoanalysis*, 5th ed. London, Bailliere, Tindall & Cox, 1948.

(10) Seidenberg, R., "Changes in the Symbolic Process during a Psychoanalytic Treatment," *Journal of Nervous and Mental Disorders*, Vol. 127, 1958, pp. 131–141.

(11) Segal, H., "Notes on Symbol Formation," *International Journal of Psychoanalysis*, Vol. 38, 1957, pp. 391–397.

4

The Code

"I'm the one that has to be careful there are no explosives."

6. [*Characteristic posture and far-away gaze.*] (You were going to tell me more about the thinking machine.) It has hitched up with another machine. (Can it be useful to him?) They can be mutually useful.

[*Pause.*] (What are you thinking about?) A gyroscope. It has to stay anchored in one place. It loses its power unless it is attached to a motor, because of the friction on the bearings unless, of course, it is off in space where there is no friction. (If it got too far out in space it would lose its usefulness.) Yes. (It is a highly complicated machine, but a valuable one. Perhaps oiling may reduce the friction.) Perhaps.

[*Pause.*] I've been up in back of the University digging around in the garbage to see if I can find some useful

equipment. If one digs around in the garbage one can sometimes find things, but it gets terribly messy. (It's worth it if
you find things you can use.) Nobody cares if I dig around
there, but *I'm* the one that has to be careful there are no
explosives. The janitor only gets excited if the mess gets
thrown around the place he's responsible for.

(If the janitor lets you poke around in the garbage, he
should be willing to see to it that the mess doesn't get out
of hand. If it does, I imagine he knows how to deal with it.
I dare say he isn't particularly worried about his own reputa-
tion. Anyway, I don't suppose you would be allowed in there
if anyone thought there was any material that would be too
dangerous.) There's an awful lot of garbage. You never know
what's in it. (A lot of good material may get mixed up with
garbage.)

One might want to keep some things that look like
garbage, but in any case, one would want some choice in
what got sifted out. (If two people got together on the sift-
ing, there are probably certain things they could agree on
which could be tackled first. By the time that was done, they
would know enough about each other's ideas to have some
basis for discussion about what should be thrown out and
what kept.)

[*Pause.*] I'd like to learn to be an engineer, but the
language is terribly technical. (Sometimes it is incompre-
hensible, but I'm sure that if an idea needs to be expressed,
ways can be found for making it clear. A teacher often has
to say things many times, in different ways, before he can
make himself understood.) The problems are very complicated. (Learning to be an engineer involves a lot of trial and
error as well as willingness to study and think about the problems as they present themselves.) I'm not sure I'm capable
of becoming one. Mentally I might not be able to solve the
problems, and there might be physical handicaps. If you had
a hand cut off, you wouldn't be able to do the work. (If you

want to be an engineer, you just have to go along and see
how well you can overcome the obstacles.)

7. [David has a bag of doughnuts with his school books. As
he lays them down he offers me one which I refuse with
thanks.]
　　　[Pause.] (What are you thinking?) Nothing. Just
wondering what to think about. (When you think of something, let me know.)
　　　[Pause.] I saw some sheep yesterday. A ram and three
ewes.
　　　[Pause.] I wonder what it would be like to be as small
as a spider. People's feet would look very big. (It would seem
that everyone was bigger than you, and able to crush you.)
Bigness isn't always so important; sometimes it makes people
top-heavy. Being as small as a spider would mean you could
get into places that bigger people can't get into.
　　　[Pause.] People don't put a dog out when they are
talking, because they don't notice him. (A dog undoubtedly
knows a lot about what goes on among people, even if he
doesn't say anything about it. He can usually sense, too,
whether people are friendly or unfriendly.) Yes.
　　　[Pause.] Little animals and insects often have protective devices, stingers and things. But if a person were as small
as a spider, he might not have such protection. What would
it be like if he met an ant? [Pause.] Perhaps he could duel
with a pin. (A pin would look long and sharp to an ant.)
　　　[Pause.] I wonder what it would be like to be a bee?
A bee can sting to protect himself, but after he has stung, he
has to die. (He must feel frightened that his destructiveness
is so lethal to himself as well as to others.) He might not
care so long as he goes down fighting. (That's true, but it
might be better if he felt he could fight to protect himself
and still go on living.)
　　　[Pause.] It is difficult to know how a bee feels. He

might not feel as we think we would feel if we were bees. (The only way to know would be if a bee could tell us.) Could—or *would*.

[*Pause. He notices wires outside the window.*] Are they telephone wires? (I've never noticed them. I guess they are.) He looks around the room and notices some indentations in the wall. What are those? (Sound proofing, so that nothing said in here can be heard outside unless we want it to. What had you thought they might be?) Outlets for pipes —or maybe places where heat might come in.

[*Pause.*] I was wondering—when the defense lawyer jumps up and says "I object," the judge sustains it. But why couldn't he save the lawyer the trouble by saying "I object" before him? (The judge has to hear all the evidence. The lawyer has his case planned. Sometimes he doesn't want to introduce evidence until he is ready. It isn't the judge's job to run the case, only to hear it. The lawyer himself makes decisions as to what he wants to emphasize, and what he wants to let go.)

[*Pause. There has been some hammering outside the office which stops temporarily.*] That reminds me of what Dad said about unions. Some guys will be putting up a door, and maybe get one hinge on, and then it's four o'clock and bang, goodbye. (Although carpenters have to think of their own interests too—get adequate rest and relaxation so they can carry on their work—still one would like to feel that they had a real interest in the job and that if something needed fixing to make it safe, they would be willing to give a little extra time to it.)

[*The hammering starts again.*] He apparently was there, even though we couldn't hear him. (It isn't always when one is making the most noise that one is working.) Some teachers at school don't care if you are working or not, just so long as you look as though you are.

[*Pause.*] I wonder if supersonic sound could drown

out other sounds? It is unpleasant to be surrounded by a wall from which sounds reverberate and you can't tell whether it is the sound you made or some other. The supersonic sound might make a dog's ears hurt, even though it was too high-pitched for people to hear.

[Pause.] If you rub the edge of a glass, you can sometimes make it sing. (Sometimes you have to rub it for quite a while. Sometimes, too, if you hit just the right note, you can get another glass to respond to the vibrations and sing too.)

[Pause.] In a chess game, if you were checked so that you couldn't make a move without losing a man, maybe it would be better to let them all be taken and start again.

(Our time is up for now.) [He turns at the door.] I'll see you Monday.

8. [David is talking even before he sits down.] Did I get here earlier this time? (Yes.) I walked instead of taking the bus. It's nice, sometimes, to find out that people are more efficient than machines. They can think things out.

[Pause.] A bookcase door puts up a front that keeps people from knowing that there is a secret room behind it where all sorts of things are going on. Like me.

[Pause.] I want to put a sink in the basement where my lab is, but I don't know if Dad will let me. I want to make some experiments. I've tried some of them with Joe, but he's at college now.

[Pause.] Some kids made some explosives and shot them off in the country. They had to stand behind trees. (If one is playing with explosives, one needs to protect oneself.)

[Pause.] When you are making gases, you have to test them with mice and plants to see if they are poisonous. A mouse wouldn't know whether it was oxygen or carbon monoxide, except by the effects. He would have to have a knowledge of the intention of the experimenter to be helpful or harmful. The experimenter wouldn't always know, either, the needs of the mouse or plant. He might put a plant in oxygen, intending to make it grow, and find out that what it needed was carbon dioxide. However, he could see if it was starting to wilt, and take it out to prevent death. (Yes. The experimenter would have to keep a careful watch to see that he wasn't doing the wrong things.)

[Pause.] I was thinking about mescaline. It distorts visual images and creates visions that can be frightening. (Yes. Do you know whether it produces auditory hallucinations too?) I don't know.

Apomorphine is another funny drug. It could be fed to someone in their food without their knowing it. (I doubt whether anyone would think it very funny to be made to vomit unless he was prepared for it. The drug is, of course, used medically to help a person get rid of something that isn't good for him, but people like to know when they are being treated in that way.) They certainly do.

[An electioneering car goes by outside the office with a blaring loudspeaker.] That candidate is certainly trying hard to sell himself. (I hope that whoever is elected will be so because of what he is, and what he does, rather than how much noise he makes.) [Smile.]

[Pause.] Some people are great practical jokers. (Most practical jokes aren't really very funny. Nobody really enjoys getting hurt.)

[Pause.] I wonder how long the earth can go on producing people without shrinking and becoming depleted. People take more out of it than they can put back. (I doubt whether the earth will be sucked dry, at least in your lifetime.)

9. [Pause.] (What are you thinking?) I've been working on the sink in the basement.

[Pause.] (Anything else on your mind?) No. (Your

father called me last week to tell me you are having trouble with chemistry at school. Is this just something that bothers your father, or does it bother you too?) I can't get myself to write up the experiments, but I'll have to do better. I don't want a poor grade. I can work the problems out in my head, but I don't like to write them down.

[Pause.] I wonder what it would be like to be as small as a molecule. (A molecule is even smaller than a spider, yet a lot goes on inside it. One can hardly imagine anything smaller, yet actually it is a whole world of atoms and electrons.)

[Pause.] Electricity goes along a spiral wire. It would shoot out the end with centrifugal force. It would be good if one could think of a way to keep it moving in the spiral. It's like planets in their orbits—forces are pulling them out and other forces holding them in. You need the outward force to keep them from bumping into the sun and getting absorbed —losing their identity.

[Pause.] Does a person who spits all the time have enlarged saliva glands? (What do you mean?) I mean would constant spitting cause the glands to enlarge so that there be ever more saliva to spit? (I doubt it.)

[Pause.] (What now?) I'm thinking about phonograph records and wire recorders. It would be nice if the grooves could be arranged so that one could play words in many different combinations but always make sense. (That would be nice.) One often has to play music one doesn't want to hear in order to get to the parts that one does want to hear. (Yes. Also, at times, a recording isn't clear, and a place may have to be played over and over in order to get it.) Yes.

[Pause.] Yogis haven't got the right idea. It would be all right to get yourself so that you could give up smoking and drinking, but I wouldn't ever want to give up eating meat. I don't understand vegetarians. (Sometimes they are people who are identified with animals; they think what it would feel like to be eaten.) Doesn't anyone ever worry about how a plant feels?

[Pause.] I'm thinking about a sighting instrument. If you have two fixed points, you can locate a goal but you have to supply the third point with your eye. (It's something like how images in the brain supply a picture from past experience, even though the eye may actually see something quite different.)

[Pause.] If space is curved, you could look through a telescope and the sight would go all around the world and come back so that you would be seeing yourself as others see you.

[Pause.] I read a story about a space ship. It had representatives of all forms of life except a human being in it. It needed a human being, so it persuaded someone to come aboard. He was supposed to come back to earth afterward and convert other people. His function was to make the space ship move faster. One can't take forever going from galaxy to galaxy.

10. [Pause.] (What are you thinking?) I'm trying to fix up a motor. I don't know whether there is anything wrong with the mechanism, or whether there's a problem of making connection with the current. I think there's something wrong with the switch. Some people might think it is important how it runs, but the important thing to me is whether I can get it to run at all. I would like to get it perfectly assembled. I don't want three black screws and one white one. I want all the parts to go together as they were intended to do by the airplane manufacturer.

[Pause.] If I get it running, its function might be to open doors of various sorts. I think it originally might have been to open an airplane door and lift bombs. Now all I care about is just to get it running. I have to experiment with various connections.

[Pause.] A boy with an air gun was shooting at a window at school. The teacher said it wasn't that she minded his breaking the window, but it was the principle of the things. (That was hypocritical. She undoubtedly did mind having her window broken, although perhaps she could have tolerated it better if it was an accident.)

[Pause.] I've got a pair of handcuffs. I could lure a kid to shake hands with me and then snap on the cuffs when he wasn't suspecting.

[Pause.] A kid got a dummy and smeared it with catsup and cheese so that it would look like a corpse. He put it alongside the road like there had been an accident, and scared people nearly to death. (Sometimes a joke like that can become so real to the person who's playing it that he scares himself. Sometimes people can tolerate frightening things better if they make a joke of them, but pretty often the joke comes too close to the real feeling to be really funny.)

[The somewhat teasing, conversational manner with which he has been telling these stories is suddenly dropped, and he stares off into space again.]

[Pause.] (What are you thinking?) There is a gadget in some museum which hangs in such a way that it doesn't move of itself, but as the earth turns, a peg is knocked over regularly. [Pause.] There is a gyroscope which is fixed itself, but operated by the motion of the earth. Even though it does no work by itself, it becomes a machine by virtue of the earth's turning, so that working together, something is accomplished.

11. [I forgot to send him a card this week. He arrives fifteen minutes late, apologizing and saying he got mixed up.]

(Did my forgetting to send the card have anything to do with it?) No. This is a part of my life now. You don't have to send any more cards.

[Pause.] I was just wondering what to meditate about.

[Pause.] I'm thinking about the junk pile I used to visit when I was smaller. It was a government surplus pile. I wonder if the government still sends stuff to it. (What did you like to collect?) I don't remember. I was small then. (What were you interested in then?) I don't know.

[Pause.] Wouldn't it be interesting if you could make a kind of electric table that could be directed by some kind of motor or beam to carry things for you from place to place. (Yes. But it would be better to keep the mechanism simple at first so that it could go back and forth between two specific points. Later maybe it could do more complicated maneuvers.) Maybe you could guide it by radar to follow a path by having it avoid obstacles and gradually find the clear space. (Sometimes it might have to go into wrong paths, and come to dead ends, but that wouldn't matter.) Sometimes things would spill in transit. You would have to be careful what you put on it.

Oh, by the way, did I tell you I got that motor started that I told you about? I took it all apart, but hadn't found the right amount of power. Now it works. I don't know what I'll use it for. Maybe to operate something like the table we are talking about.

[Pause.] I'd like to make a robot. (What could it do?) It would be interesting if it worked by putting different records onto it so that it would do different things according to the patterns laid out by the record. (What might happen if it had reasoning power like a human being?) It might not be so docile. It might decide the world needed destroying.

(Could one put in some kind of controls without destroying its free action?) Maybe it should run like those cars for beginning drivers that have two sets of controls. It could then gradually become independent, but only if its judgment proved to be good.

[*Pause.*] I wonder how much it would cost to make a robot? (No matter what it cost, it would be worth it if one could make such a potentially productive machine work well.)

I read a story about a robot that learned to do something when it became attached to a certain man. At some point it came near to making an explosion. The man got scared and influenced it to forget everything it had been taught. (One might have to risk an explosion now and then experimenting with such valuable materials, but one could work slowly, under conditions that would keep destructiveness at a minimum.)

If a car had huge tires many feet high, and the speedometer was geared to register according to the number of revolutions of the wheel, one might be going a lot faster than one realized. (One could tell pretty well by the amount of ground covered.)

12. [*Pause.*] (What are you thinking?) I'm thinking about a story I read. An explorer was trying to find his way into a buried city. He found a coin, and kept flipping it to see where he should go next. The coin eventually led him into the city. (Trial and error is often a useful way to make discoveries.) Errors waste a lot of time. (Maybe. But one doesn't always know what's an error. Anyway, even a wrong way often doesn't lead too far astray.)

[*Pause.*] How much do you suppose Cupid's bow weighs? (I don't know, but I hear there's a good deal of power in the arrows.) You might need armor against them. (Some people feel they do. Often they really wish the armor would be pierced in some way that wouldn't hurt too much.) [*Pause.*] (Have you had some experience with this?) Yes. (Tell me about it.) What would there be to tell? (You find it hard to talk about.) The question seems as hard for you to answer as for me.

[Pause.] If men with heavy cross bows shoot through armor, one can be killed. Heavy trees can be pierced. [Pause.] In medieval days they used catapults to throw rocks. They could also throw things over walls. [Pause.] I wonder if I could learn to make a catapult. Maybe an even better idea would be an electrically driven pogo stick on which you could leap over walls. However, if it got out of control, it could throw you.

[Pause.] I wonder how much distance could be covered if one rode on a big wheel. What if there was a track inside the wheel and a car could go around in it, but also use the momentum of the wheel to make it run? (It might be good to have the protection of the track, particularly if one had just learned to drive, but eventually one would want to go out on the open road.)

[Pause.] I'm thinking of a Morse Code machine. It can send messages very fast, and these can be picked up by a machine that can record them and decode them at greater leisure. It is necessary to work quickly, particularly if one has only a limited time in which to use the equipment.

[Pause.] I know a guy who needed power to run a heater. He tapped the Connecticut Light & Power high-voltage lines after he had been stopped from plugging into the school lighting system. Half the fun was the danger. He blew out several fuses, and the CL&P didn't like it, but he knew enough about electricity to tap the line without endangering himself. (You certainly do have to be careful around high voltage lines.) Yes.

13. [He starts off gaily.] I went skating yesterday. I'm stiff, but want to go again and get my muscles used to it. (Sounds like fun. [Pause.] After next week I'm going to be away for three weeks. Have you any plans for the holidays?) No.

[*Pause.*] (What are you thinking?) I got the motor working on a switch, but I can't think what to use it for. Maybe it could turn a machine gun on a mount. It would be kind of interesting if the motor was hitched up so directly that the gun would spin around fast and shoot in all directions before you had a chance to aim. Also, it might turn you by its momentum so it would push you around. (It would be more useful if it could be aimed, and you could do the directing.)

[*Pause.*] I can't focus my eyes on what's outside the window. I can only see with one eye through the crack of the curtains. (Sometimes one can see a thing more clearly if one can't see all the things around it.) Like a periscope. It would be nice if you could focus a periscope on the things in life that you wanted to see clearly. (Yes. It would be nice to be able to focus clearly on individual feelings. One might then get a better idea of their relationship to other things.)

It would be nice if you could hitch up two motors in a team. One of them could go fast, and the other supply extra power only when it was needed. (They should be mutually sensitive to what was needed in the combination to insure smooth running. If a motor wasn't hitched up to another, but was in good running order, it could be applied to whatever job needed a motor.) Sometimes a motor that isn't hitched up to anything explodes with its own power. (One would have to control the power so that it wouldn't destroy itself.)

[*Pause.*] Some guys were caught cutting down trees out in the country. The police asked if I had anything to do with it. (How do you feel about being suspected every time something goes wrong around here?) [*Laugh.*] Once I was the one cutting down the trees. Now I've offered my services to the police to help find the culprits. (Is it as good a feeling to be on the side of the law as on the other side?) Danger is exciting in itself. (What might one be needing to prove to oneself in tempting fate?) Whether one is a hard man—hard as nails.

[*Pause.*] Archimedes made a great discovery while trying to find out whether he had been gypped by the goldsmiths. Nobody ever tells you whether he really was being gypped or not. (How might it have been?) If they were "from the wrong side of the tracks," they were probably cheating the king. (What do you mean by that?) Not "of the majority." The majority has the power, and if one is in the minority, one has no choice. The goldsmiths might have had to make a crown for a price they didn't consider fair, but they had no choice, so they adulterated it. Also, maybe they didn't think the king would appreciate good workmanship. (I suppose there might have been still other factors involved in their wanting to cheat the king.) What if there were a crown like in the "Emperor's New Clothes" that only wise men could see? (In that story the hypocrites who pretended to be wise and to see what they really didn't see were the ones who got shown up.) One could make up a story about a crown that could only be seen by people with certain kinds of perceptions. It would depend on the motives of these people as to whether their perception was dangerous or not.

[*Pause.*] I read a story about the fourth dimension, where someone saw three parallel lines meeting at right angles. (I guess it's pretty impossible for a person in one kind of dimension to describe it to a person in another.) Like trying to explain what height is to a bug that only knows two dimensions.

14. [*David sits down and opens immediately.*] We won't be meeting next Monday, will we? (No. I will be away for the next three Mondays. What will you be doing?) Nothing. (How does your family usually spend Christmas?) Just like everyone else, I guess. Nothing special.

[Pause.] In chemistry there are lots of unstable compounds. Water is the basic substance in the body, and practically everything can be ionized in it. One ion can be attracted away, and then the other is discarded as unusable or built up into another compound. (Are there some compounds that are not so unstable?) One iron compound.

[Pause.] I wish I could isolate promin. I could make tear gas from it and spread it around the lab. (There are other ways of making people cry.) I wonder at what temperature gas would freeze so that it wouldn't have the effect of making tears. (You mean the warmer the temperature, the more the tears?) That's a good way of putting it. (I realize you are sorry I am going away for a few weeks, but I'll be back right after the vacation.)

Could it be possible to find a way to make ethyl chloride evaporate so fast that the flame would be blown away? It can be used on the skin to anesthetize for an operation, but it can also burn. Maybe one could make it evaporate so fast that the flame created would be blown away before the damage was done. (The same chemical can often carry out different processes at different speeds or concentrations —healing, destructive, or self-protective.) There are chemicals that form explosive substances in certain combinations and are inert in others.

(How is chemistry going at school?) I've come up from an F to a D. I do the experiments, but often don't write them up. Sometimes I look up the answers and write them up without doing them. I haven't time for both.

Chemistry certainly is complicated. Wouldn't it be good if one could go back with present knowledge and tell it to the alchemists. Then they wouldn't have had to waste so much experimental time trying to make gold. If they had spent their time discovering something like the sulfa drugs, everyone would be farther along today. (It would have been difficult for the alchemists to accept the idea that anything was more valuable so long as they felt a need to make gold. Making gold to them meant having power within themselves, and unless they could have felt they could get this power in some other way, it would have been hard to discourage them.) If only someone had been able to look into the future and assure them they would never be able to, they might have turned their energies in other directions. (True. But perhaps they gained a lot of knowledge in the search.) They could have profited by direction from someone older and wiser.

If the police were able to have foresight about the exact time a crime was going to be committed, they could watch every step leading up to that moment and perhaps prevent the crime. (Perhaps if someone were to understand the reasons why the person needed to commit the crime, it could be prevented without any supernatural foresight. The person might be helped to get the good feeling he was looking for, but in a more constructive way.)

Somewhere I read that some adult was trying to teach a child to protect himself. Every time someone hit the child, the adult said, "Hit him back." Then a dog bit the child, and the child hit back, but so hard that he killed the dog. (The child must have felt like a terribly destructive person, even though he was only trying to protect himself.)

A dog doesn't feel like biting if anyone pays any attention to him. Sometimes if a dog comes running at you, thinking you are going to attack his house, he'll chase you and maybe bite you, but if you act friendly, or maybe call him by his name if you know it, he'll realize he doesn't need to be hostile. (I know.)

15. (How have you been these last three weeks?) O.K. I joined an ice hockey team. (Is it fun?) If it weren't, I wouldn't have joined. I made a goal. I wish it were Friday and the end of the week so there would be nothing but hockey.

[Pause.] It is hard to make a goal in hockey. It would
be good if two people could get close to the opposing goal.
One would distract the goalie into thinking he had the puck,
but would quickly pass it to the other who would slip it in.
It would be nice if you could pick it up in your hand and
toss it in. (It would be difficult if a third dimension were
added to the game.) Yes. Harder for the defense.

[Pause.] A car has two sets of gears. If both were in
low, it would have twice the power and control. It would be
necessary, of course, for the two sets to be in harmony, but
in any case, the car couldn't go faster than the slowest one.

16. I smashed up Father's car over the weekend. (Were you
hurt?) No. Father said he hoped it would teach me a lesson.
Mother didn't say anything. (Was she worried about your
being hurt?) Yes.

[Pause.] (What are you thinking?) I'm thinking about
various inventions that would stop a burglar from rummag-
ing through your things or coming through the door into
private quarters. You wouldn't lock the door to prevent his
entering. It would be better to let him come partially inside
and then trap him with handcuffs that snap down from out
of nowhere. (Why not lock the door?) Too much trouble to
keep locking and unlocking it yourself. You could cause a
person to be shocked electrically if they tried to get in, but
the shocks wouldn't be strong enough to really hurt anyone.
Only enough to discourage them so they wouldn't bother to
try to get in unless they were willing to bear some discomfort.

There is a maze in which there are two possible ways
in. One looks easy, the other difficult. If you take the easy
way, you get lost, but if you take the hard way, it leads right
to the center. (These things might also apply to attempts to
get close to people. Someone might try to discourage them
unless they were willing to take some shocks and difficulties.)
Yes.

It might be interesting to find a lake of mercury. One couldn't possibly sink in it. Someone tried to patent some shoes in which he could supposedly walk on the water. (A lake of mercury would certainly be good if you couldn't swim. It would be nice to find ways to stay on the surface and not get in over one's head unless one wanted to.)

A person could stand on a rubber mat or other insulation and get an electrical current only after it had passed through another person or had been shunted through some circuit which absorbed most of the voltage. A guy made some shocking coil and attached it to a strip of copper so that there was a low voltage but high amperage; he enjoyed blowing out fuses.

[Pause.] There is an exhibit at the University in which there is a light that blinks on and off. A condenser absorbs the power and then goes out.

[Pause.] I've got a voltmeter. It needs to be tested.

17. [Pause.] (What are you thinking?) It would be nice to have a cross bow. I wonder how much force it would take to penetrate a target? (That would depend on the target.) With a cross bow you can shoot a long distance.

I read a story about some people who lived in a city surrounded by a dome charged with electricity. They wanted to atom-bomb the world, and had to protect themselves from retaliation. The hero found his way in via an underground river. He found a way to make a similar small dome around himself, and then developed a counter-ray that would destroy it. (People might need to create similar dangerous shells around themselves for fear of retaliation for their hostile feelings.) Yes.

18. [*David spends the hour talking about the problem of constructing a chain hoist that would be strong enough to lift a motor out of a car. This is apparently a real project on*

which he is working. It is unclear how he is using it symbolically.]

19. We've been working some more on the chain hoist. (The
problems of lifting a heavy load seem important to you right
now.) No. The most important thing is to get the garage
cleaned up, but I'm not directly in charge of that.
[Pause.] I wonder if an iron pipe would bend under
the weight of a motor? (You seem concerned with whether
or not the thing you are counting on for support is able to
bear the weight. This problem is important in other aspects
of life too.) Yes. (I wonder if you feel yourself to be a very
heavy load for someone to bear?) I don't think so. [Laugh.]
It's funny to think of setting up a crane to lift someone else.
[Pause.] The University really has wonderful equipment of this sort, but it costs a great deal of money. (There
are jobs that just require expensive equipment. If one is going
to take on that kind of job, one has to accept that.)

20. [More about the chain hoist. No recording in detail.]

21. I read about a musical instrument in a magazine. There
were directions for making it, and I wish I had one. It is
operated from a distance and can give out tones under water.
(Apparently you are interested in communicating from a distance.)
Maybe I had the feeling that people caused my pain,
and I had better stay away from them. (Tell me about it.)
Once my grandmother burned some of my junk without telling me. (You might not have resented parting with some of
it if you had been allowed some choice in the matter.) Yes.
(People have to feel ready for parting with things important
to them.) Yes.
[Pause.] I'm thinking about the lady next door. Everyone is hostile to her because she has been hostile to them,

but she needed to be like that to protect herself from being hurt. Maybe nobody ever gave her anything voluntarily, and this is her way of getting back at the world for depriving her. Maybe she feels that anything she can get is her due. (I think quite probably that's it.)

22. I'm on a basketball team that has won all season. (Good!)
[*The boy talks all hour about locks, and how to make a key that will fit various combinations. He speaks with animation and excitement, trying to explain the process to me in great detail.*] I tried to explain all this to my mother, but she wasn't interested in understanding. I can see why, though. I'm not interested in her work either.

23. I'm still interested in the problem of making a key. [*Pause.*] When you have a safety deposit box, you have one key and somebody else has another. It always requires two people to open it. (That's for the safety of the depositor.) One should look into a locked box now and then to see what's been forgotten. Sometimes something turns up that could be useful. Other things can be thrown away.
[*Pause.*] I wonder whether it's better to have all your money invested in one company that might make a higher profit, but could also go broke, or in several to spread the risk. Maybe in a company of one's own where one has the control. Of course, there are certain people who are bound to lose everything, but sometimes a person has to hit bottom to know what values he can depend on.
[*Pause.*] Of course one isn't expected to move faster than light, but if the sun is moving a little in its orbit, and the earth around the sun, and the moon around the earth, wouldn't there be quite a lot of actual movement, even if the relative positions didn't change much? (There is probably a good deal of movement.) Do you think anyone will

get to the moon in my lifetime? (It's certainly a possibility. I wonder what he might find if he did?) It might be more habitable than it appears to be. On the other hand, it might not. The bear could go over the mountain and just find the other side of the mountain. If the bear was hungry, though, he might have his mind so much on getting food that he wouldn't see much else for a while.

Why can't animals reason? (Too busy looking for food, protecting themselves from enemies, and satisfying other bodily needs.) Animals follow their instincts. They get very ferocious when their needs aren't met. A rampant elephant, though, might be less dangerous than a person under the same circumstances. At least people can hear him coming.

24. [*Pause.*] I've been reading about a machine gun that's controlled by radar. Even if the pilot doesn't know just where the target is, the gun can hit it.

[*Pause.*] One could invent a lock that would be controlled by a motor. This could be regulated by dials from a considerable distance. (Both those things seem to be operated from a distance, without the operator having an accurate estimate of the position of the goal.) A contraption could be invented so that one person controlled the level, and another person the position of a moving target on that level. Then the bullet would overcome its tendency to go around in a circle or to fly off by centrifugal force. It could be directed accurately by the use of both centrifugal and centripetal forces.

[*Pause.*] A scientist was trying to make some kind of fluid. Instead he hit upon a metal substance that was strongly attracted to a certain star. The force of attraction was very strong. (Such a force could be used either constructively, for communication, or destructively to the pellet.) And the star. Perhaps as the pellet approached the star, it could acquire some of the power of the star to increase its own resistance. The result might be a situation in which the forces in each of the bodies would be more nearly equal.

25. [*Pause.*] I was thinking about a revolving door. Some people are scared of them. They are afraid of jumping out, and keep going round and round. (Others are afraid the door will stick and keep them trapped even if they want to get out.) Maybe they should be controlled mechanically so they'd have to go fast and spew the people out. (I think it's better for a person to have control of his own speed, even if he errs on the side of slowness.) I guess so.

With certain kinds of locks it isn't necessary to have just the right combination. There might be a lot of movement of the dial, going around several times, and just one click of the works to open it. Some locks are opened more easily than others.

[*Pause.*] I saw a movie about a man in jail who used the state printing press to make counterfeit money. I don't see what good money would do him in jail. (Maybe he just wanted to get back at society for keeping him there.) I can't think of any other reason.

26. [*Pause.*] I'm thinking about a machine gun. Pellets are shot out by springs. [*Pause.*] I saw a small gun on a charm bracelet. (It would seem large to a small creature.)

[*Pause.*] I wonder what it would be like to make a trip to the moon? On the side next to the sun, it is too hot to support life. On the opposite side it is too cold. There might be a small strip between the two where one could live if one had on the proper kind of space suit. (It strikes me that the situation you describe isn't unlike what you feel with people at times. It's either too hot or too cold, but if you keep well insulated, and keep in a narrow area, you might survive.) Maybe.

[*Pause.*] I've been watching a TV program about

space. The only part I don't like is the ad. There's a little man who isn't real, and is always introducing phony commercials into the middle of the program. (*Laugh.* That must be what you feel I'm doing when I try to make an analogy to what you are saying. You must have resented it just then.) No. Not at all. It was a good try. If you aren't always right you can't help it. It's your job to try. I don't resent it at all.

27. [*Not recorded.*]

28. [*Pause.*] (What are you thinking?) I'm going to see my grandmother. She doesn't like mother, but she's always glad to see me and my brother. (How do you feel about that?) I can understand it. I'm more like my father than like my mother. I'm not interested in the same kinds of things she is. She doesn't help me with problems like fixing a bike wheel. (Is she more interested in her work than in the family?) No.
[*Pause.*] Last time we were at Grandmother's we dug a tunnel toward the house from the yard. It was a problem to make supports so it wouldn't cave in. Maybe we will have to dig deeper. I don't know at what point we will hit rock. (Rock makes a firm base.) Yes, but you might have to hack through it to go deep enough.
Maybe you could make an underground room to store things that might be broken or get under people's feet. Maybe a tunnel could be made to actually enter the basement of the house. (A tunnel that communicates would have more function than one just made for the fun of digging although that has a function too. It's more useful if it leads somewhere.) Yes. True.

29. [*Pause.*] I'm going to save money for a German gun. I like to collect guns as a hobby. There's one automatic gun I was looking at. I think there must be some sort of spring that prevents the barrel from being bent as it shoots.
I've been reading a story about some people who hike

into central Mexico where they come on an Indian tribe. The Indian chief wants the man's pistol. If it were me, I'd fix it so the chief wouldn't want it. I'd make it so dangerous and uncontrollable that the chief would be afraid of it. If I were an Indian, though, that kind of strategy wouldn't work with me. I'd want it anyway.

[Pause.] It looked for a while as though they were never going to come out alive, but they finally did, and found a friendly tribe on the other side.

30. My school report was better than I expected. (I'm glad.)

[Pause.] I'd like to make some kind of a switch I've read about. A needle makes contact with a certain place on the rim that crosses a connection and builds up a pressure system. The trouble is, as soon as the contact is made, it breaks again before the pressure builds up very much. I'd like to devise a way to introduce a magnet that would hold the contact until a spring has built up enough strength to pull it away. Meanwhile the pressure in the system would have time to build up.

[Pause.] Those people in the story—if they set off in a small boat they might find themselves shipwrecked on an alien shore. That wouldn't be much of an adventure. (All adventure isn't necessarily found on exotic shores. There might be some pretty interesting places to explore right around home.)

[Pause.] I read another science fiction story about a man who was held prisoner in an underground kingdom. The king wanted to marry the man's wife, but this wouldn't be legal if he had the man killed. Therefore he was just holding him prisoner in the hope that he would die. There was a cabinet of food set into a wall with glass in front of it. The lights would be turned on in the cabinet, letting the man think the food was available to him, but when he got close to it, the light went off and he couldn't get at it. Some friends on the outside finally helped him to escape. (To be frustrated to death, in the constant anticipation of food that one can't reach must be a pretty horrible kind of death.) Yes.

31 and 32. [*Unrecorded.*]

33. I was wondering about the gears on a sports car. A big wheel goes at an even pace and controls a little wheel which turns many more times, at much more speed. I don't see how three or four gear wheels could have a common center if they were different sizes, because the controlling wheel would be different distances from them. [*He speculates about it, and decides it is done by chains so that the controlling wheel doesn't touch any of them.*]

34. I've been reading a story about a man who is pulled through the eye of the needle into another dimension. He couldn't get back, and couldn't take anything with him that wasn't living. Some people who underwent this lived in a cave. Others made a new civilization. Finally all the people came out of the cave because the new world was a relatively good place to live in. The needle had originally been made to perform like surgery—if a part of you was bad, it was passed into the other dimension and could be removed without pain. (Can you imagine yourself in such a situation?) No. [*Pause.*] You could have a series of worlds into which you could go exploring, but there would have to be well-marked signs how to get back.

[*Pause.*] In another story a doctor put the brain of a man into the body of a dog. The dog had difficulty communicating with anyone to let them know of his plight, but he finally got back his identity.

We had an appointment on Memorial Day, but David didn't show up. I called up later but found him out and talked to his mother. I told her that there had probably been a misunderstanding.

35. [*David comes in without comment about the missed appointment. Talks about a bad teacher at school who doesn't understand the boys and gets teased by them. The boys don't like him because he messes up their experiments. He wonders if one could drop an atomic bomb into an engine to push up the cylinder.*] (Atomic energy can be used for other than destructive purposes.)

    [*I slap a bug that has been flying around. He looks at me sadly.*] That bug wasn't very wise.

    [*Pause.*] If all the animals in the jungle banded together, they could probably drive all the men out of Africa. But they never will. Animals can't cooperate.

36. [*For the first time he talks realistically most of the hour, about his plans for the summer. He wants to get away into a kind of life that is less complicated than the one at home. At present he feels too many different kinds of problems are coming at him at once, and he would like to be confronted with only one at a time. I raise the problem between his mother and father, whereupon he suddenly reverts to symbolism. Talks about how one could fit hooks together in some way so that four objects are all in balance.*]

    David forgets the next appointment. I call and give him another.

37. I'm working on a sports car. Something is wrong with the muffler. I'm trying to get the weight out of it. I have to get it so it can go into lower gear. In this machine you have to do three operations at once with only two hands. [*Pause.*] I can't decide which is better, hydromatic or shift. In hydromatic you have to trust the machine more, and have less control yourself.

[Pause.] I read a story about somebody who has to wear armor against his relatives. He fights his way out of a hostile city, only to die on the desert from something he wasn't prepared to fight.

The next week he doesn't appear. I decide not to call. Much later his mother calls to tell me that David got a manual laboring job out of town. His father was supposed to notify me but forgot. Four days later the boy himself calls me for an appointment. He got into trouble on the job, breaking up some property.

38. [He looks very depressed.] (Tell me about it.) I was with another kid who was just mad at the world. The kid started breaking up a motor, and I just went along with it. I really don't know why. (How did it feel when you were doing it?) It was a pleasure! A real sense of relief! (Like letting go feelings that have been damned up inside.) Yes! [He has tears in his eyes.] I'm only frustrated that I got caught, and now everything is in a mess.

(Our problem at the moment is the feelings in you that make you want to smash things. You have been telling me in various different ways about violent, destructive impulses. Apparently acting upon them always gets you into trouble, but perhaps if we talked more about what goes on in you, we could discover more what they are all about.)

[He cries and sniffs loudly throughout the hour, ignoring my offer of Kleenex.]

I've been cheated. I've never been able to trust people. [Pause.] I see a spiral. (The spiral is like your feeling of anger and the tendency to provoke more anger that increases constantly. There seems to be set up a cycle of feeling unloved, leading to anger, which in turn leads to provocative behavior and more rejection. How did all this get started?)

As a small child I got punished because I would get interested in what I was doing and stay out too long. Mother would get angry, because she was worried. (Was it something like that on the job? The officials had forbidden you boys to play around the machines because they didn't want you to get hurt, but when you were forbidden, you got mad and wrecked their motor?) Maybe in both cases I was mad because they weren't really worried about me. What they really cared about was themselves and their property.

39. [*The following day.*] I'm going back to work out the price of the property I destroyed. (I'm glad to hear it.) I've always been mad, ever since I can remember. Nobody has ever been interested in what I'm interested in.

[*Pause.*] There is a machine with two cranks that fit together so that one rotates the other. At first they move together, but once the smaller one gets going, it might go faster and swing around and crush the hand on the other handle if it doesn't get out of the way. The handle is a useless part of the machine that just gets in the way.

[*Pause.*] People want to kill when they feel left out. A man wanted to kill all the men on his side. They should put him over on the other side where he would be killing the enemy. (A friend may be an enemy at the same time. The people we need most are often the ones we hate most if we feel rejected.)

Once a machine gets going, it's dangerous to keep on cranking it. (I believe you are telling me that now you have started to think about these things, I shouldn't push you.) I hadn't thought of that.

Maybe this goes back to the time when I had a dog that couldn't point. He had kidney trouble.

One might think things were bad because one didn't understand. I'm trying to think what I might have done to produce the situation in the first place. (Have you also looked for some of the reasons in the problems of other people?) [*He looks surprised and shakes his head.*] One might have to think things were bad, because it would be so much worse if they were *not* bad!

This is the end of the first year.

40. [*Things have been going well since the last visit. He went back to the job, but they didn't want him to stay so he took a trip with his parents. Since their return, he has been working for his father for a couple of hours after school.*] [*Pause.*] (What have you been thinking about?) Electric circuits. Everything has to fit together and be running simultaneously before anything can be accomplished. This takes infinite time. (Progress can be made all along the line. One doesn't have to wait till everything is solved in order to get anywhere.) I wish I knew all about electronics so I could start doing some research. (Researchers often start out with a very nebulous idea of what they are going to find. The important thing is a desire to study something. They build plans for future progress on whatever turns up as they go along.)

[*Pause.*] It's difficult to adjust the mechanism of interplanetary ships so as to allow for the varying pull from different planets. The best thing would be to be able to adjust things so that the various pulls would tend to aid the machine in its course. (The machine itself has an optimal relationship to the various stresses and strains. One would have to make adjustments to allow for the most efficient functioning of the machine, even if this meant that some alteration in its course was necessary.) The best way is to gear the machine to the strongest pulls from the strongest planets.

41. [*Pause.*] (What are you thinking today?) About my physics instructor. [*Jeering tone.*] The guys are constantly ribbing him, and he responds by blustering. There's no way to help him. In order to get him to change his behavior, one

would have to let him know he's in the wrong, and this would put him on the defensive. (He might have gotten into a destructive pattern of behavior as a result of perfectly legitimate feelings, but now the behavior is perpetuating the bad situation rather than improving it. If he didn't feel so criticized, he might be able to look at himself and do something about it.)

[Pause.] There is a kind of motor that always keeps going, but only one part of it.

[Pause.] I'm thinking of a situation just the opposite of when you are caught in quicksand and pulling up with one foot makes the other sink deeper. This is a situation in which if you lift one foot up, you can't get it down again, and pushing down keeps pulling you further and further up, as though you were on a ratchet. You yourself would be operating the lever, but couldn't stop cranking yourself up.

There are three kinds of people. First, the regular people who are on the level and so busy with their own affairs that they aren't trying to climb or anything else. Then, those who don't care about anybody, and are climbing but don't mind. Finally, those that are climbing but don't want to. They are getting further and further away from people and can't stop themselves. (How could this process be reversed?) That's what I don't know.

(One might not actually want to go back to the ordinary level once one had done some climbing. The important thing would be to know that one had some control over whether one wanted to climb or not.) Yes. Perhaps an awareness of the fact that there are unexplored regions around the earth might make it difficult to go back to a situation where unawareness existed, but such awareness might not be a problem unless it was out of hand.

Maybe the upward rise could be checked if someone reached up from below and brought one down, or if they even checked the momentum so that counteracting forces could be rallied. [Pause.] The person being pulled might have to help pull down the force that was pulling him up.

42. I'm thinking of a mechanism to transmit code, and a long-distance transmitter. (That sounds like what you have been using here. You seem to find it easier to transmit certain feelings and thoughts in a kind of code which we both often understand quite well, but at times get lost in. I wonder why it is so difficult for you to talk directly?)

[Pause.] An accelerator keeps pulling a particle along from ring to ring, increasing the speed as it goes along. No matter how fast the particle goes, the pull is still greater. (It is difficult to gauge the amount of current necessary to keep the particle progressing.) An ideal situation would be one in which the pull exerted is sufficient to bring the particle close to the source of the pull. When it is even with it, the pull could become a push.

I was reading a story from a space comic book. An old witch doctor helped the hero get back to civilization. The man had some sort of condition in which he couldn't control his muscles because there wasn't a proper connection with the nerves. He left civilization and went out into space where there was no pull of gravity, and devised a system where, by pushing buttons, mechanical hands did things to allow him to survive. The reason the connections weren't right was because he didn't think right about things. The doctor eventually showed him how, and he was able to tap a large reservoir of energy. At first he over-reacted to release from his helpless situation by certain destructive acts, but finally went back and used the energy constructively.

[Pause.] I took a flying lesson. It was great fun. There's a gauge in the plane that tells the degree to which the plane is tipped.

43. [Pause.] (What are you thinking?) I'm thinking about flying. The controls aren't working well. There is something wrong with the foot pedal that controls direction. Even if you push hard, there is scarcely any turning. [More in the same vein all hour.]

44. I'm thinking about a compass that operates by radio, but won't work in an electrical storm. It would be good if one could find a way to fix something so that the opposing forces of the electrical storm would neutralize each other. (It sounds as though you were talking about yourself—as though you might be talking about the forces of conflicting feelings.) I am talking about an electrical storm.

[Pause.] You should have three aerials, two to absorb the opposing forces, and the third which would block out only the rays that interfere, using the ones that are constructive.

[Pause.] On a rocket ship there are two dials to test the stability of the boat. Only one is working.

[Pause.] Sometimes gyroscopes fly apart and the pieces break holes in the wall and roof by centrifugal force when they get going too fast. There is a force always a little stronger than the capacity of the mechanism to keep up. Of course, if all the pieces flew in one direction, they could act as a powerful weapon of destruction. If the energy bound in keeping the mechanism in one position could be used to make it go forward, it would be good. Maybe one could accomplish this by finding what it was pushing against, and moving that.

45. [He spends the hour discussing the conflict between forces pulling out from the earth and gravity pulling toward it.]

If two planets were near each other, the forces from each might neutralize each other, so that a person between them wouldn't feel the force and could jump from one to the other. But he might get in a place hanging between, and be unable to move. (This would presuppose that he only worked by the pull of external forces on him.) He might be able to use a shield that would cut off the force from one direction, so that he could turn to the other at will.

46. [No recording in detail. He seems to be preoccupied with the problem of how much one can trust another person without becoming engulfed, and how to establish communication without having the current get so high that it blows out the circuit. How to shift from one gear to another and regulate speed without losing control of the machine.]

47 and 48. [David is talking in terms of radar apparatus, which I understand only very dimly. It is about running a current through a filament to a plate that moves a radio wire outward or inward toward the center.]

49. [More about radar, from which I get no meaning at all. He talks about making radar apparatus with another boy, and I don't know to what extent this is true or to what extent he is using it symbolically.]

50. [Pause. Some workmen outside the office are trimming branches off trees.] I hate to see trees cut down, but it doesn't matter, because there soon won't be enough people around to care. (What is going to happen to them?) The atomic bomb. (Sometimes a destructive force is discovered but is never unleashed. The one who has it realizes he will destroy himself as well as his enemy. It is best to think in terms of making explosions unnecessary.) The cobalt has too great an after-effect to make it practical.
[Pause.] I wonder what would happen if someone printing money for the government printed fifty bills, but

made a mistake in the records so he would be held account-
able for a hundred. Would anyone believe his story? (It is
conceivable that the man's boss would trust him or give him
a break even if there was a reasonable doubt. I can imagine
a situation where, even if he *had* tried to cheat the government, someone might give him a break.) [*I tell the story of
Jean Valjean.*]

I wonder how it would have been if someone had
given him a break earlier in life? (He might now have grown
up feeling that there was no use being trustworthy because
nobody cared about or trusted him anyway.)

51. A friend of mine has gotten a motorcycle. I'd like to
have one like it so I could ride over rough trails. I like to
explore back country.

If I knew I was going to live forever, I'd like to take
up breeding. I'd breed gorillas with intelligence commen-
surate with their strength and power. Or a breed of cat that
could resist ill treatment. (A cat would be in a bad way if it
felt mistreated by the same person who also fed and took
care of it.) The cat could get out and either forage for itself
in garbage cans or find people who know how to treat it
better. (Kittens might not be able to be as independent as
cats.)

Usually a mother cat protects her kittens from mis-
treatment, but now and then you find a mother cat who eats
her own kittens, or who isn't able to protect them from a
dog who kills them. Sometimes a dog will chase a cat if she
runs, but if she turns and faces him, the dog will run away.
(Cats have more powers of resistance than one always knows
about.) If they have been scared all their lives, they may not
realize they can fight.

[*Pause.*] I'd like to make experiments transmitting
radio waves through a vacuum. It might be better if a drop

of water got in and formed a mist. Even a fog is less empty than a vacuum.

[Pause.] If you had a substance and wanted to test its reaction to various chemicals, it would be better to divide it up into many small parts and test each part separately. Certain mixtures might be explosive, and you wouldn't want to use too much of the substance. You would want to be able to control the size of the explosion.

[Pause.] I went to see a fellow who has a motorcycle, but he wasn't there. Fellows like that have no sense of time. (Sometimes they are working on something important, and it's better for them not to be distracted by the passage of time.)

[Pause.] I wonder which trails have the least hazards, bumps, curves, etc. There's a motorcycle climb that's so steep nobody thought anyone could make it. One guy did, though. If he hadn't tried, he wouldn't have known he could do it.

The following week is a holiday. He doesn't show up.

52. Grade school is useless. Teachers don't teach in the right way. They don't try to understand what children really need. Often children can understand much more adult language than adults realize. (What do you think is responsible for the breakdown in communication between adults and children?) I don't know.

(I wonder if sometimes children feel so sure nobody cares to understand them that they don't bother to express themselves in a way the teacher can grasp. Sometimes, of course, teachers don't get what a child is trying to say, even if the child thinks he is making himself clear, but sometimes the child doesn't try hard enough to make himself clear. The important thing is that they both keep trying till they can get together.)

[*Pause.*] He begins to talk in a very complicated way about an oscillograph which produces a pattern that looks like a plus sign. He offers to draw a diagram for me, but even so, it means nothing to me. [*He laughs.*] It's pretty complicated, isn't it! (Yes. I find it very difficult to understand anything expressed in terms of electronics.)

Two days later I get word from the family that David has been picked up by the police as accessory to the theft of a jalopy by a couple of friends. He had no part in the theft, but knew it was stolen, had been working on it and joy-riding. He is being held in custody until the trial.

I interview both parents together, and obtain a certain amount of information about the current situation. All the boys involved have emotional problems. They all have great interest in sports cars, and a strong group solidarity. The father is furious because the boy's loyalty is first to the other boys rather than to his family. He won't allow them to have him released unless the others are too.

Both parents agree that David is a "natural" in mechanics. He has wanted to go to radio school in the evenings, but was not allowed to do so because of poor grades. Recently his attitude toward school has been improving. He has expressed a realization that it is necessary for him to get through high school. Just before the arrest, he was trying to work harder.

The father is clearly bewildered and finds it difficult to understand David's emotional needs and problems. The mother understands all too well, but is threatened by what she sees and becomes angry. She says she thinks the boy hates her and that she is trying to stay out of his way as much as possible.

I try to explain the degree of David's preoccupation with inner problems, and his real inability to concentrate in school. I also try to get across some idea of his identification with machines, and point out the fact that this sports car has meanings to him symbolically as well as realistically. I emphasize the importance of recognizing his interests and talents in mechanical things, to help him establish some real sense of identity.

We stay in communication for several days around the problem of getting the boys to trial. I talk with local officials, attempting to help them understand. The boys are finally released on parole temporarily, in the custody of their parents.

53. [*Interview before the trial. David puts on a very bland facade.*] (How has it been?) O.K., except that all the fuss and commotion was a waste of time. (Nevertheless, I think it is very lucky for you that you get caught when you break the law. It makes it so much more necessary for you to understand the real meanings of your behavior.)

[*The facade immediately ruptures, and he talks with real feeling for the rest of the hour.*]

They don't understand how important it is for me to stay close to a machine after I have put time and work into it. It is almost as though it belongs to myself. (I know that. But it is still important for you to be able to consider the reality of the situation as the rest of the world sees it.) To work in a machine shop on something that belongs to someone else has no meaning to me. (I understand how you feel.)

[*I tell him about my talk with his parents.*] (How do you feel about all this?) Sad and depressed. I don't really hate my mother, but I don't feel any contact with her. I'd like to get closer to my father, but I don't know how. I've only recently realized that I *must* work at school, even if I'm not particularly interested. I'm never going to be in this kind of a jam again. (I do hope not!)

The court puts him on probation for a year and takes away his driver's license.

5

Starting the Translation

"It might not be necessary to stay away from the painful ones."

Tʜᴇ ᴘʀᴇᴄᴇᴅɪɴɢ ғᴏʀᴛʏ-ᴇɪɢʜᴛ ɪɴᴛᴇʀᴠɪᴇᴡꜱ, conducted almost entirely in mutual use of "code" language, comprise the first year and a half of treatment. David plunged almost immediately into a discussion of his thoughts and feelings, but had still to determine the extent to which he was willing to have them understood. Although he occasionally made factual statements and superficial comments about his outside activities, he obviously did not wish discussion to proceed on the basis of reality situations, and discouraged any attempts of mine in that direction. The time was used to express indirectly his doubts and fears about relationships, his terrible loneliness, and frightening impulses. He found it necessary to test various attitudes of mine over and over, and to struggle against the developing transference.

Meanwhile, I was repeatedly faced with a series of technical decisions. It has already been shown that topics offered by the boy for discussion often had clear meanings on a number of different levels. In conducting therapy, I constantly had to make choices as to what aspect of the material presented was most relevant to any particular moment. At the beginning, it seemed most important to pick up on the level of his interpersonal frustrations and problems of trust, avoiding interpretations of deeply unconscious material until such time as concrete clues from David should indicate evidence of a stable relationship between us. For instance, in the nineteenth interview he wondered "if an iron pipe would bend under the weight of a motor." Although a discussion of fears about impotence might have been approached in code even this early in treatment, fears about loss of support in the therapeutic relationship seemed more significant within the context of the total material.

Until well into the second year of therapy, my attempts to translate the boy's code into more direct expressions of feeling were made very tentatively, and were accepted by him very gradually. For a number of months, my occasional analogies to his symbolism about "sighting instruments" and "periscopes" (9 and 13) were ignored, as was a direct statement that I recognized talk about unstable chemical compounds as an expression of unhappiness about my impending vacation (14). However, when I later made an analogy between his ideas about possible approaches to a maze, and his attempt to get close to people, he accepted it with a brief "yes" before passing on to the next topic (16). Whether he ignored or accepted them, I continued to offer periodic translations; finally a comment that he was expressing interest in methods of communicating from a distance brought forth his first direct uncoded speculation about the origins of his defensiveness (21).

Sometimes, however, a translation threatened to clarify feelings which he considered too dangerous; he then repulsed the interpretation and rebuked me for it. For instance, it was too painful to realize that his story about a man's need for insulation and restriction to a narrow area on the moon might be a way of expressing his fear of relationships. The response to my interpretation was his comment on a TV program. "The only part I don't like is the ad. There's a little man who isn't real, and is always introducing phony commercials into the middle of the program" (26). When he could finally use an hour to talk realistically about plans for the summer, he reverted immediately to code at mention of problems between his mother and father (36).

David and I had been working together for a year before I felt I could cut into the beginning of a reversion to symbolism with an interpretation and a request for direct examination of the feelings involved (38). He responded temporarily, but when, in the next interview, we touched on the intensity of his ambivalence, said in ominous tones, "Once a machine gets going, it's dangerous to keep on cranking it" (39).

At the beginning of the second year of therapy, I had occasion to mention his use of a code and to ask why he couldn't talk more directly. The response was again a clear warning for me not to meddle. "An accelerator keeps pulling a particle along from ring to ring, increasing the speed as it goes along. No matter how fast the particle goes, the pull is still greater" (42). Again, when I suggested that in describing an electrical storm he might be talking about conflicting feelings, he replied haughtily, "*I* am talking about an electrical storm" (44). For roughly six months longer he continued to use the code almost exclusively until finally able *himself* to suggest that "children can understand more adult language than adults realize" (52). Although the work was interrupted at this point by external circumstances, it was the turning point at which he was willing to begin a consistent attempt at translation.

David's first acceptance of an interpretation from me occurred in the following session when he was willing to say, "I thought of that myself" (54). This seems to have been the beginning of a mutual attempt to translate his symbolism and discuss ideas directly. When talk about controlling high voltage clearly represented his own problem, the boy accepted a challenge to verbalize the idea in more simple terms, and expressed the difficulty he felt in controlling a desire to break probation (55). A month later came a direct statement of his difficulty in using words, and his appreciation of my value in helping him to "fit in the missing parts" of his thoughts (59). From this point on, his use of a code language was openly recognized between us, and symbolic expressions were given the character of more voluntary allegorical communications except when he was dealing with particularly frightening subject matter.

Symbolic discussion of sexual problems was obviously taking place all along but, as mentioned before, I made no attempt at direct translation of sexual symbolism until the boy himself gave evidence of readiness. He did so finally in commenting, "Nobody wants to go beneath the surface. . . . The teacher is unmarried; perhaps that's the reason. (. . . Maybe she doesn't consider the class ready to talk openly about it, although she knows problems of sex are important to everyone.) [Pause.] "I'm ready to take my motor to the shop" (65). A few interviews later I could translate fears of "leaking oil tanks" into a discussion of early bed-wetting (70), and finally begin to interpret his resistances (73). By the end of the second year of therapy,

David had begun to examine the dynamics of his conflicts and even, occasionally, to discuss directly with me his feelings about our relationship.

As they evolved in a series of changing images, David described his ideas about the participants and interactions in a therapeutic relationship. He conceptualized the respective roles of doctor and patient, the nature of the relationship, and the process by which changes are gradually effected. The development of trust and his personal reactions to the experience of therapy are at first indirectly and later openly expressed.

At first, the interactions were visualized in mechanistic terms. Doctor and patient were a "Morse Code machine" (12) or "long-distance transmitter" (42) and a "decoding machine." In the relationship between them, one machine was portrayed as more powerful, carrying responsibility for maintaining control over the safety of a mutual operation, but exerting this control only when the other gave evidence of inability to function on its own. "Two motors in a team, one to go fast, and the other to supply extra power *only when needed*" (13). A machine gun which had "one person [controlling] the level and the other a moving target on that level" (24). The subject material for therapy was held in a "safety deposit box" which, for protection of the depositor, cannot be opened without two keys (23). Doctor and patient were "a big wheel going at an even pace, [controlling] a little wheel that turns many more times, at much more speed" (33). It was not quite clear which member of the combination should control the pace of operations, however. At one moment the revolving door should be "controlled mechanically to go fast and spew the people out" (25). On the other hand, when an "accelerator" pulled a "particle" too fast (42), or the man got impatient and "looked a gift horse in the mouth" (96), they met with opposition. The ideal to be achieved was seen as a combination of two equal members, working in unison toward a common goal. ". . . two motors in complete accord, hitched together for maximum efficiency" (79).

Gradually, although the patient continued to be portrayed as a machine, the therapist assumed human form as the "good mechanic," and finally interactions began to take place between two people. Every now and then, the boy spoke directly for himself, but usually his observations were expressed through an intermediate figure or in general terms. In one way or another, his concepts of therapist and patient emerged.

According to David, the ideal therapist is objective, willing to listen, and honest in his criticism. He has a consuming interest in the therapeutic problem itself and shows scientific curiosity with perfectionistic craftsmanship. Primary satisfactions come not from money but from the knowledge that he has done a good job and is being helpful. He is, however, subject to benign human failings. "He concedes that [an] idea itself has value and evaluates it before passing judgment" (55); "I don't just tell him he's a good guy; I at least listen" (74). "I don't mind working out the proof for him because he's really interested in the kind of work I do" (105). The good doctor, like the good mechanic ". . . likes to see the wheels go 'round . . . is primarily interested in creating an intricate mechanism and wants it appreciated for its structure rather than its monetary value" (147). He "drills slowly and enjoys doing a good job" (63), and is "interested in his work and likes to make repairs so that they will last, even if it takes a long time. He doesn't care for the money" (62). "This mechanic, [however], has certain amusing characteristics. He often says things that people know already . . . but his friends understand him and treat him with affection" (62).

In contrast to this idealist, the patient appears tiresomely cautious and bungling, suspicious, devious, and secretive. He needs to make endless divisions of material into small parts, "testing each part separately to control the size of the explosion" (51). In "measuring four feet with a one-inch ruler," he is apt to "make the line crooked unless someone keeps bringing him back to the right level" (156). He tries the patience of the therapist by "sitting back and resting" between bouts of work (71), and would like to get information without admitting he had gotten it (163). No matter how much closeness he allows in some areas, he must prevent any "one person from knowing the whole" of him (187).

In the interactions between therapist and patient, roles are explicitly defined. Therapist is to provide opportunity for the patient to make use of his professional judgment and experience without exercising coercion. Patient must furnish the material for discussion and try to make it useful to himself after it has been processed. The work is a cooperative venture. Emergency measures may occasionally be called for if imminent danger threatens the patient or the interaction, and over these the therapist has control. He alone is able to "gauge the tolerance of the machine" (87). "A nation dedicated to peace must be ruthless with anyone who isn't until things have quieted down" (88). On the whole, however, the therapist's major function is to accept the proffered material and evaluate it without prejudice. "The patient has to dig up the garbage and the analyst has to sort it. . . . He has to rummage around until he finds what will be useful to the patient, and hand it back to him all cleaned up so that he can use it" (77).

In a therapeutic milieu, created by mutual functioning on this basis, something can happen. David sums it up in analogy. ". . . It's like when you want to split the current along a wire. There is a flow of electrons, and no force could make them divide, but if you put a certain potential on each part of the wire, then the electrons flow according to the

potential. You can't make a person do anything by employing force—only by making him want to. It's like putting on
first one potential and then another. He doesn't have to respond to the first, but if he does, it opens up the second. He
doesn't have to respond to that either, but it's there and he
can if he wants to. At any point he can draw back or go
ahead. It's just like human motivation; it comes along if
there isn't force, but just potential" (132).

From the beginning, the boy indicated an awareness
that communication of basic feeling is the therapeutic aspect
in a relationship. He also sensed the ambivalence in his
method of sending messages in obscure form. Although partially intended to keep the other person from understanding
his true feelings, he was aware that this method also had a
function of motivating both himself and the other to relate
to the emotional component of his intellectual formulations.
(This factor has not been stressed in the literature.) According to David, if one communicated directly, "there wouldn't
be any problem, and it's the problem that makes it interesting" (71). "Since I've been talking in English, it doesn't seem
so important. When a person has to penetrate the code, he is
bound to pick up the feelings behind it" (188).

He seemed to perceive that when emotional messages
are registered upon a receptor, changes take place in the
transmitter. "If you can transmit a thought to someone else
without putting it into words, a contact can be made that can
help clarify the thoughts and feelings that can't be verbalized" (57). "A person wants to find out about himself because of a security need, but when he does, he finds it isn't
necessary any more. When he finds he can communicate
with someone he trusts, then it doesn't matter any more
what it was he needed to talk about" (74). To sum up this
boy's view of the therapeutic process, "There was a small
universe in a capsule. You could make something happen by
communicating with it" (152).

The factors necessary to establish contact were not completely clear in his mind. David inclined to the feeling that communication can only take place between two identical psychic mechanisms. For some time he visualized contact as an indirect, non-verbal force, emanating from a machine, mediated by "waves" of some kind, and recorded upon a machine of identical construction with properly geared receiving apparatus. Even when the images took human form, there was a concept that the therapist "plugged in" on thoughts and feelings according to an intuitive recognition of the magic moment, based upon a similarity of psychic processes (154, 161). In a later metaphorical reversion to the mechanistic imagery, he described "two identical computers that have the same information fed into them and come out with identical answers" (214). A feeling for the need of psychic oneness apparently remained unchanged.

The boy was nevertheless aware that trust is an essential element in the promotion of real communication. Even at a relatively early stage of relationship to the therapist, he could make a direct expression of confidence. "I'm amazed at the clarity with which you understand my thoughts and help me fit in the missing parts . . . it's hard to know which ones to start on, but it might not be necessary to stay away from the painful ones any more than the neutral ones" (57). Rather surprisingly, at frequent intervals David was able openly to admit a consistent feeling of trust. Perhaps he could speak directly because feelings of this kind were uninvolved in the transference. At my suggestion, he considered the possibility that he might be hiding other feelings. ". . . I was just thinking how *much* I trust you, but maybe I was just covering up such thoughts" (76). There is no evidence, however, that his faith was not sincere. It was frightening at times for him to realize that he had involuntarily revealed so much of himself (81), but the "good mechanic" had seemed to him a trustworthy figure—"the

only one whose word I'll take" (87). Later on, he stated
unequivocally, "There is trust between us. We can work
together without holding too much back" (188). He recognized the importance of this feeling in his ability to communicate. "All I needed was to find someone trustworthy"
(188). Of course, it was still necessary to be wary, to check
and recheck his perceptions, but nothing occurred to alter
his attitude materially. "Actually, there does come a time
when one can say with assurance, 'This person will not damage me'" (201).

David also recognized that if a person has once experienced the penetration of his deep emotional isolation
by a sense of being truly understood, permanent changes
occur in his resistance to human relationships. When he
finds that his most frightening thoughts and feelings are not
as intolerable to others as he had hitherto imagined, he may,
with increasing ease, dispense with patterns of total withdrawal from human contact. Loneliness may at times recur if
the relationship is removed, but never of the same quality.
"It's like sending a current through a plastic block full of
iron filings. Once a path has been established through the
resistance, it becomes easier each time for the current to
follow it, and the resistance decreases in geometrical proportion. After a while, the resistance might be minimal. If you
stop sending the current through, the resistance builds up
again; never to the same extent as at the beginning, though"
(120).

---

54. I have spent most of the week digging in the basement
to make a work room. The biggest part of the job is carrying
away the dirt. So much has to be done before there is any
possibility of its being useful. (There seems to be a similarity
between that and the work you are doing here.) I thought of
that myself. (One of the things you seem to fear is that while

digging you will hit a stick of TNT and blow the place up.) [*Smile.*] Yes. That's it.

The next week he neither shows up nor calls to cancel.

55. (What happened last week?) I forgot. (I suspect that you have some rather mixed feelings about coming here. You seem to want to come, and make good use of the time, but you often forget, particularly just after you have said something that seems significant to you.) I like to come, unless it interferes with something I want to do more.

[*Pause.*] I'm working on a problem in electronics, but I can't really do it properly unless I can think of a way to handle high-voltage wires. (You often talk to me about things that seem similar to the problems you are having within yourself. For instance, I imagine the problem of controlling high voltage in yourself is important right now. Why don't you try to talk to me more directly about that today?)

It is hard for me to control the desire to just take a car or bike and go for a ride. Nobody has the right to keep me from doing it unless they can prove I can't handle them safely. (You are talking about external restrictions on your behavior, which must be hard to bear. However, I think what really concerns you more is the fight against internal impulses.) Maybe.

[*Pause.*] There's no use trusting anyone. Nobody really wants to understand my ideas or cares whether they are workable. (Nobody?) Well, there's one mechanic who is different. He may show me that my idea won't work for some reason, but he concedes that the idea itself has value, and he evaluates it before passing judgment. (I believe that with me, too, you would like to feel free to talk over and evaluate your ideas and feelings about yourself, but you are afraid of being rejected before you start.)

[*Pause.*] I'm thinking how big to make an oscillograph. If it is too small, it's hard to read. If it's too big, it's unwieldy. (I'd like to hear more about that next time.)

I am away for two weeks with a sudden illness.

56. [*The boy makes no comment on my absence. He talks factually about what he has been doing. At the very end of the hour he mentions that he and a friend have been working on an oscillograph.*]

57. [*He starts talking even before he is seated.*] Is mechanical ability inherited? (There are lots of factors involved, both hereditary and envrionmental. How do you feel about your own talents in that direction?) Hereditary and exposure. Dad always has tools lying around. (Maybe you have a desire to be like your father.) No. Not particularly. But being able to do mechanical things gives me a "place." It's something that makes me feel I am somebody.

I have trouble with things involving the need to use words. In mechanical things, and other ways too, I think I have a certain intuition. If I can work things out without the intermediate step of using words, the intuition can be turned into a feeling which can be applied to similar problems. It is difficult to communicate verbally, but if you can transmit a thought to someone else without putting it into words, a contact can be made that can help clarify the thoughts and feelings that can't be verbalized.

[*Pause.*] I'm amazed at the clarity with which you understand my thoughts and help me to fit in the missing parts.

[*Pause. He goes into a long dissertation about the curve of the universe.*] But what is beyond? I have visual pictures when I'm talking that I can't describe.

[*Pause.*] An ant is walking on an orange. The ant can't see the orange as it really is, but someone inside the orange can't see what the ant sees, nor can someone farther away. In order to see from all angles, one would have to be on a point that one can't imagine.

[*Pause.*] I don't think light is the fastest thing. Thoughts can be faster than light. Slowing them down to the point where they can be put into words makes it less useful. But maybe it's a good idea to have two people working on them rather than one.

Some thoughts might not be as acceptable as others, but I don't believe a person would have to be repulsed by someone else's thoughts, or destroyed by them. A person might understand, even if they didn't agree—at least might understand what they meant to the other person, and accept their validity on that basis. It is hard to know which ones to start on, but it might not be necessary to stay away from painful ones any more than neutral ones.

[*At the end of the hour he smiles at me spontaneously, and turns at the door to tell me about something he is making at school.*]

58. [*David took a flying lesson in the morning. He talks all hour about flying and airplanes, mostly about testing how one would know where one was heading if the plane was upside down.*] How could one tell whether the mechanism was capable of maintaining its course and equilibrium?

59. I've got a job in a filling station working weekends and part time during the week. If I save during the year that my license is suspended, I'll have almost enough for the down payment on a sports car. (That's great!)

[*Pause. Smile.*] A friend of mine says that psychiatrists have to be off their rockers themselves in order to understand their patients. I don't agree, though. I think all that's necessary is a certain amount of intuition, and that's not crazy.

[*Pause.*] A friend of mine has a 1934 car. With just a

little work, I think I could put it in good running order. [*He talks a little about various makes of cars.*] (I don't understand enough about cars to be able to follow you, but I know they are important to you.) It doesn't matter. [*Pause.*] But I was just thinking—traveling in cars at high speeds can be very dangerous.

People who ride in jalopies are "white trash." (What do you man by that?) They are sloppy people without intellectual interests who live in pig pens and are "different." Not the kind of people you would like to associate with. (I doubt whether you really believe people are trash just because they are "different," and I doubt whether you think I do. Why do you suppose it is, though, that some people have to make themselves live in houses that are uncomfortable even to them, and unacceptable to a lot of other people?) I feel insecure in any other sort of environment. I just don't feel able to live up to more exacting standards. I guess people like me defy society for wanting to pour us into a mold.

[*Pause.*] I don't like jazz. I like some of almost every other kind of music I've heard, but jazz seems a cacophony of sounds. I think an orchestra where everyone is on his own, with no regard for blending with others, makes for bedlam. When I don't like a certain kind of music, I can just remove myself from it emotionally and let it flow around me without its making any impact. (You can also do this with words unpleasant to hear.) Yes. (Do you ever find that you have removed yourself so successfully that you can't distinguish when the music has changed?) No.

60. I've got a chance to buy a car. It needs lots of repairs to make it safe for dirt trails.

Few people get hurt in sports cars. If they have an accident, they are usually killed. I wish there were some invention that would make it possible to have the momentum dissipated without dislodging the rider from the car if he suddenly hits something that stops it.

61. I got the sports car, but it needs a lot of work. [*Pause.*] I've been reading science fiction. Some people go in a space ship to a place where there are a lot of primitive people. It turns out they weren't really primitive. They had just voluntarily reverted to primitive ways because civilization seemed more complicated and unsatisfactory. [*Pause.*] I wonder about the gears on the car. [*Pause.*] There's a tall, blond, good-looking boy at school who has a car something like mine. He isn't sure whether it just hasn't learned to work yet or whether it has shot out so much stuff that it is tired. (I'd like to hear more about it next time.)

62. I'm making a new seat for the car. [*Pause.*] There ought to be a better way of arranging the gears. (Often when you are talking about the sports car I think you really are talking about it, and at other times the things you say seem more related to the problems you have with yourself. It isn't always easy to know which is which.) [*He nods.*] I certainly talk in devious ways, don't I? But I can't seem to think any other way sometimes.

[*Pause.*] I think if the people who built the car had done a better job, the frame wouldn't be so easily bent.

[*Pause.*] I know a good mechanic who is interested in his work and likes to make repairs so they will really last, even though it may take a long time. He doesn't care for the money, and often charges less than other mechanics charge for similar work. If he hasn't got the right tool, he makes one that will be exactly right rather than make shift with an inferior one. (He must really believe in his materials, and not want to waste them with slap-dash work.) This good mechanic has certain amusing characteristics; he often says things that people know already. He is probably used to working with people who aren't very intelligent and have to have things spelled out for them. His friends understand him, though, and treat him with affection.

[*Pause.*] I will have to get the valves straightened out pretty soon. (Do they leak?) [*He plunges into a complicated metaphor involving valves, push rods, etc. Ends with the comment that you have to be sure the connecting rods are O.K.*]

63. [*More about front and rear suspension on the sports car. More about the good mechanic.*] He drills slowly and with precision. He enjoys doing a good job, and likes people who appreciate his stories.

64. [*Last week he "forgot" to come. He makes an obscure comment which conveys the idea that now and then he needs to test his freedom. Then he talks on about the sports car.*]

(Your father has made an appointment. Is there anything the matter?) I can't think of anything. I'm going to pass everything in school, and I don't think he objects to the amount of time I'm spending on the car. I have to build it up practically from scratch.

The father neither shows up nor calls to cancel.

65. I'm still working on the car. I've finished with the motor and have to start on the frame.

[*Pause.*] I have a friend who got into trouble with the police. His father has no understanding of the problem, and won't send him to anyone for therapy. My friend talked to the police psychiatrist. He wants as much help as possible. He drove without insurance, and although he knew what the consequences might be, the impulse was so strong he didn't care. He felt resentful toward his father for having broken promises and not being willing to try to understand his needs.

(It does seem at times that an impulse is stronger than judgment. It's also understandable that a boy might want to strike out against his father if he feels deprived. However, although he did succeed in punishing his father, acting out his anger seems to have backfired on him as well. He doesn't seem to be able to count on his father for much awareness or help, and perhaps he will have to battle it through alone, hard as that is. It is important that he realize a need for help. If his father will not pay for treatment, there are ways in which he can get it for himself.)

The police psychiatrist doesn't waste any time finding out what's going on. He just tells him right off what's wrong with him. (I imagine the boy has heard a good deal about what's wrong with him, but perhaps not quite enough about what's right with him.) He was afraid the doctor would tell his parents what they talked about, but I assured him he wouldn't.

[Pause.] We have a class called sociology at school. It's really a kind of half-baked psychology class where you are supposed to discuss problems but in a very superficial way. Nobody wants to go beneath the surface. (There are only a few people who really care to go beneath the surface.) The teacher is unmarried; maybe that's the reason. (You feel the teacher is herself afraid to discuss subjects like sex. Maybe she doesn't consider the class ready to talk openly about it, although she knows problems of sex are important to everyone.)

[Pause.] *I'm* ready to take my motor to the shop. The cylinder needs to be bored for a bigger piston.

[Pause.] The family are thinking of moving to a farm. (How do you feel about that?) O.K. (I should be very sorry if this meant you could no longer come to see me.) Oh no! I'd keep coming anyway. I can take the bus.

[*Pause.*] There's a dog in our neighborhood who barks all day unless his mistress is there. How glad everyone will be to get rid of him! [*Pause.*] His mistress took him to the vet. There was a female dog there that looked like him, and the vet brought her out by mistake. His mistress didn't know the difference.

66, 67, and 68. [*Unrecorded. He talked mostly in what seemed to be realistic terms about the sports car, his plans for moving, and his thoughts of going to a new school. Doesn't seem to care much where he lives, and obviously doesn't expect to make any friends at school anyway. He is to be gone for two weeks on vacation.*]

69. (How was your vacation?) Fine. I've been learning etching. [*He describes the process of making plates with acid.*]
    (Your father called me about getting you into a military training program. Is that his idea or yours?) Mine. I'd like to get in. (How do you think you might feel in an authoritarian set-up where you have to take orders no matter how you feel about them?) I don't think I'd mind. Taking orders doesn't bother me if they are sincere, impersonal, and if what is said is what is really intended. What I object to are orders that are given with the unconscious purpose of getting rid of me by telling me to go and do something, or to express irritation, or to express other attitudes on the part of the giver that have nothing to do with the situation at hand.

70. A guy brought his motorcycle to be fixed. The motor is too strong for the frame, which gets bent front and back. [*Pause.*] There's another motorcycle that isn't very practical. The oil tank is too low, and if you go over rough ground it leaks.
    (Recently you have been talking about machines in

which the frame is vulnerable in certain ways, frequently in
ways where you feel there will be a leak. I wonder if you are
again talking about yourself, and fears about bodily functions?) I never had fears about physical defects. If I have
fears, they have to do with mental defects, although those
could affect physical functions. (I wonder if this fear of leaks
could be connected with the bed-wetting you used to do
when you were younger?) I don't know.

[*Long pause.*] (Tell me more about your fears of mental defect. What do you mean by that?) I don't know. (I've
never had the least worry about your intelligence.) Neither
have I. I think my school difficulties had to do with a feeling
that adults didn't understand what was important. If they
told me school was important, it was just that they didn't
know what was *really* important. I just withdrew my interest
from school into daydreams. Mother told me school was important, but I could tell she hated it herself.

[*Pause.*] It's funny, isn't it, how you can pick up a
person's unconscious feelings by intuition. You aren't conscious of it yourself, but you kind of know. (Yes. But it's
good to bring unconscious awareness up into consciousness.
It is used more effectively there.) Maybe it's used more
effectively when it's unconscious.

The important part of the problem is whether something is due to unconscious knowledge or an unconscious
fear that isn't realistic. (What do you mean?) Well, for instance, we know that a dog senses when people are afraid of
him, but do we know how? Is it because he perceives involuntary cues such as vague movements away from him, or do we
think his ability is something magical—like natives who
"know" that volcanos are going to erupt because the gods
are angry at them. This latter kind of knowledge is based on
unconscious fears that are transmitted from generation to
generation. Whether one accepts it as true depends on how
one feels about the person who teaches it. (Which kind do

you think you derived unconsciously from your mother?)
I think the first kind. (I wouldn't be surprised.)

71. [*Pause.*] (What are you thinking?) I'm working on the
sports car. Something is wrong with the generator, but I
think it will run for a while on the battery. I don't know
whether the generator broke down because of some internal
defect, or because I didn't hitch the wires together right. The
mechanic calls the machine "an old wreck," but I don't care
just so long as it can be driven.

[*Pause.*] (Have you done anything more with your
etching?) No. I got it all laid out, but I haven't gotten around
to doing it. I was planning to make a picture like the model
in the book, but I think perhaps I'd rather make my own.
(That would be much more interesting.)

I'd like to make a machine that would transmit a picture automatically onto the plate. You could transmit the
picture to the machine, and the machine would transmit it
to the plate. (Why go through all that? Why not draw
directly onto the plate?) Then there wouldn't be any problem, and it's the problem that makes it interesting. Anyway,
my way of working is to do a lot of work all at one time and
then sit back to rest in between.

(You have a tendency to want a machine as inter-
mediary between yourself and someone to whom you want to
transmit a picture.) That way if it doesn't come out right you
don't have to take responsibility for it. (True. But if it *does*
come out right, you don't get the credit.) I never thought of
it that way. That's a good point.

[*Pause.*] I've been hearing about Leonardo da Vinci.
He was one who developed his unconscious potentials to the
fullest. Isn't it too bad that the development of potentials
is often such a painful process. It would be better if man
could create out of a desire to create rather than out of a need
to rid himself of pain. (The motivation to get rid of pain is

a strong one which is often necessary to get the process started. Once it is started, a person can realize the satisfaction of creativity for its own sake. Then *that* motivation may be equally strong to keep the process in motion.)

The development of potentials is a kind of birth process, isn't it? (Yes.) But I think it's better to let things emerge out of the unconscious without being subject to conscious controls that might inhibit spontaneous expression of something powerful and good. (That's true. On the other hand, it is just as well to have some conscious control over things that might be hurtful and destructive to oneself. By bringing feelings into consciousness, one is in a better position to sort out which is which.) I guess that's so. I'm not sure.

[*Pause.*] Mother and I nearly had an accident. A man pulled out illegally from the curb and just missed us. He was in the wrong, so he had to bluster and act aggressive. (Feeling in the wrong does have a tendency to make people act like that sometimes.)

72. I've been reading a book about telepathy. I don't know whether I believe in it or not. (People universally have a desire to be able to communicate and be understood. The idea of communicating without having to verbalize appeals to you.) Yes. (The way I look at it, nothing has as yet been either proved or disproved about extrasensory perception. However, if two explanations of a phenomenon are possible, one of which we know to be true from our own experience, the other depending on a magical interpretation, we are safe in assuming that the more logical is the explanation.) Both may be logical, but based on a different way of looking at things.

[*Pause.*] I still think thought transmission is a possibility. (Maybe it is. But do you remember in Sherlock Holmes when he appeared to be reading Watson's mind?)

Yes. (The mind reading turned out to be based on a knowledge of Watson's associations and ways of thinking.) Mother says that when I was little I could read her mind. Maybe it was just sensitivity to her feelings that I picked up by tones of voice, etc. (I wouldn't be surprised. What do you think you can pick up about her feelings at present?) I don't know.

[Pause.] I wonder if someone sensitive to telepathy because of psychoanalysis could tell whether a thing was real or only the result of subjective feelings. (One can only hope to tell by seeing how the thought fits in with other thoughts and feelings by way of associations.) The trouble is, it takes so much time! I wonder if it's worth it? You need one lifetime to work things out, and another lifetime to act on what you've discovered!

(In a chemical experiment, often the longest part is setting it up—putting together the equipment, testing electrical circuits, seeing that precautions have been preserved, etc. After all that is done, the experiment itself may not take very long. I realize you have felt it necessary to do a lot of testing, and set up a lot of precautions in therapy. This has been necessary to facilitate working on what you feel is more interesting material. We only meet once a week, but things don't stop between sessions. Processes go on once they have been begun, and what seems to be time lost may not really be so.)

The next week he "forgets" to show up.

73. (It's funny about your forgetting last week. You were just talking about how little time there was, and then you forgot the next hour. I wonder if we can understand that.) I don't know.

(It seems to me that perhaps if you become aware that you feel a need for something, you then immediately have to prove to yourself that you don't need it. I've noticed before that when you have talked about something particularly important to you, you forget the next hour. It's as though you were afraid you might not always be able to get what you need, so why let yourself want it.) [*Smile.*] I guess that's it. (Does this kind of thinking operate in any other department of your life?) [*Long pause.*] I can only think of one other department—Love.

(I wonder what makes you feel it is so impossible for anyone to love you?) It isn't that. But when a person is young, he wants a partner only long enough to get to know him.

[*Pause.*] In the eighth grade I was going with a girl— but suddenly we weren't going together any more. I didn't understand what had happened. (You felt hurt and rejected.) Yes. (Whether or not this episode was the primary cause of the feeling, it must have reinforced a fear that you were unlovable, and that any relationship important to you might be lost. You figured you'd better withdraw from any need. "I quit before I'm fired.") [*Smile.*] Yes.

Maybe this feeling started when my brother was born and I had to share my mother. Maybe this is only something I've read, but it could be true. (You apparently felt if you couldn't have all of her, you'd have none.) Yes.

[*Pause.*] At a moment like this I could disappear into nothingness. [*Pause.*] I have the image of gears with their crank shafts all twisted around each other. (Do you think this might express a feeling that being "one" with your mother must involve physical contact—a sexual relationship?) [*Pause.*] I'm not aware that I want to be with my mother. (You do have a longing to be close to her?) [*Pause.*] I don't *want* a sexual relationship with my mother. (I'm sure you don't consciously. But there seems to be a fear that feelings of closeness must involve physical closeness.)

[*Pause.*] It might be that I felt my father and mother were not close, and that I had to take my father's place. (This is an idea that might be both very attractive and very frightening to a child.) I can see how it would be attractive, because a child feels secondary to all adults. (You don't see how it could be frightening?) Oh, maybe you would feel not wanted. (Or not *able*.) [*Smile*.] I never thought of *that*.

[*Pause*.] Is impotence mental? (Often.) Could a feeling of inadequacy come from parents never letting a child do anything for himself without watching over him? (Partly. Also partly from the discrepancy between the fantasies he had of being powerful and competent and the realities of being a small child. The bigger the fantasy, the greater the discrepancy and the feeling of impotence.) [*Smile*.] Yes.

74. I've been making a plan for the manufacture of a belt-fed machine gun, but it's very complicated.

[*Pause*.] I know a guy who came and borrowed some money from my family, but hasn't been seen since. I could have warned the family if they'd asked me. This is the kind of guy who gets a sense of security from getting people to give him money. He tells his family he's saving it, but tells the other guys how he goes out on big dates. (Why does he feel so insecure that he has to be inconsistent like that?) He obviously has to make the other guys think he's a big shot with the girls, but he doesn't feel like one. I guess he's disappointed in his father because he isn't a man and won't take his place as head of the family. He takes his mother's side in arguments about this. (It must be hard to have such divided loyalties.)

He can't tell the truth because he often doesn't know what it is himself. He doesn't know how he feels. He'll talk to me because I don't just tell him he's a cool guy. I at least listen. He trusts me. (He appreciates someone he doesn't have to try to fool.)

He's the one that says all psychiatrists are cracked themselves because they find out too much about themselves.

(Knowing about oneself doesn't have to be so bad.) I told him the ones who are cracked are the one who *don't* know about themselves. (He must be afraid there are things in him that are so explosive he doesn't dare know about them.)

[*Pause.*] I'm thinking about a theoretical problem. A person wants to find out about himself because of a security need, but when he does, he finds it isn't necessary any more. When he finds he can communicate with someone he trusts, then it doesn't matter so much what it was that he needed to talk about.

75. [*David starts out immediately in an animated way.*] I've been reading Dunne's "Experiment with Time." It's fascinating! I like the idea of being able to look into the future. I'd like to be able to look and see if it's good, and then if it isn't, alter the present so that it won't happen. (One could do that to some extent with one's mind alone—anticipating what can lead to certain results and thinking about how to prevent what one doesn't want.)

Freud should have been able to think up something like that in his work with dreams. (Freud's work with dreams showed us that images which might seem meaningless are really meaningful if one learns to speak the language of the unconscious mind. What are you wondering about your own future?)

I'd like to know what my occupation will be. I don't want one that will take most of my time. If I'm not free to do what I want at the moment, I'll never get anywhere. (You apparently feel a need to act on immediate impulse, and fear that your controls are not in good working order to enable you to bear the tension of resisting your impulse.) I don't want to be committed to anything. If you are, you will be punished for not meeting demands. It is simpler just not to try anything. (The only thing you feel you can be really sure of is *not* succeeding.)

[Pause.] It's funny how you are able to pick out things to discuss that bother me, when I really can't think of them myself. (Two heads are better than one at something like this. The painful things from which one protects oneself are the very things that are hardest to see for oneself. When a person is too close to a problem, he can't see the woods for the trees.)

[Pause.] I see an image, like the one about the gears. There's a stationary outer rim and a moving inner rim, with ball bearings in between. (Can you translate that?) The ball bearings have to go along, whether they want to or not. [Pause.] The outer rim may be my father, and the inner one my mother, with the ball bearings me. She is the one who is always moving and doing things. (What do you mean about your father being stationary?) I can only think of one thing—sex. Dad is completely unaware of how such drives and feelings may affect other people—not me so much as my mother. She feels unappreciated and unneeded and makes demands on my brother and me for things she doesn't get from Dad. He could fulfill them, but he doesn't want to—probably because he never got anything.

[Pause.] I was feeling sorry for myself. Society wasn't made for me. (Society includes a lot of things that are different. What do you mean?) You can never get anything without demands being made on you to give something back. You can't even get a loan unless you have collateral, and that's an obligation. (This may relate to what you were saying about your mother. You may be saying she wants too much from you—too great a return on her investment.) Yes.

[Pause.] I see a 30, 60, 90 degree triangle. (Father, mother and yourself?) [Laugh.] That's just what I was thinking, but I realize it excludes my brother. (What do you make of it?) Perhaps I don't like him. I could have thought of a square, but that has all equal angles, not a big, middle-sized, and small one.

[*Pause. Smile.*] It's interesting how the unconscious mind excludes things it doesn't like. Not first thinks of them and then ignores them, but just doesn't think of them. I would be a good convert to Christian Science. But Christian Science doesn't work, because the need to hide all feelings even from oneself makes one a very unreal person. Children of Christian Scientists are very frustrated. They realize that what's going on beneath the surface isn't at all like what's being said, but they are never quite sure what *is* real. (I know. I think children have an easier time if things are honestly presented as black than they do if things are gray but everyone tries to insist they are white.) Yes.

[*Pause.*] The hardest part of this process isn't so much thinking of what to say, but having to know what it means. (Yes. Knowing one's true feelings can be painful. But, as you just said, it isn't as painful as *not* knowing them.)

This is the end of the second year.

6

Experiments with Direct Communication

"The guy talked to him in his own language."

Ｔ<small>HE</small> <small>PRECEDING</small> <small>SECTIONS</small> <small>HAVE</small> <small>SHOWN</small>
that for two years, David could speak only in "code" about
his real concerns; even when finally able to talk more directly,
he reverted immediately to symbolism whenever dealing
with problems of bodily function or oedipal relationship. In
the symbolic mode, however, he began early and consistently
to discuss the fears about body process and sexual adequacy
which generated much of his anxiety.

To David, the concept of losing control, in addition
to derivative meanings relating to anger and aggression,
applied directly to basic body function. It will be remembered that he had been a bed-wetter up to the age of twelve.
Fears that therapy might precipitate a reversion to this

enuretic state, and that loss of emotional control in general would be accompanied by loss of urinary control, may be seen expressed repeatedly in water and flood symbolism throughout the material. The "electric table" representing therapeutic work might be unsteady; "sometimes things would spill in transit" (11). The sports car representing himself had difficulty with valves (62) or an oil tank so low that "if you go over rough ground, it will leak" (70). His troubles "might go back to a time when [he] had a dog that couldn't point—[who] had kidney trouble" (39). Discouragement in therapy was described as "like trying to finish building a house just before the dam breaks and covers it with water" (94); "There's no use building a house in a river bed that's only temporarily dry" (99). He wondered "How far one can dig without hitting water" (106), and had to be sure he could "trust the dam that's holding back the river" (166). Even at a late stage in therapy, he spoke metaphorically of the rain as "Mother Nature wetting her bed" (189). The boy felt no assurance that he could control his penis better in sexual than in urinary function. At one moment he saw it as a dangerous instrument, "an electrically driven pogo stick on which you could leap over walls, but if it got out of control, it could throw you" (12); it was a machine gun with "pellets shot out by springs" (26), or a Luger, such a "dangerous weapon that they [the Indians] wouldn't want to handle it" (30). At other times, he felt it to be a "useless part of the machine that just gets in the way" (39), or "muscles without proper connection with the nerves, to which mechanical hands did things that allowed him to survive" (42). Loss of control carried the dangerous threat of a very real, imminent, bodily reaction. One of the later interviews illustrates graphically his fear of being sexually aroused in my presence (205).

Castration anxiety was acute for David, as for most patients with his type of disturbance. He wasn't sure whether the penis was simply inadequate, "the knife too light, [so that] it wavers" (105), or whether it had been damaged either by the strength of his impulses—"An iron bar bending under the weight of the motor" (19), "A motor too heavy for the frame" (79)—or as a result of masturbation. "He wasn't sure whether it just hadn't learned to work yet, or whether it had shot out so much stuff that it's tired" (61). Right from the beginning of therapy he hinted at his fears of castration; "If you had a hand cut off, you couldn't do the work" (6); the possibility of damage was ever-present in his mind. "If a part of you was bad, it was passed into another dimension, and could be removed without pain" (34); "The center piece is held in such a way that it can't move without damaging itself," or, "the driving shaft will be pulled out of line by opposing bands that hold it" (158). Entering the vagina of a woman was visualized as braving "a door with electric sparks at the opening" (78).

Intensified oedipal conflicts and confusion in sexual identification is characteristic of borderline patients. In his first symbolic statement of a problem, following introductory testing of the therapeutic relationship, David may have hinted at a concept of reversed sexual roles which became more evident later in the material. It seems likely that "a ram and three ewes" (7) represented his view of his family, with the mother as male. In any case, a little later, a conflict around his own female identification was suggested more openly. "The vet brought out a female dog that looked like him, and his mistress didn't know the difference" (65). Preoccupation with oedipal problems also appeared early. There were stories about a king who didn't dare to kill his rival, but held him prisoner, frustrated with the sight of unattainable food (30), and the little cave man who was too incompetent to steal the big cave man's wife (96). Representations of the mother appeared as a "cat who eats her own kittens" (51), and their relationship as "The strong positive poles of two magnets [which] repel each other" (151); the father was "trying to be King of the Household, but isn't fit to rule" (92). He saw his family as "gears with their crank shafts all twisted around each other" (73). Such ideas were too dangerous even to think about directly for a number of years; gradually, however, the anxiety decreased to a point where open discussion of such problems could take place. The later stages of treatment were made up of these discussions.

———————

Here there is an interval of a month.

76. (How have things been going?) O.K. [*I had received a note from his mother saying that he got A in civics and has spontaneously gone out for a track sport, the first thing in which he has ever competed.*]

[*Pause.*] I found a rattlesnake; half the family wanted to keep it, but the senior half vetoed it. [*Laugh.*] It is at the zoo. I also wrote some lyrics to a song. The last lines have to do with people looking at a guy and thinking what a fool he is. (That seems to be what you think people will think of you.) I don't know about that.

[*Pause.*] I'm thinking of a measuring device to measure how much a piece of paper could rise if you cut it. (Can you translate?) How much I would move if I were hurt. [*Laugh.*] That's pretty good. It's funny how everything you think has something to do with your problems.

[*Pause.*] I have a new girl friend, but I don't know whether I dare to love her. I'm afraid of rejection. [*Pause.*] I was thinking—you don't respond one way or another. (You want to know whether I am also afraid that you are un-lovable?) [*Pause.*] I wonder when you will get a lie detector and test my responses. I need to keep you from knowing exactly what I'm saying, so that you can't argue with me. (You have mixed feelings about my understanding you. You have a great desire to communicate, yet are afraid I'll see beneath the surface.)

[Pause.] My girl friend was raped when she was in the eighth grade. At least that's what she says, although the girl that was with her at the time says it wasn't quite like that. (How do you feel about a girl who has had a sex experience that was not entirely involuntary?) I might not want something that was too cheap. I'm afraid she might have a need for just anyone, not necessarily me. The song about "Walking in the Rain" and the feeling that people would think me a fool, is connected with the idea that only a fool would go with a girl like that—someone who isn't "one of the crowd." (You might also be wondering whether anyone who could like you was not also a fool and a bad person.)

[Long pause.] When I was a little boy of about six, we had a baby sitter, and I went to bed with her. (Do you mean had intercourse?) What else could I mean? (There are lots of kinds of sex experience that are not intercourse.) This was. I liked it too! I've always felt like a pretty bad person because I liked it. (You must have mixed feelings—an association between a pleasant sensation and a feeling of distrust for a grown person who seduced you. There might be a strong feeling that a person might use your trust to seduce you.) Yes. That's true. (You might have similar feelings about me—that in encouraging you to stir up sexual thoughts and feelings I might also be a bad person who could harm you.) I was just thinking how much trust I put in you—but maybe I was just covering up such thoughts.

[Pause.] I'm thinking of freezing air so that it becomes solid. Some people say you can't freeze alcohol, but you can if the temperature is low enough.

77. [Pause.] I'm thinking about a car. The front wheels will operate independently of each other and flexibly with hinges

and springs so that they will adapt to the rough roads. The back wheels will be more rigid. (Why?) No reason; it's just easier to make it like that.

(Why are you talking about yourself in terms of machines again today?) [*Wry smile.*] I don't seem to have much control over the terms in which I think. (Let's see what feelings you might be expressing in that kind of an image.) I don't know. (I should think the body of a car would have to work as a whole. If one part was designed to withstand shocks and another part not, there might be difficulties.) [*Pause.*] Perhaps my desire to work on mechanical things comes out of a desire to express myself. (You certainly do desire to express yourself, even though at the same time you are afraid to.)

[*Pause.*] That seems to bring me headlong into the subject of sex again. [*Smile.*] I have to admire the way my subconscious mind brings up subjects that I don't want to talk about. Perhaps it isn't "don't want to," but that it's difficult. (Yes. They are not the same, are they?)

[*Pause.*] I have an image of a piece of wood with a notch in it and another piece fitted into it so that they dovetail. (You are concerned about intercourse?) I thought maybe that was it, but I was thinking about other things too. One notch is at an angle. (That might be an indirect approach to protect yourself.)

I was just thinking I was glad I'd never had intercourse, but then I thought of Jane. But I guess I don't have to consider that intercourse, because there was no love involved. (It must have been pretty difficult for a six-year-old to go through with intercourse.) Well, I really didn't. She told me if I were older I'd have an emission. I felt I wasn't doing what was expected of me. (You expected to have to fill a man's role when your body was only six years old, and couldn't possibly function that way. This helped you develop a feeling of impotence. You also felt you were expected to

200 Baltimore way

fill your father's role, and felt inadequate because your capacity didn't come up to your fantasies or feelings of desire.)

[*Pause.*] It must be hard to be an analyst. The patient hands him a lot of garbage; he has to rummage around in it till he finds what will be useful to the patient to keep, and hands it back to him all cleaned up so he can do something with it. All the patient has to do is dig up the garbage. The analyst has to sort it. Of course the patient has the responsibility of bringing in the material.

[*Pause.*] I see the dovetail again. It is straightened out now. Straight might be an erection; at an angle, impotence. Now I see two pieces of wood fitting together, and a third piece coming between them at an angle. It might be two feelings from the same source—impotence and potence both.

[*Pause.*] I've been tired all week, maybe because of our discussion last time. It is hard to dig up these things. I wish I could come two hours every two weeks instead of an hour every week. It's sometimes slow getting started, and then there is a whole week in which you have to close up again. (You feel these things can only be dealt with when we are together. This is tied up with the feeling that the therapist has all the responsibility. That might make you feel both potent and impotent with me.) Perhaps it isn't impossible to think of things a little bit during the week.

78. I'm going to join a singing group at school. I think it might be fun, although I don't know how good I'll be. (I hope you will enjoy it.)

[*Pause.*] My girl friend stopped seeing me. I don't know whether I was too much of a man for her or not enough. I think she wanted someone she could feel "better than." Perhaps I acted too haughty. (Anyway, I'm glad you realize that when people break up, there may be a problem on both sides.) Each time something like that happens, I lose more ability to cope. [Pause.] I have a tendency to put up barriers to make it hard for people to get through to me. (Do you remember how you once spoke of yourself as protected by a machine that would give electric shocks to anyone who came too close, so as to test whether they were willing to bear some discomfort?) That reminds me of sex. I think of sex with a woman in terms of a door with electric sparks in the opening. [Pause.] These barriers I set up have kept me from making friends, but now I have a few friends at school.

[Pause.] You are always asking me to translate my images. Isn't it possible to assume that sometimes I know what I'm talking about without having to translate it? It almost seems like your asking me to explain is evidence of distrust on your part. (It might be important to understand why you need to talk in these indirect ways, and what is the nature of the anxiety against which you are protecting yourself.)

[He looks at the clock.] It must be getting near the end of the time. I don't want to start anything new. (Are you afraid of getting chopped off in the middle of something?) Was that a slip of the tongue? I immediately thought of castration. [Pause.] I'm glad you aren't as omnipotent as you sometimes seem to be. (I'm sure it's a comfort to feel that I'm a human being who is no more infallible than any other human being.)

79. I got all good grades! I'm also playing touch football, and find it's rather fun. (I'm glad you are feeling better.)

[Pause.] If a car had two motors, and two sets of wheels, it would have greater possibilities for acceleration. The ability to accelerate is more important than running at high speed.

A friend of mine had a car in which the power of the motor was too great for the frame. (A motor should be suited to the type of car, not only in quantity but in quality of performance. What type of performance would you like for your car?) My car would want to hold well to the road like a sports car, but have a high acceleration potential. Two motors could be hitched together for maximum efficiency of the machine. Acceleration is important not only for the purpose of having quick control in getting around obstacles, but there is a thrill in increasing speed for its own sake. The best arrangement would be two people operating two motors in complete accord, but second best would be a situation in which one motor controlled transmission, differential, etc., but a second motor was available to be switched in for increased power at a moment's notice. It wouldn't be good if it had to take the time to build up power in itself. Better to have it idling so that when an electric switch was turned, its power would be immediately accessible.

[Pause.] I'm thinking of the song about how a man is made to help his neighbor, but how "with a little bit of luck you won't be home" when called upon. (You seem to have been talking about you and me working together on a problem. You are concerned about whether, if you are running more efficiently yourself, you will still be able to call on me at a moment's notice. There's a fear that I won't want to be called upon.) Ideally one would like to feel one could have help if and when it was needed, and would be willing to give help in turn if it was needed.

[Pause.] I know a guy who is getting shock therapy. I wonder if people are justified in risking the possibility of damaging him? (What damage are you worried about in regard to yourself?) You might not be justified in using devices to make me talk. (You are apparently afraid that you are being manipulated by some magic that you aren't aware of. You become anxious if you find you have talked about something that you didn't expect to tell anyone, even though you have had it very much on your mind and wanted badly to talk about it. I certainly sympathize with your reluctance to see yourself as a puppet on a string, manipulated by unseen hands. Do you remember our discussion about apomorphine, in which you expressed the fear of being made to vomit against your will? This seems to be the same kind of fear you have had all along, and I suggest that we explore further your feelings that this is what is being done to you.)

I have the feeling that some of the things I have done that have gotten me into trouble were done to bring about the gratification of someone else. (What do you mean?) I don't know. Can't think of an example.

80. [*He has only a little while longer to wait before he can get back his driver's license. Spends the hour discussing the experiences during his arrest, mainly from the point of view of group cohesion among the boys. On the whole, he feels he triumphed in being able to keep the reality in mind to help him restrain impulses to break probation.*] (It is indeed a great triumph!)

81. I plan to get a new frame for my motor. [*Pause.*] I'm thinking of a movie about keeping a poker face. Never let the other guy know when you are going to draw. [*Pause.*] I wonder what's the connection between those two thoughts? Perhaps wanting a new frame is like wanting a new body, and the other has to do with my inability to show emotion. (In what way do you feel your body needs changing?) Impotence.

[*Pause.*] I wonder if there is really something wrong with my penis, or if it's all due to feelings about the experience with Jane. (It might have to do with your feelings about masturbation. Once you told me symbolically that you didn't know whether there was something wrong with your penis or whether you had worn it out by "shooting too much stuff out of it.") [*Pause.*] I feel somewhat shocked to think I have told you so much without being aware of it. (You must have mixed feelings about that.) It's frightening to tell things without knowing it, even if you really want to tell them.

I'm afraid I've masturbated too much. Can one damage one's body that way? (No. But I'd like to understand more about your feelings about it.) I'd prefer to think my body was defective than to think I couldn't play the role of a man with a girl. I don't think I would masturbate if I had a good relationship with a girl. It's my substitute for getting close to people.

In this new town I'm getting along better, and am more nearly accepted as "like the others," but I'm afraid now of losing my individuality and becoming a freak, which is what I regard the "average American boy." (Maybe you can find a middle ground on which you can have the satisfactions of other boys without necessarily being exactly like them.)

[Pause.] I've wondered if one loses creativity in therapy? After one gets rid of the pain, there might not be any more motivation. However, to get rid of the pain is well worth it, and even the loss of creativity wouldn't deter me from going further with therapy and knowing what's in my mind.

A letter comes from David's mother, stating that there is severe financial crisis in the family. She wonders if further therapy for the boy is necessary. I reply that I do think so, and that she may owe me for the cost if it is impossible to pay at this time.

82. [David comes in quoting a joke he has just been reading in a cartoon book. A woman puts out her hand to signal a left turn, and another woman bites it.]

[Long pause.] (Is anything troubling you today?) Not

that I know of, except that I'm not allowed to stay in town because of the curfew. Mother is adamant. (Do you feel she doesn't trust you, or that she is worried something will happen to you?) Worried that I will be picked up after curfew.

(The whole problem of trust and responsibility is a complicated one for both parents and children. It is often hard for a kid your age to know whether he wants to be a child or an adult.) It depends on the kind of responsibility demanded. I don't feel ready to take the responsibility for earning a living yet. (Is there imminent danger that you will have to?) No, but it's more imminent than a year ago. [Smile.]

(What are your plans for next year?) Graduate and then the service. (Do you feel ready for that kind of responsibility—control of impulses in the face of possibly unreasonable authority?) I'm through butting my head against a stone wall. Now I have a different way of fighting which is more practical, although the hate behind it is the same. (There are plenty of things in life that justify a feeling of hate. However, it makes a lot of difference what one does with it.)

Irrational authority is when something is done for the purpose of getting a reaction from me. I think it would be hard to get me mad if I thought somebody was *trying* to get me mad. (That's understandable. However, it does seem that you often assume authority to be unreasonable and arbitrary unless it is proven otherwise. You seem to need a lot of reassurance that the person in authority is trustworthy and dependable. Your experiences have made it hard to believe otherwise.) That's true.

83. When we drive along the highway we play a game of seeing how long we can hold our breath. I don't let the com-

petition see that I increase my capacity by overbreathing ahead of time.

[*Pause.*] I've started smoking. (Oh?) Yes. I wasn't going to tell you. (Why not?) I don't know. Perhaps just because it indicates a change. If you don't know whether a change is good or bad, it constitutes a risk. (What are the pros and cons of smoking?) I can't think of any pros. A con is that it increases the risk of cancer. Perhaps it makes you more like "the others." (But you aren't sure that's a pro.) [*Laugh.*] That's a good point.

(Perhaps you wonder what my attitude might be.) Maybe I expect you to have the same attitudes as my parents. Dad doesn't say much. Mother says it reminds her of when she started smoking.

[*Pause.*] I'm thinking about various therapists I've had. (Tell me about your experiences.) One I only saw three or four times. He wanted me to do all the talking, but I didn't want to talk. (Have you been thinking of quitting here?) No. [*Pause.*] I couldn't be pushed. (Do you feel I've been pushing you?) No. There's a difference between being pushed and being helped. Anyway, I don't think I *could* be pushed. It's like if you try to make a train go too fast around a curve—it may go off the track. (You have often warned me that you have to go at your own pace, and can't go any place you don't feel ready to explore.) That's right. I can't.

[*Pause.*] A man was doing some studies on the habits of monkeys and wanted to see what they did when he wasn't with them. He left the room and peeked through the keyhole right into the eye of a monkey that was watching *him*. (*Laugh.* I guess you aren't the only one under observation here. What sorts of things might you want to know about me?)

[*Pause.*] I'm thinking again of the cartoon about the woman in the car indicating a left turn and being bitten by another woman. It probably served her right. She had created a traffic jam so that nobody could move. [*Long pause.*] That's probably me biting you for pointing in a direction that I don't want to go in.

[*Pause.*] I'm thinking about associations—how one thought leads to another, and they all seem to be connected. I wonder if when I say something, it makes you think of something too. (Like when your smoking called up associations in your mother to her own feelings rather than yours? Perhaps you are afraid I will react more to my own experience than to yours when you tell me things.) No. If I say one thing, it might lead in several directions, but the next thing will cut off some of the alternatives, and the next still more. If you just listen to me, you'll be bound to find the right direction eventually.

[*Pause.*] Therapy is like looking for gold. At first you can pick it up off the ground. Later you have to dig for it. (The richest veins lie deep.) Unless you have a fault.

84. [*Pause.*] I was thinking of a science fiction story. Some men on a planet kept back the atmospheric pressure by creating fields of force around themselves. No one field was strong enough to withstand the pressure without an explosion, but they kept replacing each field with another before it collapsed. Each new field was just like the one before it in quality and degree of intensity. (What generated the fields of force?) I wish I knew. (Tell me about yours.) Maybe it's like changing the subject. (You mean no one subject can stand too much pressure at a time?) Yes. (I imagine, though, that there are plenty of subjects that can bear a certain amount of exploration without making an explosion.)

[*Pause.*] (What's causing the atmospheric pressure?) [*Shrug.*] (Is something more disturbing than usual going on between your parents?) [*Smile.*] That's a good guess. They are fighting over money. They don't realize it doesn't bother me. It's like watching two children fighting over a shovel in the sand. Money isn't important. (Unless the lack of it means the loss of something you really want and need.) Well, yes.

(Have you been worrying about the possibility of having to stop coming here?) A little. (What have you thought about it?) When I have to stop for lack of money, I'll stop, that's all. (How do you feel about that?) Not very good. If I had the means, I would pay for it myself. (We won't stop for lack of money. Something will be worked out.) I didn't think you would.

[Pause.] One moves to where the force is weakest. It's like two guards fighting over who's to guard you. (Who are the two guards?) The forces.

[Pause.] I was thinking what I would like to do with my life. (What were you thinking?) Go to Africa. (Is that the farthest place from home that you can think of?) [Smile.] No. It's an uncomplicated place. Africa has lots of trees. I don't think about the desert. (Trees?) Security. (Perhaps an uncomplicated life that is not parched and which offers security can be found closer than Africa. It's a way of life, not a place. These are the things you are looking for in relationships.) I don't want to be taken at face value. I want to be valued for what I am. [Pause.] I was thinking about Africa again. (What aspect?) Walking.

85. [Pause.] I'm thinking about two triangles, mounted in such a way that when they turn, neither one can turn the full distance. Maybe it means carrying out a task—related to my family.

(Why do you think you are talking in this language at this point?) Young people can't talk directly about the things that really concern them. I couldn't say to another fellow that I'm worrying about what's going to happen when

I get married. Others are worried about the same things, and haven't solved them for themselves. They don't like having them brought up.

[Pause.] I'm thinking of a geometry problem. How many times can you divide an angle? (Depends on your goal. You can probably divide it an infinite number of times, but it's possible to set the problem to a useful number of operations that don't have to extend into infinity.)

[Pause.] I'm thinking of a friend's cycle. He has put a heavy motor into a light frame. He may have to change it over into a heavier frame or the motor will shake the frame apart. It may be too heavy anyway. (I suspect you are talking about the transition from boy to man. You seem to have the feeling that the strength of your impulses has outweighed the capabilities of a boy, and fear that as you become a man, you will have the power to carry out destructive impulses that previously you could only carry out in fantasy. This might extend into the sexual area.) [Smile.] That's it exactly.

86. I have a sore throat. [Pause.] (What are you thinking?) Of an iron bar, bent one way and then the other so that there are two parallel pieces. Perhaps me and my wife, or me and the world getting into step. Making a living is such a useless process. (Your father has had a hard time finding satisfaction in his work. I wonder if that colors your picture of what it is to make a living.) Maybe.

[Pause.] I'm thinking of my sore thumb. I was trying to tackle in the end zone, and it got in the way. [Laugh.]

I'm thinking about meeting my mother. (Is there a problem?) Not unless she leaves without me, and that wouldn't really be a problem. I like to wander around by myself. I haven't really had time enough to grow up in. I'm eighteen. When there's work to do, people start telling you all your responsibilities.

I read a story called "Cheating the Hangman." They

strung a guy up so that the hangman thought he was hung, but really he was being held up by a harness under his coat. He was supposed to be dead, so nobody could get him to do anything. (Appearing helpless and "strung up" served as a protection against demands. It might be the same with you, but perhaps there are other ways of protecting yourself that would be less destructive to you.) [Pause.] I wish I could cut the sore place out of my throat. (Sore throat, sore thumb.) It's a good thumb, but the throat is useless. (Are you really talking about your throat?) [Smile.] Your voice sounds different. (If you were talking about your penis, it would fit in with what you have said before. Maybe you feel that if you didn't have it, you wouldn't have to worry about impulses being too strong, or about having to protect yourself from demands.) If I didn't have it, I wouldn't have to worry about being helpless and incompetent. (You don't have to get rid of it. All you have to do is get rid of the feelings that interfere with your ability to function.)

He doesn't show up for the next appointment. Didn't leave enough time to get back from a visit to the shore.

87. I was nineteen last week. [Pause.] (Do you finish school at midyear or in June?) I don't know—when the other seniors do, I guess. (You don't like to think about it.) I'm afraid of the future.

The world is getting so mechanized that you become dependent on a single source of food, and if anything happens to that, you don't really know how to get along. (Are you afraid of being dependent on someone?) My parents for food and shelter. (Are you afraid of being unable to take care of yourself?) I don't want to. I can't see any point in working. (Can't you imagine something from which you could get satisfaction?) Something that would combine brain work with physical and mechanical skills. But nobody wants new ideas. (The world is crying for new ideas.) I'd like to make some improvements on a jet engine.

(I think one thing you have to do is learn to disentangle your ideas about machines, so that when you are working on a machine, you can see its problems as separate from your own.) I use facts and ideas like a handrail. (To hold on to in the face of shifting realities around you.) Maybe it's because of the unsuccessful love affairs.

A man in a story tried to escape from a crime by taking a lie detector test. He thought he could get away with it, because he could control his reactions, but eventually someone else testified against him. They turned up new evidence.

[*Pause.*] Yogis can control their bodily processes consciously, and even stop their hearts. (A heart is a pretty good thing to have working.) I can't control mine. The Yogis can make themselves appear dead. (The heart pumps the blood that keeps the brain going. Heart and brain work together.) It's sometimes useful to appear to be dead, or hibernating. (For protection.)

[*Pause.*] Mickey, the good mechanic, is the only one whose word I'll take if I'm told another way is best. Sometimes he'll say your way isn't best, but go ahead and try it anyway. Sometimes I do, because I want to see how it will work. But if it involves a bearing that's essential to the whole machine, it would be too important if I made a mistake. He's the only one who knows the tolerance of the machine.

88. I just tried out a motor that my friend has been working on. He didn't put it together well enough, because he was in a hurry to try it out. It didn't work very well. I looked it over afterward and found that a rather minor adjustment would have made a lot of difference. (What was the hurry? Why didn't you work on it until you were sure of it?) Oh well, the

main value is working on it anyway. Once it is running smoothly, we'll probably be bored with it anyway.

(I think you might again be talking about yourself and therapy—feeling that if you get functioning well, there will be no more interest. Also the fear that you have to hurry to be ready to go into the army. What's the hurry? Why not continue treatment for a while and get a deferment until you feel more sure of yourself?) I don't know if I can. (I'm pretty sure you can, and I'm not sure you feel ready to work in and with a group.) I don't feel like taking on the problems of a group. It's all I can do to handle my own.

[Pause.] A man went to Mars on a space ship owned by America. Something happened to it, and the Russians sent one after him. He wondered who would own him under those circumstances. (Have you a feeling that your family and I are in some kind of competition to "own" you?) No. (It occurred to me you might feel that if I think you should stay and continue treatment, it might be that I wanted to have you tied to me.) I don't believe that about you. If I did, I'd just go my own way anyway. In the story, the first thing the guy did when the space ship landed was to spit on the ground.

[Pause.] There was another story about some guys from the future who went to teach a child new ideas about what to do with the past. But they left some stuff lying around that was dangerous, and the child got into it and was blown up. (You want to be sure I'll take care of you, and see to it that you don't get into anything explosive.) If it were that dangerous, I probably wouldn't be able to think of it anyway.

[Pause.] I read a story about two space ships. They meet on a galaxy, and both feel friendly, but each fears the other will find out where it comes from without its getting corresponding information about the other. They fear attack without the ability to retaliate. (You apparently feel I "have something on you" that I might use against you unless you get something on me that will insure my neutrality.) It would preserve peace if one nation strongly dedicated to peace would be ruthless with anyone that wasn't, until everyone quieted down.

[Pause.] There might be only small things acting as impediments to therapy if one could see it as a whole. But when you can't, small things look big, and you might not dare approach for fear of the pain. (I know.)

89. [This hour was not recorded in detail. By circumlocution, David discussed a fear of loving me because it is a professional relationship which might end just at a point where he allowed himself awareness of a need. He expressed the feeling that one must have all of a person or nothing at all. If love is shared, it can't be worth anything.] (What you are saying sounds like when you have a frozen foot that is beginning to thaw out. It hurts so much while it is thawing, that you wish it were frozen again because it is impossible to believe that it will ever not be painful.) In spite of this, I would rather have the pain than be frozen.

90. I've got a trig exam coming up. Tells of various kinds of problems and how to solve them. (How does all this apply to attempts at solving your own problems?) [Smile.] That reminds me of a riddle. How are an elephant and a toothbrush alike? Neither of them can ride a bicycle. (You must feel it is very far-fetched for me to try to apply everything you say to your own problems.) No. Not to try. Even if there isn't always a similarity, at least it might present an interesting problem.

[Pause.] A sphere is balanced on a point by equal weights hanging on each side. In order to stay in balance, one can change the positions of the forces even if the weights on the two sides are not changed proportionately. Greater weights can be balanced by lesser ones hanging farther from the point of balance. It is the same with psychic forces. You can change their direction without necessarily lessening their intensity, and reach a better balance internally.

[*Pause.*] Life has no real purpose, but I'm willing to concede that I may not continue to feel so. I'll wait and see.

At present I see therapy as a narrow path between a sheer bank on one side, which represents the demands of society, and a sheer crevasse on the other, which represents insanity. The bank that is society keeps moving inward, making the path narrower all the time, and there is no way over the top, and no foreseeable end to the path where it would open out into a field. Originally the path was wider. In a young society, you could do more what you wanted about expressing hostile impulses. If you wanted to kill someone, there was a chance you would be overpowered by him or his friends, but at least you had a chance. Now society has, so to speak, taken away your knife.

(Why does the contest between aggressive impulses and acceptable outlets seem so hopeless? Maybe this picture has a defensive function. The acceptance of hopelessness might make it unnecessary to face feelings that might be painful.) Yes. You don't have to sweat. If there is no goal, you can just enjoy what you see along the path. (Enjoying things as you go along doesn't need to mean that you won't reach a goal. You fear your impulses would be so overwhelming that there's no use trying to find an outlet.)

[*Pause.*] I wonder where the universe comes from? It's hard to imagine a "nothing." Even space is something.

91. I'm starting a course in "family living," which is a duplication of sociology in the other school. They try to make generalizations about things like "preparation for marriage,"

but if one fits, it's only by accident. (You mean you can't call a spade a spade.) If one could, the course wouldn't be necessary.

[*Pause.*] I'm thinking of a book called "The First Two Thousand Years." A guy is present at the crucifixion of Christ. Christ says to him, "I go, but thou must tarry till I return." (How does that apply to you?) I don't know exactly.

[*Pause.*] I worked out an ingenious proof in solid geometry, but the teacher won't accept anyone else's idea. He's like me—he has devious ways of communicating. (These might have a value. What might the value be?) You keep people from getting close to you. It might be more comfortable not to have to be aware of people. If you have to live two thousand years, you might not want to have it end. You might not want to be like everyone else. You learn a lot in two thousand years. You can look down on people. (You might also have to experience unmanageable emotions like love and hate and jealousy and pain. It's like we were saying the other day about unfreezing. The obscure communication could be a protective device to preserve the relatively more comfortable isolation, bad as that is.)

Maybe if you had all the time in the world you might solve your problems. (You have a lifetime.) I don't know whether what you find is worth the search, unless there is value in the search itself.

[*Pause.*] Making a living seems futile. You lose your creativity unless you can do what you want when you want. (Why the connection between creativity and limitless freedom?) Perhaps I'm confusing creativity with getting knowledge. (You feel one can only learn if one is completely unrestricted. That is a little like what you were saying the other day about feeling that love has no value unless it is limitless —if you couldn't completely devour everything, your hunger could never be satisfied.)

There are so many things to know, that if you are directed into learning certain things, you can't have others. It's like being almost full and having to choose between all your favorite desserts. (You are talking as if there was only going to be one meal, and if you didn't eat everything at once, there would never be another chance.)

No matter how hungry you are, you might have to refuse food if it is forced. (That's true. Even little children react strongly to forced feeding.) Sometimes they throw the mush on the floor. But when they get older, they learn to smile and act as though they were eating it, and wait till later to spit it out. Otherwise they get into jail or a mental hospital.

[Pause.] I'm thinking of a political cartoon. A giant is standing on the globe with a big hammer, and there is an indentation on each city where he has smashed it. He is saying, "How I grieve over the strife of humanity." [Pause.] In that book there was an analogy saying that religion is like a vase that has been smashed in pieces. Everyone worships a little piece, and condemns anyone who worships another piece.

[Pause.] Why is it that people who can't indoctrinate a person want to kill him?

92. [As David walks in, he points out that he has a new coat. It is so heavy it can almost stand by itself.] In six days I can get back my driver's license. The period of probation is nearly up. (That must be a good feeling!) Not particularly. Probation didn't bother me. In some ways it had face-saving aspects. It was a good excuse for not doing things that might get me in trouble, and still let me preserve status with the crowd who don't seem to care whether they get into trouble or not.

[Pause.] I'm thinking of a water turbine. It goes the

wrong way. (You have mixed feelings about identifying with that crowd. You feel theirs is a "wrong way," yet it fills a need in you.) Yes.

[Pause.] I'm thinking about my friend's relationship with his father. His father is trying to be "King of the Household," but he isn't fit to rule. If Joe is delinquent, it hurts his father, but it also hurts his mother and grandmother who are good people. (And himself.) It's like trying to break down a stone wall. You try to save the good bricks, so you don't want to use dynamite. (Unless a person uses dynamite very carefully, he's apt to blow himself up too.)

[Pause.] I'm wondering what sort of a person Joe's grandfather must be to have produced a person like his father. (Joe's father seems to have a lot of problems of his own that make him act the way he does, but I guess that doesn't make it any less painful for Joe.)

[Pause.] I'm thinking about a book I just read called "Here come the Martians." Some Martians came to earth, but nobody could see them or make any contact with them. The hero of the story is a writer of Western stories. He is busy writing, and one of the Martians comes up behind him and says, "Hi Ho Silver!" It scares him into a catatonic state. (What scared him so much?) The guy talked to him in his own language. When a person is threatened by another who tries to break through his isolation, it often makes him feel very angry at that person. (I know.)

[Pause.] I'm thinking how one can bring the conscious and the unconscious minds closer together. What keeps them apart? (Sometimes things get pushed into and held in the unconscious mind at times when the organism is too young and vulnerable to cope with them. He gets used to keeping them there in certain ways, even when he is no longer so vulnerable nor so unable to cope. Feelings from the unconscious do come up into the conscious, though, although they sometimes express themselves in devious ways.)

93. A friend of mine got into difficulty with the police again. The families thought we had all ganged up against his father, but it wasn't so at all. (How do you feel about having it assumed that you were involved in something anti-social when, as a matter of fact, you were not?) Well, I often have been. I suppose it's natural.

(It must annoy you that if there is a choice of loyalty to your friends or to the adults, the adults assume you should be on their side.) Adults don't always understand about loyalty to one's friends. (It's difficult to make a choice of allegiances.) Yes. (There might also be situations in which guilts might make one feel there was a conflict of loyalties, even when there might not actually be one.) Yes. That's true.

94. I may get my license soon. Dad has to sign it, but keeps putting it off. (How do you feel about this tendency on your father's part?) I learned long ago not to take him seriously. (A child might have difficulty recognizing that a father had problems of his own. He might feel that if his father didn't pay attention to the things that were important to him, he must be of no consequence to his father and therefore bad.) Yes.

One couldn't count on Dad for anything important, but his department was things like summer vacation. (The fun department?) Yes. (That might make it harder to be mad at him for not being trustworthy in other ways.) Yes. (Both your mother and father could be counted on for some things but not others. Divided loyalties again.) Yes. The things that weren't essential you might get from your parents, but you couldn't count on them for anything essential. That you had to get for yourself. (Could you always?)

[*Pause. Anxious smile. He starts to revert to symbolic language.*] (Why the code just now?) You pushed me into a corner where only one answer was possible. This seems to be embarrassing for me. (You felt angry at being in such a position.) I don't know whether I did or not. [*Pause.*] One can go deeper, and be more thorough, if one doesn't try to go too fast. If one is trying to bend an iron bar—if the arms are close together, one doesn't have to exert as much force as when they are farther apart, at an angle. (If one exerts force directly, it is more effective than when it is applied indirectly.) Once momentum has been gained, both increased force and increased speed may be possible.

[*Pause.*] (What are you thinking?) I escaped into a feeling that there's no use anyway. A rather negative attitude. (A protective attitude. If there's no use anyway, one doesn't have to waste energy in trying.) It's like trying to finish building a house before the dam breaks and covers it with water. Few people would try to build a house in a river bed that's only temporarily dry.

(What is the rush of water you fear?) Maybe revolt. (Maybe something more literal—from the eyes or from the bladder.) I was just thinking that maybe it was the bed-wetting. (Maybe revolt and bed-wetting aren't too far apart. Maybe a rush of water is the only weapon a child has to express a rush of feelings.) It's frustrating that nobody recognizes the reasons.

A child might feel that the only way to put out a fire is to pee on it. The parents might come along and see only the puddle, not realizing there had been a fire. Parents might go crazy if they could know the thoughts of children. (Children's thoughts and feelings might be painful for parents, but if a child could tell them, it might not be destructive. It might help the parents to be able to help the child.)

95. I can get a car for thirty dollars, but have to get my license first. It hasn't come through yet. I have to start think-

ing about how to get some money. Eventually I'd like to be a flyer. (Do you think you are ready at this point?) No. I need more time to be a boy. (I agree with you.) Now all we have to do is convince Uncle Sam. [*Laugh.*] (We will if we need to.)

[*Pause.*] I read a story about a guy who knew a word that would destroy the world if he said it. At the end of the book he hadn't decided whether to say it or not. (To possess such a power must be very frightening.) The most frightening part would be to find out that you had said it, and nothing happened. You might want to destroy the world because you felt so helpless, and to find you couldn't would make you feel even more helpless.

There should be opportunities for kids to do road racing under safe and legal conditions. Most of the kids wouldn't break the law if they could get rid of their impulses to race and speed in controlled ways. They wouldn't even mind supervision by an adult if it was someone they respected—perhaps someone who had done road racing himself, and could tell them what things were too dangerous. The way it is now, it's difficult to get insurance, but the impulse to drive is greater than the fear that someone will get hurt if you make a mistake. You hope nobody will get hurt, but you would rather drive anyway than stay safe and never take a chance. (Better to have safeguards so that one can drive safely, have the satisfaction he wants, and still protect himself and others.

(Do you mind if I ask your mother to come in and give me some more of your early history? I think we are at a point now where I need to know more facts about your past.) O.K. with me.

Between this interview and the next I meet with his mother to obtain historical material on early development.

7

Resistance

"It is like looking a gift horse in the mouth."

T HIS CHAPTER SHOWS HOW AN OPPORTU-
nity for displacement of angry feelings onto a reality-based
complaint may temporarily prevent both patient and therapist from recognizing the real source of the patient's aggression. It also begins to show that in David, this source was a
struggle against feelings of dependency and rising sexual
stimulation.

Within the framework in which he viewed therapy,
David had a realistic cause for annoyance with his therapist.
A momentary counter-reactivity in me, caused by interest in
historical material, resulted in the introduction of a distraction from the boy's current train of preoccupations. (See

the chapter on countertransference and reactivity.) David objected, and I at first missed the point of his communication (96). However, my recognition and interpretation of the feelings a few interviews later did not stop the flow of anger; instead, an immediate reversion to symbolism after the interpretation gave evidence of anxiety which suggested that aggressive feelings had actually been stimulated. It then began to appear that the anger focused on this incident was probably displaced from a more significant area of conflict.

David's fears of leaving treatment were projected onto me (and his mother) in the form of a need on our parts to hang onto him and force him into a dependent position (100). His own feelings of dependency on therapy had to be seen by him as my need to make him into a "successful case" (99). The ambivalence about his own ability to function independently is graphically expressed in an image; ". . . someone trying to pull a man away from a cliff with a rope. He's so resentful of being pulled that he falls over the cliff. . . . I suppose it would depend on how great the emergency was, and whether he had to be pulled in order to save him" (99). It was difficult for David to admit that I had not forced him to stay out of the army, because he had then to face his own guilt for wanting to remain in treatment (100). It also threatened him to become aware that his view of me as a co-conspirator had, to him, implications of sexual seductiveness emanating from me—projections of his own rising sexual wishes. The boy made an unconscious equation between his dependent and his sexual needs. As soon as such needs entered his awareness, they had to be pushed back, like ". . . an electronic rat that was made so as to be attracted to the light, but also repelled. As its batteries ran down, it came closer to the light and got recharged; then it became repelled and backed away . . ." (102). The need to fight with me can be seen as a defense against the recognition of these feelings.

The expression of aggression was also, however, a

direct outlet for frustration accumulated as a result of his real life experiences during this period. The importance of this factor becomes evident in the fact that my offer of pocket money did not stimulate his fears of seduction or the defenses against them, but reduced the aggression and allowed him to get back to work. (See Chapter 12, on the fee.)

---

96. [*He comes in carrying a metal Chinese puzzle.*] Learning to solve it has been interesting. (How do you feel about the process of solving your own puzzle?) I don't know.

By the way, Mother says to tell you she's trying to get hold of the Rorschach. (Your mother told me some interesting things about your early experiences. Can you tell me something about your own outstanding memories?) I can remember once exploring around a dump where old scientific equipment was abandoned. [*I initiate a discussion of some events related by his mother; he cooperates for a time.*]

[*Pause.*] My teacher at school doesn't care whether what I learn has any meaning to me just so long as I memorize what she wants and get it down on paper. (That doesn't sound like a very good teacher.) I can learn math better than English, because in English you just get the stuff that bears no relationship to anything interesting. (Poets often say things that everyone feels, but one has to understand their language.) I never had a teacher that made poetry interesting.

[*Pause.*] I read a story about a little cave man who wanted a wife. There was a big cave man who had twenty wives. That would have been O.K., except there were no other women in town. The guy was too little to fight the cave man for one of his women, and decided to steal one. He made a cart to run away in; the trouble was, he made square wheels, and the cart wouldn't go. After about five years, he sawed the corners off one wheel, and it still wouldn't go. After another five years, he realized he had to saw the corners off all the wheels. It was a very funny story. (I guess it didn't seem very funny to the little man who was so frustrated.) I guess not. (It is easier to laugh at one's own problems when "once removed.") Yes.

97. [*Seems more reticent than usual. Starts only after a very long pause, and has to have every statement initiated by a question from me.*] (What are you thinking?) Of a "Peanuts" cartoon. Charlie Brown's kite is caught in a tree; Lucy keeps telling him to shake the tree, and finally to kick it. When he does, he hurts his foot. Then she says, "Why do you always do everything I tell you to do?" (For a couple of weeks now you have been bringing up similar ideas of people not being helpful in frustrating situations. I think you must be referring to something that is going on between us.) Maybe so. I don't think I'm making much progress. (Do you think I have been unwittingly reassuring you, or giving you the feeling that "you shouldn't feel like that?") When my father helps me with math problems, he asks me what the difficulty is. When I tell him, he tells me I shouldn't feel like that. (If I have been giving you that impression, it is a mistake on my part.) [*Pause.*] I don't like the idea of putting you "in the wrong." (Why is it so necessary to have me infallible?) I don't like to be put in the wrong. I want everyone to be happy and leave me alone. (I see you feel I've been pushing you.) It is like looking a gift horse in the mouth. But perhaps I need to be pushed. (The gift horse was giving a gift every day, but the man got impatient.) [*Smile. Pause.*] I overheard a conversation between Mother and Dad. Mother said I should be doing something; Dad said not to push me. Mother

said I was pushing the family. I don't know how I do it, but I know that if people push me, I push back.

98. Mother is writing to my first therapist. (What feelings have you about my having asked for this early information?) I don't know.

[*Pause.*] My teacher is a fool. He ignores the interesting part of the course, and is always being concerned with foolish things like how to make out tax forms. (I rather think you are talking about my interest in tests and information from the past. You might be feeling discouraged in your attempts to talk about things that are current and meaningful if you think my major emphasis is on other kinds of material.) Maybe.

[*Pause.*] I feel bitter at the idea that the volume of a prism is determined by multiplying the area of the surface by the altitude. I can see this intellectually, but my *feeling* is that the volume is decreased if the prism deviates from the straight up and down position. A tin can's sides come closer together if the can is tipped on its base, and it seems impossible to imagine that it has the same contents. (Could you be trying to express something about yourself?) Maybe. [*Pause.*] Geometry isn't as absolute as people think. (You might be talking about psychiatry.)

[*Pause.*] "Family Living" is a bore. The teacher refuses to let me out of the course, even though I covered the same material in a course at the other school. (I wonder if you are angry about my having told you I didn't think you were ready to go into the army?) Yes! I don't like the idea of anyone else keeping me out, even though I don't want to go. I wouldn't mind getting out of it on the basis that I didn't *want* to go in, but I resent being kept out on the basis that I'm not *able*. I may have doubts about my own capacities, but I resent being considered inferior. A runner in a race stops because he's out of breath. Even though he knows he will be better able to finish the course, he resents the knowledge that he'll never catch up enough to come in first. (A runner has to go into training before he can race. Maybe you have to run in a later race, when your muscles are toned up, regardless of what others do now.) Why race at all? Why use up the energy? (Your energy seems to be all tied up in holding down feelings.)

[Pause.] I drew my teacher a cartoon of a man in jail who had to break a pile of rocks into pebbles with a hammer. The guard is telling him that if he doesn't do better, another rock will be put on the pile. [Pause.] People are always trying to set goals for other people. (What is your goal for yourself?) [Smile.] To go where I'm top dog.

[Pause.] Being denied something increases the desire for it; being forced decreases the desire. (Do you feel that the idea of my having used force in some way has heightened a desire in you to quit therapy?) No. Therapy is like being stuck with a hook; you resist the pain of having it pulled out, but you go through with it because you want to be rid of the barb. (But sometimes you get discouraged and feel maybe the barb is too deep, and you can never get it out anyway.) Yes.

99. [Long pause. Vague smile.] (What were you thinking?) How some delinquents got off the opium habit by discovering heroin. All it did was rid them of some physical symptoms. (But they were still slaves.) [No answer.] (I wonder what this has to do with the feelings we were discussing last time?) I guess it's the same. Therapy shows you that some feelings aren't right, but doesn't give you anything to replace them. (Aren't right?) Like being anti-social. But it doesn't tell you what to do if you don't feel like being social. I don't know what I'm going to do.

[Pause.] I'm thinking about exploring—a space ship. [Pause.] (There's a lot of unexplored territory. Let's start by exploring what might be a good world for you to live in. It might not be the same world that some others prefer, but the important things is what's best for you.)

[Pause.] A man in a space ship lands on a satellite on top of a tall building. It is all filled with filing cases, and the thing that holds it up is a pillar of light. The guy who runs it gets to feel he owns the guy who landed there, and makes a file on him and files it away in his case. (Just like what you were telling me about feeling that I want to file away material on you, and that my only concern with you is whether or not you are a successful "case." You feel, perhaps, that I have a goal for you in terms of what kind of a patient you are, and that I want you to satisfy me regardless of your own needs.) If you satisfy people, they leave you alone. It's like protective coloring; they don't notice you any more, and you don't have to use your energy being what they want you to be. (It might also work the other way; if you want to stay visible, you have to keep people dissatisfied with you for fear that if you don't, you won't be noticed.) [Smile.] Yes. But the main thing is to disappear so that you won't have to be bothered with other people's demands.

[Pause.] In order to be satisfied yourself, you have to be better than anyone else. But as soon as you are better, you don't care any more. Then you lose something of what made you feel better, and you have to start all over again. (Perhaps it's important to explore why you feel you have to be better than anyone else in order to get that kind of satisfaction. You seem to feel that you have to feel better in order to feel equal.) If you are best, you can call the terms.

[Pause.] I'm thinking of someone trying to pull a man away from a cliff with a rope. He's so resentful of being pulled that he falls over the cliff. (It would certainly be better if he could be persuaded to cooperate and back away from the cliff voluntarily.) I suppose it would depend on how great the emergency was, and whether he had to be pulled to save him. (It seems possible that some of your fear that I am pulling you arises from a sense of urgency—a feeling that time is slipping away.) Maybe. (Actually, you know, time isn't running out, even though it may often seem to be.)

I don't feel anything is worthwhile. There is no use building a house in a river bed that's only temporarily dry. (Tell me more about your fear of losing bladder control.) It's embarrassing. (I imagine there are lots of thoughts and feelings that are hard to talk about.)

This morning I wanted to go into town with Dad, but he drove off without me. I said "piss," and Mother nearly had a fit. Such a lot of fuss about a word, when I had a thousand times more anger inside me! (Which you would have liked to let out in a stream of words, just as you used to let it out in a stream of water when there was no other way to express it.) It's funny how mad people get about words, when they are quite understanding about bed-wetting. (Too bad you can't get the understanding when you use the words instead.) [Smile.] Actually, a river bed might not be a bad place to build a house if the river had been diverted to other channels.

Everything seems pointless, though. It's like building a wall across the beach, extending into the sea, and trying to throw water across with a bucket. (You seem to feel there is a never-ending supply of pent-up feelings.) You might not accomplish much except to develop your muscles.

100. [Long pause.] (What are you thinking?) My sports car is almost ready to run, but Mother wants me to sell it. (Why so?) She thinks it's too dangerous. But she's not concerned for my welfare. She just wants to see herself as my protector. (What makes you think so?) I don't know, but it's true. (I think your mother does feel somewhat guilty because she feels she hurt you when you were small, and it could be that some of her self-esteem is tied up in keeping you safe. However, I don't think that is her only reason. I can see how

difficult it must be for a boy to feel on the one hand so isolated from a woman, and on the other hand so involved with her that it is hard for both of them to see themselves as separate at all.)

[*Pause.*] I'm still mad at my "Family Living" teacher for making me take the course. I drew a cartoon of a hand in an iron gauntlet, with the caption "the continuing guiding hand of our teacher." (This suggests that the guiding hand needs considerable protection. Someone might want to bite the hand that's trying to guide him.) Yes. (I think the teacher is a stand-in for me. You are still mad at me for telling you that you should remain in therapy right now. You said last time that even if one might want something oneself, it might make one resistant to feel forced to accept it.) Yes. (One thing we need to explore is your need to see yourself as forced by me, when actually we agreed mutually that you were not ready for the army.)

I think I feel guilty for not wanting to go in. (In your eyes I have become a "co-conspirator" to protect you from what you feel you should want. We are the "bads" versus the "goods" like the cowboys with black hats on TV.) [*He flashes a quick smile at me, which he immediately suppresses, going back to his impassive stare.*]

101. Joe got his license back, and his father and mother are tolerating each other. (Does that make it easier for him?) Yes. (How are things between your parents these days?) There is no sweat between them at the moment. I don't worry much. (Perhaps your worries in the field of divided loyalties are reduced. It struck me last time that something like what is happening with me might be happening at home. You feel you should be what your father wants you to be, and that if your mother doesn't go along with this, it makes you and her co-conspirators, lining you up against society in general and your father in particular.) Could be.

[Pause.] All the various people I know want me to be something specific to suit their ambitions, but those things are not the same. I feel pulled in many different directions. If you try to be something different for each person, and then get into a crowd, you will die. What each one wants me to be is determined by the needs of that person, not my needs. It's a matter of trying to find out what I have to be to each person in order to have them like me. (What do you think you have to be for me?) [He flashes a smile which is again immediately suppressed.] I don't know.

[Pause.] I need to resist the pattern of values anyone tries to impose on me. It's like trying to feed a baby. You have to feed him when he's hungry, not sit him up at some special time and scold him if he doesn't eat.

[Pause.] Communication is difficult. Language is only a part of what's said. (There is a lot of non-verbal communication. Sometimes the unconsciouses of two people communicate on quite a different level from that which they think they are on when they are talking.) It's like listening to the radio in French Canada. I didn't know the language, but could get the gist of what was said by tones, inflections, and certain words that are similar to English.

[Pause.] A man could try to make a machine that would function independently, but he could only make the mechanism to function according to his own value system. He could judge whether the machine was functioning smoothly according to its physical adjustments, but he couldn't tell whether it wanted to work with another computer machine in some complicated calculation. (That's where communication would be helpful. If only the machine could have a way of making its wants known!) In order to do that, the machine would have to have a sensory apparatus to find out what it did want, in order to be able to communicate.

[Pause.] A robot was designed to make war unnecessary, but it drove its inventors crazy because it came to a standstill. All it could say was "Want!" It didn't want anything, but to want nothing was to want something, so it went against its own mechanism. It couldn't solve the problem it was designed to solve, so it went against everything.

The next week he called up shortly before the hour to cancel.

102. Last week I was out of town buying a car, and forgot what day it was. (I wonder if you really forgot, or whether there was something interesting to do so that for the moment you didn't care.) I forgot until my plans were made, and then there was a conflict between the immediate pleasure and the long-term gain. (It's often true that to give up immediate pleasure, one has to be pretty sure that the long-term gain will really be forthcoming.) It is also important how you feel about the person you are disappointing.

[Pause.] I'm thinking of a story about a machine that could reproduce itself if the parts were fed into it. I would like to invent one that could go even further, and mine the ore for its own parts. (So that it could exist completely independent of other people for its survival. I suspect that's the way you feel about yourself sometimes, but the reason seems to be that you are afraid of needing anyone. If you need someone, you are afraid of the anger you would feel if they disappointed you, so you think it's better to stay away from people entirely.) Machines are like that because they have to be.

[Pause.] I'm thinking of an electronic rat that was made so as to be attracted to a light, but also repelled. As its batteries ran down, it came closer to the light and got recharged; then it became repelled and backed away, so it was oscillating between two lights. (Which two are you oscillating between?) Not two; many. There is no one thing I really want to do. All are negative choices. It's a problem, because in every situation the important thing is to be able to conform to the rules that are made for somebody else's benefit. Everything has some factor I don't like. (Which makes you feel that the things you do like aren't important enough. You seem to feel that if you have any negative feelings about something, or someone, no positive relationship is possible.)

I have an individual way of approaching problems, which is unacceptable in any formal educational structure. I want to start with the interesting part and then when I feel the need for some basic step, find out about it at the time that it has become meaningful. If I could find a person with the same way of thinking, who could help me fill in the missing links, I could maintain my interest. (I agree with you that, for you, your way will probably work better than the traditional way. This kind of approach is more and more possible the higher you go in the educational scale. The tragedy would be if, by being unable to accept some other approach at times on a lower level, you cut off your opportunities to work creatively a step further along.)

It isn't always so good to convince someone you are right. If you do, you may have to uphold your point of view. (You obviously have some doubts about it yourself. Although in some ways your approach works well for you, in others it doesn't. You don't want anyone to agree with one side of your ambivalence because this would mean they are opposed to the other side. You seem to be afraid of situations in which you feel you are doing things someone else's way, even if this might coincide with your own desires. Sometimes in order to satisfy yourself, you have to satisfy someone else, and it's almost worthwhile to defeat yourself in order to defeat them.)

103. [*For most of this hour he carries on a realistic discussion of his feelings about getting a job.*]

No money would be enough to pay me for work that is valueless to me. On the other hand, if I were interested in what I was doing, and able to be creative, anything that covered my minimum needs would be enough. I can't imagine an employer, though, who would take me on the basis of my self-evaluation. Therefore, somebody will have to pay for my food and shelter. (Nobody *has* to. Many parents would tell a boy of your age to work or get out. Obviously, people want to help you, even if they don't always know how. My feeling is that you are yourself unsure of the value of your output, and seem to be afraid of not meeting your own standards.) That could be so.

104. I want to get away from people who don't trust me—people who don't understand that it isn't my intention to do wrong, even though I may go around with people who break laws. (It strikes me that one of the people who doesn't trust you is you yourself.) Yes. But I'd like to be out of a situation where people don't approve if I don't conform with the crowd. What I do is O.K. with me, but it isn't with others. (And the approval of others is important to you even though you pretend you don't care.)

　　Nobody believes in my good intentions. They don't realize that I might have to act in certain ways in order to be accepted by the only group that will have me. I wonder how you would feel if you saw me with a law-breaker. (How would you feel if I did?) I would feel like a dog caught wetting the rug. (A dog wetting the rug is scared and anxious unless he is a very young puppy.) I'm afraid I wouldn't be able to resist doing what the group wants me to do. If I didn't, they might let on to what I don't want people to know. (What are you afraid you would do to avoid being exposed?) Maybe fight somebody, so they wouldn't think I'm a coward. (Maybe you have to fight to keep from exposing other feelings.)

[*Pause.*] Pain is intended as a warning against physical damage. Now I'm beginning to feel more sensitive to emotional pain than to physical pain. (Emotional pain can often be pretty physical. It's hard to know which is worse, fear of physical damage, or the pain of feelings like love.)

[*Pause.*] I read somewhere that the human being is just one big chemical reaction. That would be very deflating for a lot of people who think they are a lot better than anyone else. (You think that in order to feel equal, you have to feel better.)

[*Pause.*] I'm thinking of a machine. It is just using up energy and not going anywhere. (Better have it hitched up to something so that the energy will be useful, and in turn will feed energy back into the machine.) Physicists have been trying to invent such a machine for centuries. (Every machine needs an outside source of energy because of the friction within it, but if it is greased and cared for the friction will be minimal. Just like people. There is no such thing as a conflict-free person, but if the conflict can be managed, the internal friction is cut down. In each individual there is an optimal amount of outside energy needed for his best functioning.)

105. [*Pause.*] I'm thinking about Gandhi. He certainly beat the whole British Empire. (Passive resistance is certainly the most active resistance.) He thought his way was best for everyone, but I don't agree. (He thought his way was best for Indians, not necessarily for everyone. The Indians didn't like to have to live according to what the British thought was best for them, when they felt the British were most concerned about what was good for the British.)

[*Pause.*] I'm thinking about a problem in math. How many lines go through "n" points? I have to work out a proof for the teacher. (Perhaps you feel the teacher wants you to work out something that is more for his benefit than yours.)

No. He's a good guy. I don't mind working out the proof for
him because he's really interested in the kind of work I do.

[*Pause.*] I'm thinking about taking a trip to Florida
for part of the summer. I was wondering about the food
supply.

[*Pause.*] I know a wonderful beach, but it's off the
beaten path. (It isn't everyone that is adventurous enough to
go off the beaten path.) You don't always have to be alone
because you are off the beaten path. There are fewer people,
but they are selected, and better company.

[*Pause.*] I'm making a knife for my brother. I promised to cut a groove in it—a blood gutter so you can get the
knife out after you have stuck it in. [*Smile. Pause.*] I'm thinking of a machine that holds the knife in a kind of vise. The
knife goes back and forth and cuts on the forward motion,
but the knife is too light. It wavers.

[*Pause.*] A community shouldn't be able to make laws
to punish an individual when it made him what he is. I
know a guy that acts very unlovable, because he feels unloved. Sometimes a person like that has too much pride to
give in and show any affection. (You empathize with his
problem because you have some of the same conflict in yourself.) Yes.

[*Pause.*] I'm thinking of a level. You could make it in
the shape of a square. It would show if you were off the level
in any direction. It might not work well with a rectangle,
but it would work fine on a square. [*Smile.*] (What other
meaning could this have?) I don't know. (Being on the level
—being square with someone—maybe you are wondering if
someone is being honest with you.) I got that for myself.
(Do you know what is bothering you about that?) The only
thing that's bothering me is that I've got a sore throat.

[*Pause.*] I'm thinking of the movie "Lizzie." The girl
had a personality split three ways. I wonder if things are as
clear-cut or work out as fast as they do in a movie. I should

think the personality changes were probably more subtle. (They usually are.)

[Pause.] I've been working on my sports car. I drilled a plate, and got all ready to solder another piece onto it. Then I found the plate was made of stainless steel and can't be soldered onto. Now I have to make another piece out of the right kind of material, but I hope to be able to use that piece somewhere else. Drilling is the hardest work you can do.

106. I have to pass "Family Living." It isn't fair, because I passed the state requirement in another school. It would be a moral victory to hold out, but I don't know if it's worth it.

(You are obviously sensitized to the idea of being discriminated against. You may be fighting someone else through the school. Remember the poem of "Walker J, who died defending his right of way?") [Laugh.] (There are all sorts of things that aren't fair in this world. Each individual has to make his personal decision as to whether a cause is really worth fighting for, or whether he is fighting just for the sake of fighting.) I know that not graduating from school would restrict my freedom to choose my own course in life. Perhaps it wouldn't be worth it to buck this particular requirement. I don't know, though.

[Pause.] I'm probably going to visit my grandmother this summer. There's nothing to do there but sit around and dig tunnels, but I like to go there. I enjoy digging. I wonder how far down I can dig without hitting water? There is a layer of hard stuff part way down, but if you get through it, you can go a lot farther. The biggest problem in digging is to get rid of the dirt. Maybe a stream of water would carry it away. Water isn't always bad, if there's a system of drainage.

107–115. [Detailed recordings not kept during this eight weeks. David was almost totally blocked and dispirited. For *six weeks each interview consisted almost entirely of long pauses and monosyllabic grunts in response to my attempts at getting him started. I gathered that things were in turmoil at home, with quarrels between his parents almost constantly, and pressures on the boy to get to work. These were expressed in angry outbursts, with periods between in which he was ignored. Finally, in the seventh week, he began to talk about it.*]

I haven't got so much as fifty cents in my pocket. All the extra money buys things my mother needs. On the other hand, I'm refusing to get a job, and I don't really deserve anything different. (It must be a terribly difficult period for you, and also for your parents. I can understand how bitter you feel if you think your mother is feeding herself when you are unfed. On the other hand, I think you should realize that things may seem almost as great a necessity to her as money does to you. Both of you are feeling very deprived. Feeling deprived is painful, whether you think you deserve it or not.

(I have thought over some of the things you have been telling me, and I've decided to give you some pocket money. I'm not doing it because you deserve it, but because a boy your age needs a little something to spend. At this point I know you have conflicts about working, and I know that the feeling of being forced into work by not getting any allowance is making the conflicts worse. I know you will have mixed feelings about my giving you money, but I really don't care, because I am convinced that it is the thing to do. What you use it for is of no importance to me. I don't expect you to repay it, I don't expect you to be grateful, and if you want to blow it, that's up to you. You don't have to tell me what you do with it. You can tell your parents or not, just as you wish. You are under no obligation to me. You haven't asked for it, and I am giving it to you only because I think

it is necessary. If you want to discuss it, you can, and if you
don't want to, you don't have to.) [*He smiles and pockets
the money without a word.*]

[*Pause.*] There is just no point in getting a job. My
father has done nothing but work, and where has it gotten
him? (You empathize a lot with your father's unhappinesses
but don't have quite so much sympathy for the effect that
troubles between them have on your mother. They have a
lot to do with the way she is feeling too.) [*Shrug.*] What can
he do? He just gets so frustrated that he has to strike out.
(I know it, but it has become a vicious circle. The more he
strikes out, the angrier your mother gets, and the angrier she
gets, the more pressure she puts on him. It isn't at work that
he gets all his dissatisfactions; it's in the interaction between
them.) I guess that's right.

[*Pause.*] I want to build a short-wave radio to receive
and send obscure communications. It has to have a certain
kind of socket, to fit an unusual type of plug. (Perhaps you
are talking about finding someone with whom you can have
intercourse.) Yes.

Love is like a stalagmite—delicate when it first begins
to form, but later very strong. I don't believe in marriage,
though. It is an artificial structure holding together two people that don't want to be held. If they don't want to, marriage is no use. If they do, it's unnecessary. (It's true that
marriage is an institution developed in civilized society to
furnish a little glue for keeping people together and giving
children two parents. On the other hand, I think your concern about marriage has more to do with your fears about
having intercourse, with or without marriage. What you
want is to find a girl who will have intercourse with you, and
with whom you will be successful in this as well as in human
terms.) Yes. But girls run in packs. They want to be one of
the herd. (That's often so, particularly of young girls. But not

always.) I would have a better chance to get a girl if I wanted to be part of the herd, but I have a better chance of finding what I want if I'm not.

116. [*He continues in the same vein, and quite directly.*] Does closeness mean control by one person over another? How do people really communicate, and to what end? [*He speculates a bit about telepathy, but agrees that one doesn't need this theory in order to understand non-verbal empathy.*]

117. I'm worried about having to go into the army. It would be such a waste of time. There are so many more interesting things to do. (What have you in mind?) Electronics research. My unfinished course is holding up my diploma. (I know how you feel about that. However, I'm inclined to believe that in spite of your feelings about being forced to do something meaningless to you, you should do it in order to make possible the things that will give you satisfaction.)

[*Pause.*] I'm thinking of a German gun. Its sound is too high in frequency for human ears to hear. (I realize you don't want to hear my voice added to all those others that are urging you to do something about which you have such strong feelings.) You are like my mother. (I know all too well how feelings may weigh on a person, even to the point of blocking him from doing the very things he wants most to do.)

[*Pause.*] Two opposing forces are not only pulling in opposite directions, but are interwoven in such a way that some of each are on both sides. You couldn't cut off either one without cutting into the other. I know that the hatred I have put onto the school is really from somewhere else, but it is the same kind of hate I would feel if I saw someone mutilating my wife. [*Pause. Half smile.*] I feel better. [*Pause.*] You can't go on fighting all your life.

[*Pause.*] I think that soon now, I can be more stable

without a feeling of submission. [*Pause.*] I feel there may be a real source of energy. [*Pause.*] If you have such power, you have to have a controlling power, and then more power to control the controlling power.

118. [*Pause.*] Did I tell you that I had an auto accident a couple of weeks ago? (No.) I swerved to avoid a rock and hit a car that was passing me. It rolled over, but the woman who was driving wasn't hurt. (I'm certainly glad of that.) She was a lousy driver. (You know, whether she was or not, I think you have a tendency to get mad at a person if you are afraid you have hurt them.) I know. As a matter of fact, I was terribly scared.

This is the last interview before both of our vacations. It ends the third year of treatment.

8

Case Management

WHEN A DISTURBED ADOLESCENT LIKE David is treated by out-patient psychotherapy, practical problems of case management invariably arise. Upheavals in the boy's life are frequent, not only as a result of his intrapsychic conflict, but also as a result of conflict situations in his external environment. Modifications of therapeutic procedure, which might be contra-indicated in working with a neurotic patient, often become necessary in order to maintain effective contact and promote communications.

Many difficulties arise from sources in the environment over which the patient has little or no control. Some stem from parental ambivalence, which is always present in varying degrees. A young person's need for psychiatric intervention usually threatens parents with feelings of inadequacy in their parental role. Guilt, defensiveness, and fears about loss of influence over their own child almost always accompany realistic feelings of concern and desire to have the child helped.

Parental ambivalence may arise from sources within the parent. Intrapsychic conflicts of many sorts tend to be expressed in feelings about the child and/or the therapeutic relationship. The disturbed behavior of adolescents and children frequently meets unconscious needs of the parents, and therapy threatens to upset some kind of internal balance within one or both of them which has hitherto been preserved by the child's behavior, no matter how objectionable or distressing the behavior may seem to them by conscious, rational standards. Even when they are overtly cooperative with the goals and plans of treatment, parents often express unconsciously their ambivalence toward both participants in a therapeutic relationship.

It should be stressed here, however, that the very presence of a disturbed person in any family tends to disrupt not only the intrapsychic balance of other individuals but also a balance of forces in the group as a whole, creating problems which tend to accentuate any that already exist. Hostility is a normal by-product of such a situation.

A family is put under great pressure by having a disturbed child, no matter what may have been the causes of the disturbance. Fear of public censure or ridicule almost always creates parental defensiveness; this has been increasingly evident since the recent trend of articles in popular literature which tend to blame parents for everything that goes wrong with a child. The patient's behavior itself may be a source of considerable anxiety. Bizarre actions or thinking processes can often be very confusing to people who are not used to them, and may foster equally bizarre and irrational responses. Sometimes, if a patient has a tendency to act out violent impulses, actual physical fear of him may be aroused in family members, making it more difficult for them to act firmly or reasonably. Passive resistance by the patient can be equally irritating, and "may bring the whole British Empire to its knees," as David himself pointed out a number of times. Everyone else in the family may feel that his rights are jeopardized by the disturbed member.

Needs of the patient may encroach upon the needs of parents and other children in a family. While guilt or sympathy for his disturbed state may predispose parents to stress his interests over and above those of others, conscious or unconscious hostility may be generated against him.

Cost of treatment may be a major item in any family budget, necessitating curtailment of many legitimate expenses that could otherwise make life easier or more pleasant for everyone. When therapy must continue over a period of years it often runs into thousands of dollars, which few families can afford without considerable sacrifice of other important activities and material possessions. The treatment of one child may mean that another cannot have the car he badly needs and feels entitled to. College may have to be deferred for one, and another cannot go to camp. In other families, the whole standard of living may be changed to an appreciable extent by the need to pay large psychiatric bills. Resentment by parents and other family members under these circumstances is only natural, even though they may be willing to undergo sacrifice to help the patient.

Another way in which the treatment of a child may create intra-familial hostilities is to arouse dissension between adult members. One parent who favors psychotherapy as a method of dealing with behavior problems may encounter opposition by others who disapprove or do not understand psychological treatment. Grandparents may scoff at the idea; conflicts of generation are stimulated, activating whatever difficulties the parents may have in dealing with dependent attitudes toward their own parents. There may be religious differences within any one family, immediate or extended, and what seems to one to be a recognized method of medical treatment may seem almost sacrilege to another. One member of a family may not approve of medical treatment in any form. Important philosophical differences between parents on this matter may add to other sources of friction between them, or between one of them and the patient. Even when one parent allows treatment of which he disapproves, his attitude may arouse fear of rejection in the other, damaging his relationship to the patient. Or the opposite may occur: opposition by one may tend to foster overconcern by the other toward the patient.

One last factor should be mentioned. Often in the families of disturbed patients, more than one member would like to have help with his own problems. Although the patient's need may have to take precedence because of the nature of his symptoms, others may consciously or unconsciously envy him his opportunity for relationship with a therapist, and react negatively toward him for that reason. This is particularly apt to be true if the patient seems to value his therapy and take comfort from it. In our culture, emotional disorder is sometimes thought of as equated with immorality, and it often seems grossly unfair to others that the child who has been "bad" is given privileges that are withheld from the "good" children who give less trouble. If a member in such a family has had some contact with therapy himself, finding it useful or comforting, he may feel an especial antagonism toward the one who is now getting what he has had to give up.

The expression of parental ambivalence may take various forms of unconscious punitiveness toward child and therapist, or may show itself in inability by the parents to comprehend matters of vital importance to the child and his treatment. Any one, or any combination, of such factors unwittingly sabotages the treatment, and may bring it to an end unless both child and therapist have strong motivation for weathering the storms that occur. Conflicts between parents and therapeutic personnel may occur even when the patient is in a hospital, but usually do not have as much direct impact on the relationship between patient and his personal therapist. Hospital structure and routines offer protection, and the course of psychotherapy is determined largely by variables that lie in the direct interaction between patient and doctor. In an out-patient setting, both patient and doctor come into direct contact with the attitudes of parents, and may feel manipulated by them. Pressures upon either the child, the therapist, or both may be reflected in a breakdown of the therapeutic relationship.

A therapist who is not prepared to deal with expressions of conflicting motivations in parents, and to make concessions over a long period of time, should think twice before assuming psychoanalytically oriented therapy with a borderline adolescent. At times, parental motivations have more influence upon the conduct of therapy than the patient's own motivation. Parents are responsible not only for emotional support, but for actual practical support of the young person's treatment. They must make it possible for him to keep appointments, cooperate in modification of the environmental situation when necessary, and continue to assume financial responsibility, an important consideration when therapy is undertaken in private practice. The fate of the treatment relationship hangs upon parental attitudes toward these practical matters. Unconscious hostility and punitiveness toward the therapist may be expressed in various types of withholding. Information about intercurrent events having considerable bearing upon the treatment is not communicated. Constant "realistic" reasons make it impossible to keep regular appointment times. Financial crises occur with great frequency to complicate the regularity of fee payment. A therapist's refusal to be manipulated may be considered grossly unreasonable, and used by the parents as an excuse for termination of treatment. Guilt for failure can then justifiably be projected onto the therapist. If the therapist feels a commitment to the patient, it may be necessary for him to make numerous adjustments to the whims and vagaries of the parents.

Withholding, in the form of unreasonable deprivations and restrictive conditions, may also be visited upon the patient, and make for difficulties in his relationship with the therapist. Sometimes punitiveness goes under the guise of cooperation with therapy. For instance, whenever the child attempts to discuss plans or problems with his parents, he is told to "take it to the doctor." Parental support is thus subtly withdrawn, while at the same time the child is made to feel his alienation from the family. He is expected to depend upon the therapist for gratification of *all* his emotional needs. If the therapist will not, or cannot, accept responsibility for parental functions as well as his own, the child may feel threatened with a feeling of total abandonment before he is at all ready to assume responsibility for himself. At other times there is a more purely manipulative goal. After the therapeutic relationship has taken on emotional importance for the child, his parents may explicitly or implicitly threaten termination as punishment for undesirable behavior, or make continuation contingent upon certain types of performance at school or home. In either case, the young person's own ambivalence toward therapy is increased. If the price of treatment for him is abandonment by parents upon whom he still feels dependent, or submission to authority which he needs to resist, the result will probably be hostility to the therapist and a stalemate in the relationship.

Other forms of injustice, inconsistency, and punitiveness may occur within the family setting, and may have such an incapacitating effect upon the patient that all therapeutic progress ceases unless direct action is taken by the therapist to mitigate or counteract the emotional response. Intolerable frustration may disrupt the patient's best efforts to carry on the work. When parental attitudes threaten to disrupt a child's ability to work in the treatment, active steps must be taken by the therapist either to effect changes in the parental attitudes or to counteract their effect upon the therapeutic relationship.

The attitudes of parents toward a young person's treatment are determined at least partially by the degree to which their own needs are met by the therapist. Permission for the child to continue in a therapeutic relationship can be given only so long as the parents are not themselves too threatened by anxiety and hostility. If the therapist overlooks or ignores their concerns and wishes, or does not make some provision for dealing with them, he may invite premature termination of the case. Sometimes underlying negative attitudes can be modified by therapeutic attempts of various sorts with the parents themselves, either by the child's therapist or another to whom they may be referred. More often, parents are too unmotivated, or too frightened, to deal with their own conflicts. They resent the implication that they have any problems except those aroused by the child's behavior. If, as in most clinics, a condition is set which makes it necessary for parents to accept personal therapy in order to obtain help for the child, the parents may remove the child from treatment in order to protect their own defenses.

Attempts may be made to effect changes in parental attitudes by other means. Sometimes their reactions toward a child will change when his viewpoint is explained by the therapist and feelings behind the behavior interpreted. Often, however, interpretation is impossible, either because it violates the patient's confidence or because the parents are incapable of understanding. Blind spots in ability to comprehend the child's feelings are commonly encountered. Parents may need to ward off empathy, either because a young person's needs clash with their own or because awareness of his feelings would awaken painful, repressed adolescent conflicts of their own. In the unconscious of the parents, a child may represent hated or feared aspects of themselves or others in their past experience; they may need to express toward him unconscious hostility aimed at the object he symbolizes. In spite of a real desire to cooperate, parents may be unable to modify their behavior very much. When it becomes clear that this is the case, the therapist must learn to ignore or circumvent evidences of their hostilities without retaliation. If he acknowledges their conscious, helpful intentions toward the child, and displays a helpful attitude toward *them*, most parents will cooperate with him to the best of their ability. Effects of their behavior which are destructive to the patient may then be minimized by active support by the therapist throughout therapy.

Sometimes interpretations of parental attitudes can relieve the patient. At other times, compensatory gratifications of some kind become necessary within the therapy. Such activity may create difficulty in the therapeutic relationship. Interventions by the therapist will have transference meanings that cause trouble unless they are immediately or eventually worked through. Remarks by the therapist about parents may be transmitted back to them, arousing anger and retaliation. Nevertheless, a young person who is already swamped by pressure within himself needs real help in combating destructive environmental pressures. The success of treatment may depend on a therapist's willingness to run whatever risks are incurred in offering such help.

Parental behavior and attitudes are, of course, by no means the only sources of problems which may require intervention or adjustment by the therapist. The young person's *own* ambivalence toward therapy may cause him to raise challenges which must be met until a stable relationship has developed. Before the patient can relinquish any part of the armor of hostility that protects him from vulnerability, trust must be firmly established. No matter how strong his motivation for help, he will need to make repeated tests for tolerance and interest on the part of the therapist. As David said himself early in therapy, "If a burglar were trying to rummage through your things, . . . you could cause a person to be shocked electrically if they tried to get in, but the shocks wouldn't be strong enough to hurt anyone. Only enough to discourage them so they wouldn't bother to try to get in unless they were willing to bear some discomfort" (16). Willingness to bear some discomfort is, to a boy like this, an important index of the therapist's concern. Until the intensity of emotional hunger has abated, and defensiveness decreased, it may be necessary for the therapist to make flexible adjustment to quite a bit of hostile or uncooperative behavior designed to test him.

Disturbing interactions also take place between the patient and his external environment which are brought about by his behavior toward others. He has poor control of impulsivity; to be aware of a feeling is to act upon it immediately, without thought of consequence. His perception of reality is governed by needs to satisfy a massive emotional hunger, and may be quite distorted. On the other hand, the values of authority have often been truly inconsistent and unrealistic in his experience. A boy who feels so unsatisfied himself, and who feels himself to have been wronged, has little motivation to satisfy others at the cost of any more frustration for himself. He may act destructively in rebellion, provoking legitimate anger and punitive actions from contemporaries as well as authority figures.

The borderline adolescent sees himself as a hostile, destructive person. He expects retaliative hostility from the environment as much for his feelings as for his behavior, and makes no distinction between the two. He nevertheless feels justified in his own anger, and reacts with extreme resentment to any criticism. Thus a vicious circle occurs, in which feelings of rejection provoke anti-social behavior which, in turn, inevitably has hostile repercussions upon him that generate more feelings of rejection. Any attempt to break into this circle by putting restraints upon the behavior will be met with firm resistance. Although he is well aware of attempts by authority to protect the environment from *him*, the boy has little comprehension of attempts to protect *him* from the environment. Restraint is seen as restrictive, never as protective.

The therapist must come to represent a new kind of authority to the patient—one who accepts the validity of angry feelings without condoning anti-social actions, and who maintains a sympathetic attitude even when destructive actions have incurred retribution from others. He must hold a position opposed to *unreasonable* authority, but upholding the legitimate demands of society.

Assumption of such a role poses complicated problems of management. Although the therapist has little ability to control the patient's behavior, he must often assume responsibility for it and take the blame if things go wrong. He must, at times, make value judgments of environmental demands upon the patient, encouraging in him attitudes which, although desirable from a therapeutic point of view, may cause criticism at home and school. The therapist must also be willing to assume the risk of a possible outbreak of impulsive misbehavior when, in the course of movement in a constructive direction, the patient may possibly be threatened with more anxiety than he can tolerate. If the parents cannot be helped to understand the boy's needs, full responsibility will fall upon the therapist to support him and protect him as much as possible from the anger he arouses. Often, too, eruptions occur which cannot be foreseen either by therapist or the patient himself. Legitimate punishment for law-breaking cannot be prevented, but continued acceptance from the therapist for *feelings*, as distinguished from *actions*, may be an important factor in enabling the child gradually to increase control over the impulse to act destructively.

The therapist in a case of this kind walks a narrow path between rigidity and seductiveness. He must be ready to give freely whenever giving is appropriate, and stand firm when demands are unrealistic. To determine what is realistic, not only from his own standpoint but from that of the disturbed adolescent, is often a complicated decision. A boy's picture of "reality" in a relationship may differ markedly from traditional psychiatric concepts of interview structure. A boy who can barely distinguish his own identity from that of a machine cannot be expected to make realistic evaluations of therapeutic conventions. When a person is overwhelmed by unmet needs, he can find little "reality" in a therapist's desire to maintain structured verbal interchange under "neutral" conditions. The burden of frustration is already too heavy. He requires that the therapist be willing to lighten it by offering certain gratifications. One source of gratification for the patient is freedom to manipulate therapeutic procedure in small ways. He is, however, exceedingly sensitive to "phony" attitudes, as has been mentioned previously. Concession to demands which he himself knows to be unrealistic arouses intense suspicion. Seductiveness is projected onto the therapist by this kind of patient whether or not it is actually present in the therapist's behavior. The therapist must learn to give neither too much nor too little. Hitting the correct balance requires much experimentation within any particular relationship.

Sometimes tangible gifts may be needed to further the progress of therapy. This is true with adolescents as well as small children. In such cases, a therapist may be influenced to some extent by countertransference elements, and may find it difficult to estimate a realistic degree of therapeutic need. However, even if personal factors play some part in the therapist's readiness to offer gifts, there are times when such gifts are necessary on a rational basis. The therapist often has no guide other than his feeling about the immediate situation.

A successful outcome to analytically oriented psychotherapy with a borderline adolescent involves considerable effort and the assumption of responsibility by both participants. The young person must be willing to make a major commitment to treatment in order to work through his problems. Treatment is a long-term endeavor, involving a careful test of the adult for dependability, and a gradual erosion of resistances to trust. Only after much time and struggle can a boy feel free to communicate honestly and directly with an adult.

The therapist must also be willing to make a long-term commitment. In assuming a relationship of this kind, he encourages the patient to drop a strong protective armor of unhealthy defenses in return for promise of help in relieving the anxieties which make it necessary. If and when a patient is finally able to risk exposing himself, he becomes vulnerable to deep emotional hurt until the capacity for new kinds of interpersonal adjustment has been achieved. While he is in a vulnerable condition, allowing himself to trust an adult for perhaps the first time in his life, the therapist has a responsibility not to let him down. A doctor interested in working with this kind of patient knows from the start that the working contract between him and the patient becomes binding until a reasonable therapeutic goal has been reached, and that no external force may be allowed to interfere except under unavoidable conditions. Preservation of a therapeutic relationship after it is firmly established may, at times, subject the therapist to some inconvenience, but he has assumed that dedication to a therapeutic goal in this type of case requires willingness to be personally involved when necessary. He has accepted an obligation to carry on to the end by agreeing to work in this way with a borderline boy.

Many of the factors mentioned above entered into David's case during the course of treatment. Frequent upheavals occurred, requiring practical adjustments and departures from a strictly psychotherapeutic approach to forestall stalemates in therapy. The parents were often unable to see how their efforts in behalf of the boy conflicted with those of the therapist. Needs of the family as a whole frequently took precedence over matters that the therapist considered vital to David. A therapist who works with young people frequently has his attention centered on what is good for his patient, and may react negatively toward any action of the parents or others that has what he considers to be a destructive effect upon the patient or the therapy, no matter how aware he may be that everyone is acting in good faith according to the way they see things. I had this problem at times. David had a tendency to react to feelings of deprivation with paralysis, and I was annoyed when events or attitudes occurring in his environment seemed to be impediments to therapeutic movement. When the flow of therapeutic communication was interrupted by extraneous factors, steps had to be taken to eliminate interference or reduce its impact on David and me.

In this case, the needs of the parents could be met sufficiently to prevent defensiveness and hostility from arousing overt opposition. In spite of realistic hardship in the family, the mother assumed responsibility for support of the treatment, although she might have brought about termination many times during the four and a half years before David became a legal adult. Her cooperation was maintained by a policy of "reasonable permissiveness" on my part, defined according to what I feel is accepted by the general public as standard professional practice. It is my belief that a more rigid structuring of procedures would have furnished justification to this family for termination of the treatment relationship.

Certain rules were explicitly stated both to the parents and to the boy at the start of treatment. Regularity in keeping appointments was expected, and a charge was to be made for cancellations without good reason and adequate notice. I did not, however, demand that therapy appointments take precedence over all other legitimate activities. No charge was made for vacations that did not happen to coincide with mine, hours were changed for good reasons, and make-ups allowed for appointments missed through parental mistakes whenever this could be done without serious inconvenience to me. When David skipped an appointment on his own responsibility, I also allowed make-ups if possible, and did not inform his parents that an hour had been missed, even when a charge was made. This latter policy involved a calculated risk. An adolescent may sometimes try to manipulate his therapist by asking him to juggle appointments, or his parents by making them pay for missed hours. Had there been any evidence that David was staying away from interviews for the purpose of interpersonal manipulation rather than as an expression of intrapsychic conflict, I would have altered my tactics. As it was, he showed clearly that he valued the appointments, and I demonstrated that I wished, whenever possible, to avoid having him deprived of them. Parental wishes in regard to practical matters were also gratified by me. Interview time to relieve personal anxieties around focal issues was granted to either or both upon request. Considerable latitude was allowed in regard to financing. Exploitation of my efforts to meet their practical needs would also have demanded a change in policy, but this did not occur.

My efforts to alleviate environmental pressure upon

David by influencing attitudes and behavior of people in his environment toward him were remarkably unsuccessful. Attempts were made to interpret some of his problems to courts and probation officers when he got into trouble. I had no intention of helping him to avoid all punishment, but hoped that an understanding of the complex reasons for his delinquent behavior might enable officials to ameliorate penalties. In no case did my explanations have any perceptible effect upon the outcome of legal procedure. In all these instances, it became obvious that disasters emanating from David's interaction with his environment could not be prevented by interventions from me. The fact of my attempt to intervene was, however, important in the relationship with David, and therefore useful.

When David's response to external pressures interfered with his progress in therapy, it was necessary to take steps *within* the therapeutic relationship to reduce destructive effects of parental attitudes and official punishments. Reactive hostility on his part could frequently be relieved by interpretation of the motives of others. An open discussion of his parents' problems often mitigated the impact of attitudes which he perceived as hostile. As previously mentioned, permission for such discussions had been granted by the parents. David was himself expressing anger and rebellion in many of the same ways as he felt his parents were doing, and found it therapeutic to see that destructive behavior can be criticized without loss of sympathy for the underlying feelings.

It was also possible to dissipate by interpretation some of David's anger toward "the law." Legal penalties for lawbreaking, although anticipated as inevitable, are often seen by young people as meaningless nuisances which serve no constructive purpose. Full of hostility themselves, they expect retaliative hostility from society for any expression of their anger, but see no distinction between retribution and revenge. A boy who feels himself to be at the mercy of over-whelming impulses can have no concept of a preventive "example." Imposition of a penalty after the event is equiva-lent to "closing the barn door after the horse has escaped." It makes no sense to him. In order to have an internalized value, punishment must be seen by the individual as con-structive to *him*, not for society as a whole. For David it was necessary to have it demonstrated that "getting caught" aided therapy. He was able to see that if he got away with acting out impulses, he might be hampered in his efforts to understand underlying feelings. An acceptance of this idea took away much of his resentment for the process of law and allowed him to undergo punishment with resignation. As he himself said, "It is just a temporary setback, not a defeat" (136).

Interpretation alone was not always sufficient to allay the quantity of anxiety generated in David by extreme frus-tration. When he was incapacitated as a result of feeling deprivation in his environment, some degree of direct grati-fication was occasionally necessary to restore his ability to function in treatment. A boy like this often needs from the therapist restitution for deficiencies in relationships with others. For instance, there was an eight-week period of stag-nation in therapy caused by David's extreme feeling of deprivation and anger at his mother. In order to break the block, I decided to give him five dollars for pocket money on one isolated occasion (107–115). He had been saying bit-terly, "She feeds herself, but refuses to feed me." I answered, in effect, "It is hard for her to feed you when she is so hungry herself. I will temporarily take care of some of your need, so that you will both have relief."

This kind of action may be criticized if it is taken without due consideration. I thought about it for a long time, and decided that it was necessary. My conscious intent was to increase David's empathy for his mother. By giving him something in reality, I hoped to ease the sense of immediate deprivation. By showing sympathy for his mother's feeling of need, I hoped to relieve his own guilt for difficulty in giving. The possibility of a negative reaction from him was anticipated, but did not occur. Actions of this kind may sometimes be interpreted by young people as seductive or manipulative; if disclosed to parents, they may stir up guilt and anger with repercussions on therapist, patient, or both. The whole interaction was another calculated risk. Fortunately, David perceived benign intentions and reacted, as I had hoped, with prompt return to work in therapy.

Demands for concessions or gifts symbolizing love are often made with great intensity by patients in this diagnostic category. David was remarkably restrained in his expectation. He seldom asked for anything concrete, but nevertheless proceeded on the assumption that I would not allow him to be deprived of treatment. When, at a time of financial crisis in the family, I told him we would not stop for lack of money, he answered with assurance, "I didn't think you would. [*Pause.*] One moves to where the force is weakest. It's like two guards fighting over who is to guard you" (84). He obviously saw me as competing with his mother for the privilege of assuming his care, and it seems possible that some unconscious competitiveness was involved, but he seemed to respond with immediate progress in therapy when "the forces" of deprivation were weakened around him.

One great hazard in the management of David's case was my own reactivity. Like most therapists working with this kind of patient, I felt constant need to be aware, and to lessen the impact upon me, of hostilities from the patient himself and those that I felt from his external environment. Empathy with his strong motivation for help tended to arouse frustration in me when resistances occurred in treatment as a response by him to external rather than intrapsychic forces. On the other hand, empathy with the parents' conscious desire to have him helped, in spite of all the difficulties entailed in keeping up therapy, decreased the anger with which I periodically responded to what I felt as their unconscious hostility. I was aware that some countertransference elements were involved, but I tried to control them. For reasons related to my own life experience, I liked and sympathized with all members of this patient's family; everyone knew it and responded with confidence. My knowledge that both parents wanted to keep the boy in treatment despite their own conflicts about it enabled me to make adjustments without too many of the punitive reactions that sometimes impede the relationship between a young person and his therapist when difficult working conditions are imposed upon them from outside. I could not avoid them all.

It took David nearly five years to reach a point where he could more or less consistently make direct communications to me. Only at the sixth year of therapy was he approaching the ability to attack underlying conflicts which prevented him from loving and working according to his superior capacity. In six years of living, an adolescent boy faces many crises under the most ideal conditions. A boy like David was frequently in a potentially explosive condition. Tension between him and his environment necessarily interfered at times with his ability to work constructively in therapy. In order to facilitate the psychotherapeutic process, attempts had to be made to keep disruptive extraneous elements from damaging a relationship between the boy and me. Many active interventions and departures from the ideal of a purely verbal interchange will appear throughout the material.

It is not within the scope of this book to discuss in detail a philosophy of the therapy employed in David's case. The text speaks for itself, and only a few general remarks will be made here about conduct of the interviews themselves.

There are almost as many ways to handle therapy

with patients like David as there are therapists working with them; methods of technical management depend not only upon the kind of professional training, but upon the personalities and individual styles of different therapists, even those operating within the same theoretical framework. It has already been mentioned that David's therapist subscribes to Freudian psychoanalytic theory, adapting analytic therapy techniques to the special requirements imposed when varying degrees of autism characterize a patient's problem. Most analysts agree that the technique of classical psychoanalysis without parameters is seldom useful with schizophrenic or borderline patients, particularly those in the adolescent age group which is notoriously difficult to treat by that method in any case. There is, however, considerable disagreement over the number and types of variation from a standard "analytic attitude" that may be employed by a therapist. Much has been written on this subject which will not be quoted here. It is sufficient to say that the same theoretical principles may be employed in different ways to achieve somewhat varied goals for a patient's "adjustment."

In working with autistic patients, particularly children and young people, some therapists actively induce regression in the hope of enabling a restitutional experience to counteract defects in original object relationships. At the other extreme of therapeutic method is an attempt to produce social recovery in the patient as quickly as possible. This may result in sealing off pathological processes without eliminating the core problem. In my opinion, both of these extremes are to be avoided. Necessary regression must be permitted at the same time that appropriate growth is encouraged. David's case is a good illustration of the fact that this balance is difficult to achieve.

David needed to regress to a more primitive mode of communication, and had to be allowed the protective armor of his "code" until he felt safe in relinquishing it. Consider-

able degrees of dependency and infantile impulse gratification were necessary to him for quite a long time. His ability
to progress from one stage to another could be gauged only
by periodic therapeutic attempts to "push" interpretations,
suggest more direct communication, and encourage more
age-appropriate behavior. Some of the attempts to encourage
more direct communication have already been described.
The problems caused by failure to gauge his readiness for
more adult behavior are illustrated by the results of my participation in premature attempts by parents, and by one side
of David's own ambivalence, to urge him into a job before
he was really ready. Had this succeeded, I believe it would
have been a social recovery incompatible with his emotional
requirements at the time. However, intense pressure upon a
patient from people in his environment demanding that he
act in certain socially approved ways, may frequently be
transmitted to the therapist, causing anxiety which interferes with ability to determine whether such behavior is
actually appropriate to the patient's present psychological
state of readiness. I believe that my somewhat prolonged permission for David to remain irresponsible toward the end of
treatment related not only to the countertransference factors
mentioned in another section, but to a reaction against my
earlier experience in misjudging his readiness for independent action. Such conflicts are very common in working with
patients who have David's type of personality disorder; the
therapist must try at all times consciously to evaluate the balance between regressive and progressive needs in the patient.

PART II

From this point on, the original quasi-verbatim material has been abridged in the interest of readability. Repetitious passages have been deleted, and some interchanges condensed. There has been no change in the sequence of topics or in the essential content of communications.

9

Suspense

"Practical experience has to go into the computer."

THE WHOLE FOURTH YEAR OF THERAPY WAS a period of prolonged suspense for David. At the start of the period, his father was conducting negotiations to get the boy a machine shop job in a distant city. David had mixed feelings about the whole project on many counts, but on the whole was looking forward to it. Right at the moment when it seemed likely that the plan would go through, the boy was involved in a minor automobile accident in which the other party, although uninjured, instituted a law suit. Since it was considered legally unwise for him to leave the area until this matter was settled, David waited—and waited! Weeks and months passed. Meanwhile a serious financial crisis occurred at home, his mother and father were engaged in a crescendo of open strife, and the atmosphere became increasingly intolerable to the boy. His resentment and frustration mounted to a point where some form of emotional blow-up was inevitable.

Throughout the year, David nevertheless worked in therapy. There were twenty-four interviews, during which he talked, sometimes in code, sometimes directly, about all the matters that were of real concern to him. He discussed feelings about the value of treatment, ambivalence concerning his progress and the degree of his stability, worries about his ability to function both sexually and on the job, cut loose from ties to me and to the family. Periodically he exploded and vented, in various ways, intense feelings of frustration and aggression.

Discussions of therapy reflected both his fears of ultimate failure and his sense of the value which treatment had for him. "I want to build a calculating machine, and then a decoding machine, but the number of units required are so costly, and so numerous and complicated to put together, that I wonder if the results will be worth it. I wonder if anyone would want the machine if it finally got working" (120). A good part of his ambivalence about taking the job was related to the necessity for interrupting treatment, and he openly resented my statement that there might be advantages to getting some practical experience which would outweigh his loss of therapeutic time (121). There seemed to be little doubt in his mind that "this is a lot more useful than a lot of things one could be doing. It's important to be able to face one's problems" (123).

At the various times when David thought he was on the eve of departure, he could only let himself hint at hopes for continuation of the contact with me. "If I go, I might want to send word to the good mechanic. (Friends like that will undoubtedly be glad to hear from you.) It's good to know that if things don't work out, I can always come home again" (124). Later, "If a person knew that someone realized he had a hard job to do, and was doing his best no matter how it looked, he might really succeed. (If he felt someone was 'with' him, and didn't require that he prove himself.) Telepathy would be a nice moral support" (128). Many weeks later, when he finally did leave, he could state unequivocally, "This is a good time to stop the puzzle contest. . . . I doubt that there will ever be another that offers so much promise of gain" (142).

David was not at all sure of the degree to which his ability to function had improved, but it was clear that he felt ready for a test, and was not without hope that things were put together more firmly than he sometimes felt. "No matter how good the workmanship is on a piece of equipment, it is necessary at some point to see how well it functions when it is in actual use. One can then see where the stresses come, and what changes need to be made to improve the operation. . . . Once, a few years ago, my friends and I were building a cabin in the woods; although the police eventually insisted that it be demolished, everyone was amazed at the solid way we had put it together" (125).

The scrape that got him into serious trouble with the law can hardly be considered more than a most unfortunate accident. Although the boy undoubtedly derived some vicarious release of aggression through the delinquencies of his friends, he was sentenced for a crime which he committed only by virtue of a legal technicality. His conviction, on a charge involving a penalty under an adult statute, was a farce under the circumstances; all the boys involved were roughly the same age, but David alone had just passed the birthday that removed him from juvenile jurisdiction. The fact that he did not let the experience embitter him was a great triumph, and evidence of real progress in the ability to accept even the most irrational "realities" of the adult world.

119. [Pause.] I want to fix up an old car. It's in pretty good shape, except it has no motor. (I wonder if the motorless car you are talking about is yourself.) Yes. The only thing that's lacking is the ability to function sexually. (Tell me about that.)

I'm not only afraid of not being able to get an erection; I'd even be afraid to take my clothes off. I'm afraid I couldn't satisfy myself or a girl either. I don't think I could take any rejection of love in my stride, even as part of a learning experience. (Again you seem to be expressing feelings about yourself that indicate you see yourself as a small child, trying to function in relation to a grown woman.) That's so.

120. The woman in the accident is suing. (Oh my! I hope it will come out all right.) Well, I'm pretty worried, but it's in the hands of the insurance lawyer. At the moment I'm not driving at all; I want to avoid the possibility that anything could happen.

[Pause.] I want to build a calculating machine, and then a decoding machine. But the number of units required are so numerous, and so costly and complicated to put together, that I wonder if the results will be worth it. I wonder if anyone would want the machine if it finally got working. (You seem to be talking about treatment again. Apparently, when you have any real feelings about something, you use this kind of code.) Things come to me in those terms; although I'm vaguely aware that I'm talking about something else, I can't translate into more direct expression ahead of time.

[Pause.] I'm thinking about sending a current through a plastic block full of iron filings. Once a path has been established through the resistance, it becomes easier each time for the current to follow it, and the resistance decreases in geometrical proportion. After a while the resistance might be minimal. However, if you stop sending the current through, the resistance builds up again. Never to the same extent as at the beginning, though.

[We continue to talk in code, and at least once he looks directly at me and laughs a little, accepting our mutual use of it. We discuss the expense of treatment, and he speaks bitterly of how few people will extend credit or assume a risk.] (People will often invest in research if they think there is a good project. They are willing to assume the loss if it doesn't work out.) If I didn't have credit, I suppose I would have to go to work to pay for it. (I know you will go to work when you feel able. At that time, we will talk about payment.)

121. I have a possibility of a job in a machine shop down south run by a friend of Dad's. (That sounds fine.) I'm not so sure about that. (What are the cons?) I'd have to stop therapy. (I know you would regret that, but it might be worth a temporary interruption to know you could master a real situation that could promise satisfactions in itself.)

[Pause.] People are anxious to have me prove I can do a good job because they want me to do it, not because it will give me any satisfaction. I know I can do a good job; I'll only get satisfaction if the work is satisfying. I doubt it will be, but perhaps the money will be worth it.

122. [He talks to me in code about wanting to make a gun that will work, even though he doubts anyone will find a use for it.]

(After you leave here, do you ever try to make translations for yourself of the things you talk about?) When I'm alone, I can face my unhappiness more directly. I only need the code to communicate. A problem of communication is that often adults can't stand a child's pain. [Pause.] There was a robot. In order to avoid long-range pain, it was necessary for him to endure immediate pain, but the immediate pain was so acute he had to spare himself from that, even if it meant greater suffering in the end.

123. [*He talks about applying for a job, even though he doesn't want it.*] I might have to use more aggressive ways to get back at the people who are trying to force me into a job. (You apparently feel people are interested in getting you into a job not for your own good, but to get you out of their hair.) [*Smile. Pause.*] Most people are just running around like ants on an anthill, each one thinking he's doing something important, whereas he's really just doing some useless, boring job, talking about a lot of unimportant things, and getting nowhere. (I wonder if sometimes you think that's what we are doing?) No. I think this is a lot more useful than a lot of things one could be doing. It's important to be able to face one's problems.

(If you weren't talking about us, it must have been something else close to you.) Mother and Dad are typical examples. Not Dad so much; he doesn't let anything bother him. But Mother can't do anything useful, and doesn't even want to learn. She can't unlock a door, open a can of food, or drive a car so as to get efficiency from it. These are things *I* can do. An adult should be able to do better than a child, so that he could learn and get support. (You feel disappointed and guilty that in some ways you function differently than she.)

[*Pause.*] I'm thinking of how to drill a bore so that a penny can run in the groove without vibrating. (Can you translate?) Maybe I want to know how I can stop leaning on my mother without losing control. (Both of you see in each other the things you fight in yourselves, and get terribly angry at each other. At the same time, you feel an unusual closeness and understanding.) [*He speaks sadly.*] We could both do the things that interest each other, but just don't want to. (Yes, but this relates more to emotional relationship than to activity.)

124 and 125. There is a good chance that I'll get the out-of-town job; I might leave soon. The only problem is that the suit hasn't come up yet. [*Pause.*] If I go, I might want to send some word to the good mechanic. (Friends like that will undoubtedly be glad to hear from you and keep in touch.) It's good to know that if things don't work out, I can always come home again. [*He smiles, and then quickly averts his eyes from me.*] I haven't finished the work on my gun yet.

(This job venture can be a trial period rather than a final commitment.) Yes. No matter how good the workmanship is on a piece of equipment, it is necessary at some point to see how well it functions when it is in actual use. One can then see where the stresses come, and what changes need to be made to improve the operation.

This is a kind of moratorium period for me; there's no feeling of crisis—just waiting to see what comes next.

Once, a few years ago, my friends and I were building a cabin in the woods; although the police eventually insisted that it be demolished, everyone was amazed at the solid way in which we had put it together. They thought one man could pull it apart in an hour or so, but it took several men three days.

126. [*After a mix-up the day before, he arrives right on time.*] I woke at 6:30 for fear of being late. (Would that have been so frightening?) Mother's major complaint about Dad is that he's always late. (Is it that you fear antagonizing people, as your mother is antagonized, or that you fear being like your Dad?) I don't know. I do some things the same as my Dad,

but I'm much more worried about them. He takes things easy, and so do I, but *I* don't like it.

[*Pause.*] I get a big kick out of my friends baiting the police, although I've learned that for me it's too dangerous to do it any more. (A lot of your activities against the police have been in the nature of a game of cops and robbers. I think you are trying to prove something about your masculinity in these terms.) I have to be on the side of the rebel or I have no side at all. That's the only way I can get noticed. If nobody cares what you do, why bother to do what they want? I might as well get pleasure out of annoying them.

127. [*He brings with him some metal parts of the gun he's making; he talks in terms of machinery or methods of meeting specific problems about the work on it.*] (What feeling makes it necessary to talk in these terms?) Maybe I'm bored because life is so dull and routine; this might be a way of making it more interesting. (Another form of cops and robbers? "Come and get me, and I'll hide in the bushes"?) No; "Come and get me, and I'll be so close to you that you can't see me." Some of the cops get so they can't see the woods for the trees. (I wonder if you are telling me that I'm so busy looking for an obscure communication that I'm missing something more simple and direct going on right under my nose. Perhaps you are communicating with me directly about these things, and are disappointed that I don't take pleasure in your pleasure, but seem to be wanting you to be more interested in my line of interests than in yours.) Yes. I've had some feelings like that. I think maybe today I needed to prove to myself as well as to you that not everything I think is a coded message.

[*He seems relieved; stretches his arms and shoulders, quite stiffly at first, keeping his head turned away, then relaxes and unstiffens his position in the chair. This is one of the few times he has made any marked muscular movements*

*or changes in position. He suddenly begins to talk quite
freely about when he was younger.]*

128. I definitely have the job, but the suit is still pending.
(Do you know any details of what you will be doing, or where
you will live?) [*He discusses some of his practical plans.*]

(Where is the balance between plus and minus in
regard to the work itself?) I'd like to have my cake and eat it
too. (You haven't had much cake in your life, and I hope
you'll get a piece.) [*Smile.*] That has a double meaning.
(Yes.)

I'm doing some machine work. Great accuracy is required, or the consequences will be disastrous. (You seem to
be talking about the need to be exactly right or everything
will fail.) [*Pause.*] I think I'm afraid of the responsibility of
taking on a man's job—both at work and sexually. In the
sexual area, almost any girl will be more experienced, and will
laugh at my efforts. (Again the small child, expected to cope
with the emotional needs of a grown woman.)

[*Pause.*] If God knows the future, he should know
whether one is to be saved or not. He shouldn't need the
proof. (He might know that a man was going to be saved,
but not know in what way.) If a person knew that someone
realized he had a hard job to do, and was doing his best, no
matter how it looked, he might really succeed. (If he felt
someone was "with" him, and didn't require that he prove
himself.) Telepathy would be a nice moral support. (A person doesn't always have to be nearby to be "with" someone.)
[*Pause.*] (I know you will find yourself eventually, but I'm
not sure in what way. It will be your own way, and it is not
possible at this point to relate success or failure to any particular job. Your problem will be in terms of inner mastery,
and confidence to handle the intensity of your feelings.)

[*As he goes out, he turns.*] I'll let you know what
happens on the job. (I hope you will.)

129. [*Things are still pending. He looks disheartened.*] I did something I wish I hadn't—acted destructively on a frustrated impulse. [*He tells the incident.*] (You seem to have difficulty in restraining an impulse long enough to give yourself time to decide whether or not you want to act on it.) Often I wouldn't do things if I were able to think a minute, but when I feel frustrated and left out, the tension immediately becomes unbearable. (You have to work on increasing the time span between impulse and action.) There is no thought involved; I feel and act simultaneously. (That was a painful situation which would naturally arouse strong feelings. I do hope, though, that eventually you will learn to control the *actions* that get you into trouble.) I hope so too. I wonder if I ever will be able to.

130. [*Pause.*] I'm thinking of a machine tool; it's a compass with a third leg. (That suggests a man with a penis.) I thought of that myself. Actually, any machine tool could be the symbol of a penis, and working with tools a way of playing with yourself. [*Pause.*] I'm thinking of a blabber-mouth. (You are ambivalent about wanting to communicate feelings about this.) [*Pause.*] I'm reading a story about a man who wanted to shoot rockets to the moon. (You are talking about sexual worries.) I don't know what I'm trying to say, but it *feels* unhappy.

[*Pause.*] I saw "The Jet-Propelled Couch" on TV; I didn't like it. (It bothered you that the analyst entered into the fantasy with the patient?) The patient wanted the fantasy accepted, not made real to him. (You can't quite believe in your fantasies, but hate to relinquish them for fear that nothing will replace them.) That's right.

Some African natives were forced by the English to have the Englishman's religion imposed on them, but it didn't suit them. In any case, it was phony. The English preached that everyone was equal in the sight of God, but they didn't really accept the Negroes personally, and the Negroes could see that the acceptance wasn't real.

131. I will be leaving soon . . . I don't know for quite how long. (Since I will be away for three weeks during the holidays, there is a possibility that our next meeting will be the last for a while.) [*Nod. Pause.*] I finished the gun I've been making. I had to remake various parts a number of times before I was through, but now that it is made correctly, it works. [*Smile.*] This is the first time one of my projects has come out successfully.

132. I'll be leaving soon. (Do you know any more definitely?) No; maybe Dad does, but probably not. (Anyway, until we know more, we have to assume this will be our last meeting for an indefinite period.) [*Yes. Pause.*] I'm thinking about milling a piece of metal. I don't know whether it's better to make shallow cuts that might be uneven, or deeper cuts to be sure they are even. (Are you talking about cutting the ties with home?) Yes. I wish I could cut off the past, but I'm afraid I can't. (The past is only important as it is reflected in the future.)

[*Pause.*] It would be nice if the job were nearer to the family. (I know you will miss many things in your present life. You have mixed feelings about being on your own.) I'd like to be near the family, but not *of* it, nor *in* it. I want authority to change to support if I need it, but I wouldn't like to be enveloped by it. [*Pause.*] I want to be able to survive alone, and leave people behind. (Without loss of contact.) Yes.

[*Pause.*] I'm thinking of a story about the U.S. wanting to avert war with Russia. They sent some bombs filled with truth serum instead of explosive; unfortunately, the factory where it was made got filled with it, and that was bad. Nobody wanted to use it on themselves. (You are afraid that if I maintain an interest in you, I will expect some kind of return that you won't be able to make.) Not that *you* will, but that *I* will. I feel a gift must be repaid, while a loan can be ignored.

(You and I have done a meaningful piece of work together, and I'm sure it has a place in both of our lives. Under such circumstances, nobody is obligated to anybody. There will be a relationship, even if we never see each other again.)

I feel it is a priceless interchange. The money that is paid to a doctor is what it takes to run his business, but what he gets out of it is the satisfaction of his desire to help. What the patient gets can't be paid for in money. (That makes sense. It is a mutual interchange.)

[*Pause.*] It's like when you want to split the current along a wire. There is a flow of electrons, and no *force* could make them divide; but if you put a certain potential on each part of the wire, then the electrons flow according to the potential. You can't *make* a person do anything by employing force—only by making him *want* to. It's like putting on first one potential and then another; he doesn't have to respond to the first but if he does, it opens up the second. He doesn't have to respond to that either, but it's there, and he can if he wants to. At any point, he can draw back or go ahead. It's just like human motivation; it comes along if there isn't force, but just potential.

There is a month's interval, during which I talk to both parents and then leave for a vacation. There is apparently no question but that he will still be here when I return.

133. (How have things been going?) Status quo. The suit is still unsettled. (Is your father working on it?) I think so.

[*We spend the hour talking about plans and living arrange-*
ments in the new city, if he ever gets there.]

134. I'm in the process of building a jet engine. The main
problem is getting the fuel into the explosion chamber. (It
must be terribly irksome to wait so long and not know what's
going to happen.) Yes. But actually, I don't know what the
job is going to prove. What's the use of taking a job to stay
alive, when there isn't any reason to? (Do you have to have
a reason right now? Why not just take one step at a time?)
Someone has said that the point of life is that it's a learning
process, and the process is the goal. (That's a good idea.)

I hope to find there is some reason for life. There is
no sense trying to build a bridge from one side of a gulf unless you know there is land on the other side. (Sometimes, if
it is necessary to get away from where you are, you have to
start on the bridge just in the hope that it will reach something. In the meantime, the work of building might keep you
from getting anxious about the dangers you are trying to put
behind you.) Yes. But nobody would want to build a house
on an island that was going to be used for an atomic bomb
test. (No, but nobody knows ahead of time which islands will
be used for tests. People just go ahead and build houses because they need a place to live; when they find their island
will be bombed, there is usually time enough to take the next
step.) That's so.

I don't know whether the job will really be the kind
of work I'm most interested in. (I know you are very much
interested in the work of solving your inner problems.) The
unconscious mind is really the one thing you can trust, but it
has the hardest job of all. It has to sort out the perceptions
that come to it, not only from other people, but from the
conscious mind. Sometimes the perceptions that come to it
are erroneous. Sometimes I have to wait a while until it de-

cides which ones are valid. (It is particularly difficult when contradictory messages come through at the same time from different levels.)

Not only from yourself, but from other people. Sometimes they want two different things from you at the same time, but they don't always know it.* The unconscious mind has to decide which one to respond to. Sometimes you hit it right, but they don't think so, so you're wrong anyway. (I think you have just stated a major problem between you and your parents. Both of them are unconsciously sending out messages that are opposite from what they send out consciously, and on both levels there are mixed feelings. Love sometimes comes out expressed as hate, and hate sometimes comes out expressed as love. It isn't surprising that often you get your signals mixed.) It's better just to sit back and wait. I try not to respond at all, either way. Then I'm safer.

135. I'm building a jet engine. (Tell me about it.) It doesn't work, because there are some leaks; but you get the feeling it *wants* to. (What are you going to use it for?) I don't know. (I guess the main problem at the moment is just to get it working.) I guess so.

[*Pause.*] We found an unexploded rocket. (Even a live mine can be explored and made harmless if it is handled carefully and the job is done slowly.) The teacher wasn't scared of this one, but the kids were. (One has to understand the mechanism, so as not to fool with something until it's safe.) Funny thing; when we got it apart, there was stuff that looked like gunpowder, but the teacher said it was only sand. (I think you sometimes feel like an unexploded rocket that will go "bang" if it's jarred.) Only sometimes.

* See Don Jackson's theory of the "double bind," as set forth in "Toward a Theory of Schizophrenia," *Behavioral Science*, vol. 1, October 1956.

[*Pause.*] It would be fun to refuel that rocket; I think maybe it could be converted into another kind. I'd like to attach a turbine that could be moved from place to place. (You mean a built-in self-starter of some kind?) Yes. (Just as you would like to feel able to get going from within yourself, no matter where you are.) Yes. (What would be necessary for building this self-starting mechanism?) I think maybe the mechanism is in, but hasn't been connected up yet. Perhaps it isn't connected because it's never been needed. (I think that's a strong possibility.)

[*Pause.*] I was thinking about government missiles. The people that make them either don't care, or they are stupider than I think. They use solid fuel, whereas everyone knows you need liquid fuel for space travel. Solid fuel gets them moving. (You mean all they care about is to get them off the ground, but they don't care what happens after that.) [*Smile.*]

[*Pause.*] I'm wondering if the rocket will work. (As you said, perhaps one can't tell until there is a need to connect it up and try it. If there are then parts that need adjusting, they can be worked on until the whole mechanism is in running order.) I think the problems will be in the control mechanism. (Yes. I think you will have to work at interposing a layer of thought between impulse and action.)

Two days later, I get a call from his mother, saying that David has been picked up by the police, along with a gang of kids who have committed some vandalism. He was not involved in the actual crime, but had invented an ingenious method of committing it and told the others about it. Since some of them are under eighteen, and he is just over, he is held on an adult charge.

The father has gone away on a business deal that he "couldn't get out of." The mother says she doesn't think she can go to see the boy in jail "for fear I'll break down." I suggest that there's nothing terrible about breaking down, and maybe he needs to know she feels like that. When I ask whether I could get permission to go and see him, she refers me to the lawyer.

Nobody informs me what happens next, but when I call, David himself answers the phone. He asks to come and see me before the trial.

136. (How do you feel about all this?) It seems very unnecessary. (Tell me about it.) I worked out a plan as a "project," and they wanted it. (Didn't you realize what kind of trouble that might get you into?) Yes. I thought about it, but it didn't seem important. Being with my friends seemed more important, but I know now that it wasn't. (What about the "layer of thought" that might have saved you?) It came too late.

(Do you think you have been treated unjustly by the authorities?) No. But it doesn't do any good to put me in jail. (That's true. On the other hand, the police are in no position to understand your feelings; they can only react to your behavior, and it's their job to administer the law. From their point of view, this is the only way to protect the interests of society. I am very sorry this had to happen, but I don't think you have been wronged, and I hope you can come through whatever happens without any more bitterness. Let's see if we can figure out how to prevent your feelings from running away with you another time.)

I think this is a temporary setback, not a defeat. (I think so too. I wonder if some part of you was trying to say in this way that you didn't feel ready to go so far from home.) Perhaps I didn't feel ready for such a big step all at once. (Should we be considering a less drastic move? Something like living away from home and taking a similar job nearby?) No. I think at this point I might be able to take the job down there as a preparatory step toward taking one nearer home.

I was afraid that if I went there, I wouldn't be welcome back, but I'm not afraid of that any more. I've been talking to my family, and I think I understand a lot of things better. (That's a big step. A lot of the trouble has been a difficulty in communication.) Yes. It's not so bad any more. I think I can go away and try to prove to myself that I can make it; then I can come back. (Yes. Others can say they believe in you, but you must learn to believe in yourself.)

(What can you do to make the jail experience constructive rather than destructive?) Finish my high school course. But I dread the inactivity; I hope there will be some work to do on the farm. (I hope so too. Anyway, good luck.)

137. [*This session took place after his stay in jail. We discuss his experiences on a realistic level, with free communication on his part. He expresses some bitterness about the living conditions, with enforced inactivity and no attempt at constructive rehabilitation. I sympathize with his feeling.*]

I didn't mind too much, though, and hold no grudges. I was released on the understanding that I'll soon be leaving for the job. I'm not sure I want to go so far away. I like being on my own, but not being gotten rid of.

[*At the end of the hour, we again recognize that this might be our last meeting, for a while anyway. I assure him that I will be thinking of him, even if there is no more direct contact, and hope that things go well for him. He expresses some doubt, and fears being a disappointment to people.*] (You may be a disappointment to yourself, but I consider this one kind of step that is desirable, even if it doesn't work out. You aren't committing yourself for life; just for the immediate future.)

I'd like your address, just in case I might want to write. [*He stands rather uncertainly by the desk while I write the address. When I offer to shake hands, he does so without apparent shyness.*]

There is no word from anyone until over a month later. Then the mother contacts me about something else, and mentions that the boy hasn't gone yet. "If I had known it would be so long, I would have sent him in."

I immediately write David that I hadn't known he was still in town. I offer to see him if he feels like coming in, although I state explicitly that he might not want to start in again for only a short time. About a week later he calls, just at a time when I am out with flu. I tell him so on the phone, and promise to call him as soon as I am out of bed. There is about a two-week interval between his call and the next appointment. In the interval I receive a note from him saying "Dear Doc: I hope you get well soon. You are one of the few people that we need around here."

138. [*There is a striking change in David's appearance. He has on a clean shirt; his hands and face are clean and deeply sun-tanned. He is smiling and quite relaxed, talking freely but superficially.*]

The first job has fallen through, but there is another prospect in another shop up north. (Another friend of your father's?) Yes. (Another uncertainty as to whether it will materialize?) Yes. (How do you feel about these long waits?) I don't let myself think about it. (It must be discouraging at times.) [*Smile.*] There's no point in worrying. (It's hard to keep being worked up to something, and then have nothing come of it. I did it to you myself when I offered an appointment, and then had to keep you waiting.) You couldn't help it. (No, but it's uncomfortable anyway.)

[*Pause.*] I've been working with Mom and a friend of

hers on finishing the high school course. We make a game of it, and it isn't so boring. (I'm glad you will have it out of the way.) I'm also working on a puzzle contest. The prize is thirty thousand dollars, and I'd sure like to win! [Pause.] With a computer many millions of computations could be turned out in a short time; the human mind is limited by its slowness. It may be very accurate, but each computation takes so long that one can turn out relatively few in the time allotted. (Perhaps it isn't necessary to turn in every possible combination.)

The next week we have to change the day of our appointment. He doesn't show up. Later in the week his mother calls to say he "forgot" until the following day, the day of his usual appointment.

139. I got mixed up because of the change in the day. I'd gotten to think of Wednesday as "my" afternoon. [Pause.] I'm still trying to get hold of a mechanical computer.
(We can come back to that if you wish, but right now I want to ask you something that seems important to me. How did you feel about my getting in touch with you about coming in again, after you had presumably quit therapy?) I was glad. (I wonder if you didn't have mixed feelings— glad, but also a little afraid I had some need to hang onto you.) Perhaps. But mostly I was relieved. (You had wanted to come in?) Yes.
(Then why didn't you get in touch with me when you found you weren't leaving yet?) I think I was embarrassed. About still being around. (You thought I would feel, "Oh my God, is he still around?") Yes. (You feel as though people are blaming you because the job fell through?) Or maybe blaming Dad. [Pause.] Mom is upset because he has quit his job again. (Your father has a problem about that; it isn't your responsibility. I think, though, that you are reluctant to

take the responsibility about something that *does* concern you, like calling me for an appointment.)

It's better if it just happens. If I wish for something myself, something will go wrong. It's better not to wish for things. (If you "will" something, you will put a jinx on it?) Yes. I try not to "will" anything good. (I see. If you admitted to yourself that you wanted to come in, something would be made to prevent it.) Yes. But I was glad you said I could come. (I've noticed that sometimes, when you have given some indication that you really want an appointment, you "forget" the next one; maybe this is the explanation.) Perhaps.

140. I went to New York this week to see a hypnotist. I'd read an ad saying that he could break blocks to learning that exist in the unconscious mind. I asked if he thought he could bring out the combinations for the puzzle contest that I'm sure are in my mind if I could only get at them quickly enough. He said he pretty surely could.

[*We have a long discussion of hypnotism, in which I urge him not to play around with it. He asks the dangers.*] (I feel there are good reasons why it is difficult for you to uncover all your unconscious feelings and emotions speedily, and that you would do better to take them at the pace for which you yourself feel ready, not have them dragged out of you by force. It is a great temptation for you to be passive and have things "done to" you, as we discussed last time, but you also have a strong need to defend yourself against the pos- sibility of exploitation. I think you will do well to trust your- self to people who know you well, and whom *you* know well enough yourself so that you're willing to risk *voluntary* revelations at such a pace, and under such conditions, that you feel safe. Although under scientific conditions hyp- notism is useful, it can also be abused. Someone who puts ads in the paper guaranteeing miraculous discoveries might not be a very responsible person. In spite of the temptation to passivity, you should keep yourself in the position of being an active, voluntary agent in whatever therapeutic process you are involved in.) That makes sense.

141. [*Another fruitful discussion of the "double bind." Also of whether it is possible to hold an unsatisfying job and still find other sources of satisfaction. He is trying to formulate a philosophy for living without feeling defeated.*]

142. [*An emergency appointment in response to a call saying he can leave tomorrow.*]
(How do you feel about the situation, now that it is actually upon you?) Good. I didn't dare let myself anticipate it till it was final. [*We discuss his realistic plans, and his feelings about leaving home.*] I'm not too worried; I want to feel I can come back, but I like the idea of being independent. (You want to have a choice.) Yes.
[*Pause.*] This is a good time to stop the puzzle contest. (You have more immediate problems at the moment. Later, if you want to enter another puzzle contest, you always can.) I doubt there will ever be another that offers so much promise of gain.
[*Pause.*] I'm thinking of a problem about centrifugal force. When a particle spins around a central point, each degree of motion really involves a change of direction at an angle of infinite smallness. This means there must be a force producing acceleration, even though the particle seems to be going at the same rate around the point. I'm interested in what makes the force. (The reason the acceleration hasn't been greater is that centripetal force has balanced centrifugal.) Yes. The pull to get away from home has been balanced by fear of being on my own. I don't know whether one has gotten stronger, or the other weaker—or maybe some of both.

Maybe in proving the importance of emotion and intuition, I am trying to prove that I have something worthwhile in a line that interests me. (There is no doubt about that in my mind, but there seems to be some in yours.)

There is too much unhappiness in the world, and not enough pleasure; there should be a better balance. (Yes; it shouldn't be all striving, nor all pleasure. One should be able to have a productive place in the world, and still have satisfactions and pleasures.) I'm going to find where the best balance lies. (I hope you will.)

Nobody likes to work, but being lazy isn't the answer either. Practical experience is a factor that has to go into the computer, or the answer isn't valid. If you are working with nothing but theories, the margin of errors gets larger and larger, like going out on an angle.

(We've said "goodbye" a couple of times now. I guess we don't have to say it again.) I'll write. (I'll be thinking of you.)

1 0

The Risk of Suicide

A<small>T THE BEGINNING OF HIS FIFTH YEAR OF</small>
therapy, David suddenly gave unmistakable indications that
he was preoccupied with the thought of his own death. Such
preoccupation in an adolescent must always be considered to
indicate the *possibility* of a seriously intended suicidal attempt. Effective therapeutic measures of some kind are
almost always required promptly, but the therapist in a
private office practice is posed with a crucial decision as to
what kind of measures he must take. He must not only be
able to make an accurate evaluation of immediate risk to the
patient's life, but must sometimes be prepared to assume a
calculated risk for the sake of the patient's future.

The therapist faces a delicate problem. Suicide is a

common symptom of maturational crisis and a frequent cause of death in the adolescent age group.[1, 2, 3, 4] On the other hand, adolescent patients as a group characteristically present florid pictures of transient symptomatology which do not necessarily indicate the same ultimate grave prognosis that similar pictures would imply in adults. The expression of suicidal thoughts does not always indicate a real desire or intention to die. Evaluation of the real danger to life rests upon exceedingly fine points of judgment, and a mistake may be serious either way. Overestimation of suicide risk may be almost as damaging to the patient as underestimation. In protecting him from possible loss of life, a therapist may jeopardize the patient's capacity for developing a self-concept compatible with future health and autonomy.

Action by a therapist which signifies to the patient that he is recognized as a definitely suicidal person may confirm the young person in making final commitment to a role with which he has been playing somewhat tentatively. One may paraphrase what Erikson has said about adolescent role experimentation in general, and say that an adolescent toying with suicide is "leaning out over a precipice [experimenting] with experiences which [may become] more amenable to ego control provided they are not prematurely responded to with fatal seriousness by [overfearful] adults."[5] Expression that the therapist believes loss of control to be inevitable may confirm the patient's own feelings of worthlessness and weaken his ego defenses against impulsive action. Despair, mingled with guilt for resentment and rebelliousness toward the therapist, may contribute to the strength of a self-destructive impulse which has arisen at least in part from similar conflict of feelings toward the parents.

Action by the therapist which in any way extends beyond the limits of interaction with the patient himself may result in damage to the patient's confidence in the therapeutic relationship, and often to its termination. On the other hand, failure to take such action as suggesting hospitalization, or at least warning parents of the young person's condition, may have grave consequences not only to the patient but to the therapist himself. Two risks are thus precariously in balance—the risk of failing to give adequate protection which is temporarily necessary to save a young person's life, and the risk of either actually precipitating self-destructive action or robbing the patient of confidence, not only in his own capacities, but in any future therapeutic relationship which might help him to understand and master his impulses. It may be a win-all or lose-all gamble.

A solution to the problem depends upon the therapist's competence in assessing the clinical picture. It may also depend to some extent upon whether his personal philosophy places the highest possible value upon preservation of life at all costs. Conflict will be most acute for the therapist who believes that a human being has the right to choose to risk his life in order to gain its fullest realization.

Accurate assessment of the total clinical picture is aided by some previous knowledge and understanding of the patient's psychodynamic patterns. A therapist's knowledge of past history and current events may clarify for him precipitating factors in the suicidal reaction. A young person's feelings of discouragement at failure to meet standards of performance set by himself or others, or his difficulty in adapting to conflicting environmental demands, may tax his self-esteem and bring on depression. However, the importance of precipitating events may lie largely in what unconscious meanings they have to the patient. Increased aggression arising from intensification of unconscious conflicts is far more apt to tip the balance of control over self-destructive impulses than conscious feelings about task failure or inability to perform adequately. It is important that a therapist be aware of the kinds of situations which tend to increase aggression in any particular patient, in order to evaluate the strength of forces with which he is contending.

He must also be alert to minor indications of change in mood swing. Rapid fluctuations in psychic balance are characteristic of adolescents in general and of emotionally disturbed patients in particular. The nature of psychic functioning in suicidal adolescents is often quite different from that of adults with similar tendencies. Even though in early developmental stages they may have suffered psychic traumata creating an anlage for the classical states of depression and psychosis seen in suicidal adults, young people are at a developmental stage that introduces many variables to alter the final picture.[6, 7]

In adolescence, physical and psychological growth is still active. Permanent defensive and characterological patterns have not solidified. Basic interests and skills for adapting to real life situations are still in the process of formation. Young people who are still to some degree truly dependent upon adults, no matter how violently they may be struggling for independence from parents, are amenable to help from adults outside the home in finding models for identification and verifications for their own sense of identity. They are capable of sudden swings in psychic equilibrium which make successful therapy at any particular time both more hopeful and more precarious. Adolescents often move rapidly toward either greater stability or greater eruptiveness. They can sometimes handle conflicting urges more flexibly than older people, but they may also be more impulsive and unpredictable in their actions. A therapist must be ready to perceive quick changes in the clinical picture.

To take the risk of proceeding in therapy without recourse to other forms of intervention, a therapist must believe that the patient will gain enough ego support from the therapeutic relationship to counteract whatever forces are working against him, and that the patient's confidence is sufficient to allow time for mutual exploration of the dangerous impulse before he commits himself to action. Such a belief must be built upon an accurate evaluation of the balance between positive and negative transference factors if it is to be valid. Don Jackson says, "It is doubtful if suicide . . . can ever occur where adequate communication exists between patient and therapist." [3] However, he also points out that blocks in communication may be interpreted by a patient as death wishes toward him from the therapist and may precipitate suicide by increasing the patient's feeling of abandonment. A therapist must be very much aware of the state of the transference if he plans to stake everything upon his interaction with the patient.

A final decision on whether or not to risk acting through the therapeutic work alone may be determined by nothing more than a therapist's confidence in his clinical "feel" about the young person's emotional state. Objective clinical signs of dangerous depression, which usually serve as a warning in adults, are often absent in young people. Even with considerable knowledge of a particular patient, it is easy for a therapist to underestimate the likelihood of sudden impulsive action. Clues to guide him are nebulous and few, making it necessary to rely largely on relatively subjective indicators. However, this subjective "feel" by a therapist who is experienced in treating young people, may be the most valid criterion in estimating immediate danger. [4] Knowledge and intuition together often allow a quite valid estimate of the patient's suicidal potential.

A number of factors enter into the production of suicidal impulses in young people. Bender and Schilder have pointed out that the feeling underlying overt attempts by children is most frequently fear and a feeling of unbearable tension arising from real or fantasied love deprivation. The aggression which results is turned inward with unconscious hope that a self-destructive act will force the parents to restore love and at the same time punish them for having withheld it. Coerciveness and spite are thus strong elements in the suicidal urge.[9] Similar feelings may play a part in the motivation of some adolescents.

However, the onset of puberty introduces unique issues productive of conflict for which a young person may seek solution in self-destruction. The young borderline patient in particular is at or near the "identity crisis" described by Erikson.[5] Conscious and unconscious conflicts, heightened at this stage of development, may cause seemingly unbearable tensions from which ideas of death offer the only possibility of relief.

Sexual impulses are apt to be extremely intense at this stage, and frustration of genital as well as oral wishes may cause a sharp increase in self-directed aggression.[7] Disturbances in direction of libidinal impulse may also arouse conflicts leading to a self-destructive drive. The concept of "being dead" may unconsciously become associated with pleasurable fantasies of passive gratification or the regaining of infantile omnipotence by oceanic blending with a preambivalent mother. A strong urge for relaxing gratification and an intensification of aggression resulting from guilt for wishes unacceptable to the superego may overwhelm protective forces of a patient's ego and allow loss of control over impulsive action.

Erikson suggests that suicidal trends in young borderline patients may be in part a product of diffusion in time perspective.[5] Adolescents characteristically tend to feel a sense of great urgency combined with a feeling that each moment is interminable. This tendency is accentuated in those who are psychologically disturbed, and may result in a decided disbelief that time will bring a change mixed with a violent fear that it might. Need to end the conflict between wishes for improvement in their condition and equally strong fears of what improvement might entail may be expressed by the adolescent patient as a wish for death.

A borderline patient who has reached a certain point of improvement in therapy may feel this conflict most acutely. Destruction of a protective fantasy adaptation, and puncture of infantile feelings of grandiosity, may bring about an acute crisis if reality conditions do not immediately offer strong reinforcement to a rapidly dwindling sense of self-esteem. As Fenichel puts it, "The desire to live means to feel a certain self-esteem . . . when this feeling vanishes, the original annihilation of the deserted hungry baby reappears." [10]

When David returned to therapy after six months of attempting to "put practical experience into the computer" (142) I was alarmed at the change in his condition. Certain objective signs, along with a strong subjective "feel" on my part, suggested that he was potentially suicidal. A vague appearance, dull stare, and affectless voice were characteristic of deeper withdrawal than any he had previously expressed. The content of communications about need for "blending individual consciousnesses" (145) had a flavor of psychotic fantasies about individual reunion with the cosmos which frequently lead young people into impulsive attempts to "seek a new state of consciousness." When a boy like David starts to speculate on the nature of death, there is always a possibility that he will try to obtain first-hand information about it. After considerable experience on a University student health psychiatric service, I feel some confidence in my ability to sense nuances of emotional tone in the philosophical ruminations of adolescent patients in general. I had also worked closely for four years with David. Never before, in all his goal-less periods and emotional upheavals, had I sensed in him such an authentic feeling of hopelessness and resignation to defeat. He appeared ready to give up the struggle against conflicting forces within him.

Elements in David's psychodynamic history were consistent with a possible swing toward suicide. He had always been inordinately ambivalent toward all love objects and confused in the direction of sexual impulse. Fluctuations between guilt for, and acceptance of, pleasurable fantasies involving passive gratification had been frequent in his communications. It is not unusual for the concept of death to become erotized in conjunction with such feelings and fantasies. David had, in the past, exhibited sudden ego-alien impulsivity and a tendency to act self-destructively in periods of heightened rebellion. An unconscious impulse to obtain libidinal gratification through self-annihilation might well be put into action under the pressure of stress.

The boy had returned to treatment with mixed motivation. Underlying aggression toward me was obvious. His bitter description of our relationship as an "exchange of waste products" (146), and the caustic comment that "it's easy to be nice to a person . . . if it's the last thing you will ever have to do for him" (146) had an ominous ring. It seemed likely that a strong element in his decision to come back was the need to show me how completely I, as well as every attempt of his own, had failed to help him. I felt that his voluntary renewal of therapeutic contact was also prompted by the opposite—a positive bond with me, and a hope of being dissuaded from his intentions, but David gave an impression that the scales were precariously balanced and ready to tip in a negative direction at the slightest provocation.

Ambivalence toward me had contributed to growth of the anxiety which seemed to be reaching a climax. Even before leaving therapy for the job in another city, David had had mixed feelings about my agreement with his decision to do so. He derived from my attitude both self-confidence and a sense of rejection. Strong elements of negative and positive transference were in opposition. Identifying me at least partially with those whom he saw as trying to force his capitulation to "demands of society," he gave evidence of anger and resentment which conflicted with feelings of love and reliance upon my faith in his capabilities. Hope of finding new sources for satisfaction through realistic accomplishment temporarily held in abeyance his dependent and erotic needs, but when new life experience proved disappointing, aggression toward those who had encouraged him mounted along with the frustration. At a time when he most needed ego support, interruption of therapy had withdrawn it. David felt lost and betrayed.

As a matter of fact, his present condition was, in part, a direct result of therapy. For years he had maintained a semblance of self-esteem with protective fantasies of grandiosity and infantile omnipotence. Therapy had punctured these fantasies and forced him to relinquish defensive mechanisms of withdrawal from all emotion by which he had previously adapted to unpleasant reality. After a prolonged and vigorous resistance, he had finally agreed to comply with the wishes of others and try a new approach to life. The new approach had failed. Compliance had led only to further decreases in his self-esteem. Fantasy adaptation had been destroyed, and reality offered nothing to replace it. At the time the boy returned to work with me, a full force of rage against the betrayers was unleashed within him and directed primarily against himself. There was some doubt in my mind whether sufficient support could be obtained from positive elements in the relationship between us to give him strength for combating aggressive impulses.

I nevertheless knew that it was necessary to take a chance upon resumption of therapy without resorting to any other form of intervention. The boy had come to me willingly, able to discuss feelings before committing himself to action, and I had to trust the strength of his motivation for self-understanding to tide us over the crisis. David already had strong feeling that others wanted to protect him for their own good rather than for his; rebellious self-destructive action had, in the past, been instigated in response to this feeling, and a move on my part to call in outside help at this time might have precipitated a suicide attempt. Whether it did or not, any act by me which betrayed his trust would have been highly destructive to our relationship just when the relationship was potentially his source of greatest hope.

A move to warn his parents would indeed have been taken largely for my own protection. I believe that to preserve an individual's physical existence without offering hope of future possibility for emotional satisfaction is no service to anyone, particularly a boy with such intense need for awareness and autonomy. I felt that for David, the only hope of real happiness lay in working through his problems, and David knew this. Loss of my faith in his capacity to do so would have removed the last vestige of self-esteem and hope for the future. A move by me toward limiting his right to make a free choice of life or death would have been interpreted by him as a complete loss of my confidence and would, I am sure, have resulted at the very least in termination of therapy. Although I never lost sight of the fact that an impulsive suicide could occur at any time, even in the course of treatment, I dared not risk destroying the hope that lay in our work together. There was no real choice except to believe in David and support his own efforts.

Decisive therapeutic aid to the boy had to be made available immediately, but help had to be offered without threatening David's sense of autonomy. The forces within him which were fighting for control of aggression had to be strengthened and time gained for decrease in the frustration that was generating such violent feelings. What he needed most was a rapid reinforcement of self-value and a stabilization of his time sense.

"Time diffusion" was a striking characteristic of David's thinking. He fluctuated between feeling like the "man who has lived two thousand years" (91) and one whose sand is about to run out at any moment. Constant emphasis in therapy had been placed upon the importance of immediate experience, and the lack of necessity to anticipate the whole future before taking a step. Now more than ever, this concept seemed to need firm reiteration. Stress on the value of "here and now" might hopefully decrease unbearable anxiety about future capacities.

A basic sense of self-value in any individual grows from the experience of being loved and cared for in infancy and of having his special qualities appreciated by those who matter to him throughout childhood and adolescence. The feeling is confirmed when realistic accomplishments and creative contributions are recognized as worthwhile by those people in the environment whose opinions are respected by the individual himself. David had had rather sparse experiences with unambivalent love and appreciation in early life or with recognition of valued contribution later. His self-esteem had been bolstered largely by omnipotent fantasies before treatment, and was presently at its lowest ebb. A meaningful relationship with me had, however, developed throughout the past four years, and had made me one of "those who matter." The boy had become convinced that my basic goodwill and interest in his welfare were honest, and knew, even when negative transference was at its height, that I respected his own special quality. Such knowledge had

now to be firmly re-established, and my concern unequivocally demonstrated. I knew that speedy action might be
important, but also that unless I was willing to raise the
alarm by urging extra interviews at a time when money and
transportation difficulties barely enabled him to come in
once a week, our working time was limited to the usual fifty
minutes, separated by an interval of seven days. It was not a
comfortable situation for either David or me.

Under these conditions, I did what I could to put my
ideas across without creating a sense of urgency or panic.
Responding to his expressions of goal-lessness by firm emphasis upon present functioning and the value of knowledge
for its own sake, I implied faith in the therapeutic work itself (144). In answer to rambling abstractions about the goal
of life, I merely stated a belief that the goal of life was to
live it, and stressed the value of David's capacity for maintaining awareness (145). By the third week, his tone of bitterness had deepened, and speculations about death were gaining momentum (146). At this point it seemed necessary to
make a direct statement that I would care if anything happened to him, but also to play down any obligation on his
part to act or not act for my sake; I stressed that playing with
the idea of death might be jeopardizing his own capacity for
future gratifying intellectual and emotional experiences. I
was trying to increase his feeling that the special "ability to
be aware" which he possessed was a quality to be valued. At
the end of this interview, however, I was extremely worried
about his clinical condition.

Three days later I was in the hospital with a sudden,
acute infection that promised to incapacitate me for some
time. A vital decision faced me. The outcome of our entire
work together might depend upon my judgment of David's
ability at this moment to respond realistically to an emergency. It was necessary to decide immediately whether his
transference feelings and autistic fantasies about possible

meaning of the interruption would be strong enough to over-throw his already delicately balanced tolerance for frustra-tion. For some indefinable reason, probably based upon a feeling for the basic strength of our relationship, I decided to trust David. Although I telephoned him from the hos-pital to tell him what had happened, and followed up with a note specifically asking him to take it easy until we had more time to talk, the situation was left in his hands. I be-lieve this was the turning point of his crisis.

In the interview after my return, David continued with philosophical speculations on the value of living, but there was a distinct change in the tone. He expressed in-directly but clearly the feeling that my concern and trust had given him a sense of value, even though at the same time he rebuked me for putting him under obligation to stay alive for my sake (147). The danger seemed definitely past, and he was soon re-engaged in research on "the storage of mem-ories" (148). Although a few weeks later, under the pressures resulting from his mother's illness, there was a resurgence of desperation and explosiveness, with temporary reversion to the use of code (151 through 155), the suicidal *quality* was lacking in his communications and attitudes. David was able to admit then that recognition of my concern was what kept him from "going off on my own somewhere, away from security" (155). He was able to respond directly to an appeal for control by commenting with assurance, "I dislike people who panic" (155). At that point, he felt capable of landing his plane eventually, even though the wing might tempo-rarily be on fire.

During the last years of therapy, pressures periodically increased and created periods of severe anxiety for David. However, there was never again a real threat of self-destruc-tive action. Once in a disgruntled moment he said, "If it weren't for therapy I would be more interested in suicide. The world is a grubby place." Immediately afterward he added, "Unfortunately, I can't quite wish not to be experiencing" (191). Even when things looked dark he had become "stuck with being committed to wanting life" (186).

REFERENCES

(1) Bakwin, H., "Suicide in Children and Adolescents," *Journal of Pediatrics*, Vol. 20, 1957, p. 749.

(2) Parrish, H. M., "Epidemiology of Suicide among College Students," *Yale Journal of Biology and Medicine*, Vol. 29, 1957, p. 585.

(3) Parrish, H. M., "Causes of Death among College Students," *Public Health Reports*, Vol. 71, 1956, p. 1081.

(4) Raphael, T., et al., "The Question of Suicide as a Problem in College Mental Hygiene," *American Journal of Orthopsychiatry*, Vol. 7, 1937, p. 1.

(5) Erikson, E. H., "The Problem of Ego Identity," *Psychological Issues*, Monograph No. 1. N. Y., International Universities Press, 1959.

(6) Josselyn, I., "The Ego in Adolescence," *American Journal of Orthopsychiatry*, Vol. 24, 1954, pp. 223–237.

(7) Zilboorg, G., "Considerations of Suicide with Particular Reference to That of the Young," *American Journal of Orthopsychiatry*, Vol. 7, 1937, pp. 15–31.

(8) Jackson, Don, "Theories of Suicide," in Shneidman, E. S., and Farberow, N. L., eds., *Clues to Suicide*. N. Y., McGraw-Hill, 1957.

(9) Bender, L., and Schilder, P., "Suicidal Preoccupations and Attempts in Children," *American Journal of Orthopsychiatry*, Vol. 7, 1937, pp. 225–234.

(10) Fenichel, O., *The Psychoanalytic Theory of Neurosis*, N. Y., W. W. Norton, 1945.

11 ·

Danger

"It doesn't hurt if one pebble drops on your head,
but a whole sackful may crack your skull."

THREE MONTHS PASS, AND THE FOURTH
year of treatment ends. Then I get a letter from David, saying that he is coming home and wants to see me.

143. [The job convinced him of the value of going back to
school. He did hard physical labor; it was tiring, boring, and
led to a dead end. With a note of irony he gives the impression that school doesn't seem worthwhile either, but if he is
going to have to make a living, he might as well try to prepare for something that leads somewhere. There is no use
going on with therapy or anything else until he has gotten
himself settled.]

Another three months pass; then comes a brief scrawl asking if he can start in again.

144. [*The boy looks vaguer and more withdrawn than he has looked for a long time. He has nearly finished a semester in junior college, but can't see any practical use in what he's learning, and has no real interest or desire to learn. He has a part-time job bringing in a small amount of money but no satisfaction.*]

On the whole, I'm just drifting around and absorbing information; that's all I'm good for. I can't see that I am able to—or for that matter want to—put my knowledge to any use. (One doesn't always know ahead of time what use knowledge will have. Most research starts with learning for its own sake. The use may evolve later.)

145. He spends the hours in a hopeless, spiritless, abstract discussion of whether living is worthwhile. He seems already to have made up his mind that it isn't, but is in no hurry to commit himself pro or con. (I don't know what the goal of life is myself, but in my opinion, the goal of life is to live it. Since we aren't in a position to know whether or not there is anything else to it, experiencing and maintaining consciousness are important in themselves for people who are as capable of awareness as you are.)

It is too difficult to establish communication between individual consciousnesses. It's like someone attempting to establish an even level in three glasses of fluid. One can spoon liquid from one to the others, but the most accurate way would be to connect all three with tubes beneath the level of the fluid; they would immediately find their natural level. (You feel that in order for people really to establish empathy, they have to become part of each other.) I think this is slowly happening in the consciousness of mankind, but the process is too slow. The world is filled with millions of glasses of fluid at different levels, with everyone madly spooning from one to the other. Eventually the consciousnesses must all blend by making connection at another level.

146. [*I keep him waiting fifteen minutes.*] I'm sorry; I guess I made a mistake in the time. (If anything goes wrong, you apparently take it for granted that it was your fault. This time *I* made the mistake.) I guess I do feel relieved that other people can be wrong sometimes. On the other hand, I don't feel too bad about it; I assume you are friendly, and if you made a mistake, there is no malice in it. Perhaps the person ahead of me needed extra time; I can sympathize with him. I assume you are interested in your patients, and get satisfaction from doing what you think best. I'm getting something for nothing anyway.

(There seems to be a discrepancy. If you feel I get satisfaction from my work, you must feel I am compensated for whatever you get from it.) Animals and plants have a reciprocal need for each other's waste products; nothing of value to the one who is giving it out, but it is necessary for the other.

[*Pause.*] I've just come from my grandmother's funeral. The minister eulogized her. It was interesting to hear a few nice things said about someone who has never been called anything but a bitch. It is easier to be tolerant of people if *you* aren't the one they have injured. Also, you can afford to do something nice for someone if you know it's the last thing you'll ever have to do for them.

[*Pause.*] I wonder what death is like? Is it an enlargement of consciousness or not? (Since we really don't know, it's better to concentrate on enlarging consciousness in the life we have. An experiment with death is pretty final. Even if others are *extremely sorry*, the one who loses his life is the one who doesn't get another chance to find out what happens next.)

Just at this point, I fall ill and am in the hospital for a month. I call him personally and tell him what has happened; I also write a note, telling him how sorry I am to have complicated things just when we have an important piece of work to do together. I tell him I'll see him as soon as I am back on my feet, and in the meantime, I hope he'll take it easy.

147. [*He sits and stares.*] (What are you thinking?) I solved a problem for a friend. It can't be solved by math, but you can see by logic what the answer is; you can't work it by formula, but the answer is clear by just looking at it. (Sort of like something one gets by intuition.) Yes.

[*Pause.*] The letters on the book titles can be read upside down or backwards. "t-i-o-n" backwards looks like "n-o-l-l." Nolla is a word for non-Aristotelian logic. (You seem to be concerned with problems of logic. Anything specific?) No. (It seems like what you were talking about the last time we met—concern with solving problems by logic that can really only be solved by feeling. Things like the meaning of existence, or whether life is worthwhile.) That's true.

[*Pause.*] I can't really find any reason to go on living. (Do you have to have a reason?) It would make things easier to bear. If there isn't any reason, there is no point to the struggle. (Unless the process of living is in itself the reason.) I have my doubts about whether the pain and difficulty of life are compensated for by any satisfactions that can be derived from the mere process of living.

[*Pause.*] When I was a kid, I had an old clock. It was of no use to anyone except somebody like me, who liked to see the wheels go round. It didn't keep good time. The best person from whom to receive such a thing would be someone who was likewise interested primarily in creating an intricate mechanism, and wanted it appreciated for its structure rather than its monetary value.

[*Pause.*] I have very mixed feelings about giving and receiving, owing and being owed. To feel that a person is willing to give makes the one who is given to have a sense of value, but it also puts him in danger of being possessed. If a person fears he will get nothing, he needs to grab everything he can get. If he is sure of getting what he needs, he might not have to take so much, and could even give a little. But there is a great difference between giving voluntarily and giving because something is demanded or taken for granted. One might not want to do something because the doing of it would hurt another person. He might feel differently if he thought it was expected of him.

(You might refer to the idea of going on living purely because your death might hurt someone else like me, rather than a desire of your own to live.) If one did it voluntarily, it would be different than if people expected it. One should have freedom of choice.

(Freud said that to many a man, life has become tolerable because of the knowledge that it can be ended at will. On the other hand, there are times when a desire to end life is symptomatic of other problems, and temporary. One needs to feel that under such circumstances, one will be protected against taking a step which precludes any change of mind. Death is irrevocable. If one achieved it, one doesn't get a second chance.) That depends on one's personal beliefs. (True. However, we have no way to know for sure whether there is an after life, no matter what one may hope or believe. We have to reckon in terms of the life we have.)

The problem is lack of drive to survive. (I understand the feeling very well. However, the drive to survive is a basic human drive; if it is absent in an individual at any time, there is a blockage which it is important to explore. Sometimes it is necessary temporarily to borrow drive from someone else if the sense of personal value that's necessary to keep it going is temporarily depleted.)

It is better to be owed than to owe. The person who is owed always has the privilege of canceling the debt, but the ower hasn't. (Putting the person who is owed in a position to make the ower feel inferior.) That, of course, depends on the attitude of the person who is owed. He might be able to manage without creating resentment. (That might not be easy to do, and certainly couldn't be done by formula.) I imagine the best way to do it would be to proceed as has been done so far. If it worked out in the end, the assumption would be that it was the right way. If the ower paid the debt, it would be because he wanted to, not because it was demanded.

He "forgets" his next appointment.

148. I planned to take some deep breaths before climbing the stairs so I wouldn't be panting when I came in. (Are you anxious?) Not exactly; it's more like an alertness.

(I suspect mixed feelings. You seem eager to come, yet sometimes forget your appointments entirely.) I didn't exactly forget last time; I forgot the time of the appointment, and then was reluctant to call. It seemed like a reprieve to have forgotten. (So there was *some* desire not to come.)

Perhaps it was because I was wild last time—almost out of control. (Tell me about it.) I had the feeling people are just stupid—everyone talking at cross purposes. (You felt we were talking at cross purposes?) No. [*Pause.*] I think my saying that was a sort of test—a question mark. (Tell me more about how you were feeling and what was going on in your mind.)

[*Smile.*] Your questions are always completely open-ended. Sometimes I find a need to misinterpret what is asked, but with you there is nothing to misinterpret. (You sometimes misinterpret to protect yourself from communicating what you feel.) Yes.

(What have you found so frightening in what you've discovered about yourself?) Nothing has turned out to be so terrible. But it's like if a man is approaching a dark cave; if he sees two eyes staring out, he becomes wary. If, as he gets closer, and the light falls in a different way, he sees they were only two beer cans, he wonders how he could have been so scared. But the next time he's in a similar situation, he's just as scared. (Particularly if his previous experience has often been painful; then he is more apt to anticipate that "two eyes" will be hostile rather than friendly.) You only have to be hurt once by the dentist's drill to have some fear of it, no matter how often it has not hurt you. (That's true.)

[Pause.] I would like to be able to help people with their problems, but there are some kinds I wouldn't want to help. (What kind?) Those who wouldn't want to hear. (When people don't want to hear, it's part of the problem. You have to find out why they are so afraid to hear.)

[Pause.] I'm thinking about storage of memories, and what is the best way to go about locating the ones that are important. If you put a monkey at a typewriter, it is possible that by chance, if he had enough time, he would hit the right combination of keys to write Shakespeare. But there have to be more systematic ways to approach the problem. I've heard that every thought is connected with every other, but it has to be narrowed down. (Everything is connected with what has gone before it by associations. One can follow the train of associations and see how things are related.) Sometimes wrong memories are stored too; new connections have to be learned. (Sometimes reactions are connected with feelings that were appropriate to the condition of a small, helpless child; they may not be necessary to an adult who doesn't really need to be so helpless.) [Smile.] I have to relearn a lot.

[Pause.] All my friends are individualists. (The world needs more people who think for themselves.) [Ironic smile.] That usually means, "Think for yourself, so you'll do it my way." (Yes; often people do feel that anyone who is sensible thinks as they do.) [Pause.] If something is half good, is it half good or half bad? If the world is half water and half earth, is it a lake or an island? [Laugh.] I guess it depends on whether you're an optimist or a pessimist.

I had to change his hour, and the following week he doesn't show up. He calls later in the day to say, "I was working on a brass coin, and got so absorbed that nothing else was important." I offer him an appointment the next day.

149. [He walks right up to me and puts two metal medallions in my hand to show me what he has been working on; then he sits down and stares into space.] (Working on coins was pretty absorbing?) Yes. (Can you describe the feeling that was sufficient to make you miss an appointment that presumably was quite important to you?) [Smile.] There was an acute conflict of interests. I made some mistakes in casting the metal, but felt the errors are not irreparable.

[Pause.] I will soon be able to fly solo. The instructor thinks I'm good. It's good to know that someone you think is very good thinks you are good. (What does it take to be a good flier?) What does it take to be a good tricycle rider? Mother says I was very good at that; I didn't hit the furniture. She says I did things like walking and talking very early. I wonder why? (Lots of factors enter into something like that; intelligence, motor activity level, and coordination are built into body potential by native endowment.)

I can't believe heredity is the prime mover. (Sometimes emotional factors prevent a person from using his native endowment; I think that's what happened to you. You had all the potential for good motor coordination, but feelings about yourself slowed you down and kept you from using it. You felt, "What's the use?")

People have different degrees of adaptability for sur-

vival. If a mouse sees another mouse walk into a trap, he
may be able to avoid it. (But he may have an even stronger
impulse to eat the cheese that baits the trap.) I would try to
figure out how to get the cheese without getting caught in
the trap. (You are a man, not a mouse.) [He looks directly
at me, with an intense, jeering look.] The only way to avoid
a trap is to spring it from a distance. I read about two mice
who worked together and figured out how to spring a trap.
I would be willing to share the cheese under those circumstances. It was sad, though; someone figured out how to stop
them. (Someone must have been very eager to trap them.)
      A mouse's needs aren't very great. If people would
stock the mousehole with enough food, the mouse wouldn't
have to interfere with their needs. On the other hand, there
might be an overpopulation problem among mice if they
were freed from dangers; then they would outnumber people,
and people would become the endangered minority. I wonder if people and mice could ever learn to live together without endangering each other? I think a better way than trap-
ping mice would be just to keep them out of the house. Then
they wouldn't bother anyone.

150. [Pause.] (What are you thinking?) There wouldn't be
any reason for you to get sick except overwork. (I can't catch
a germ like everyone else?) People don't get sick unless they
need to. You have been working too hard. (You seem to feel
you are an awful burden to anyone who has anything to do
with you; I wonder if this isn't the source of your feeling
about the pressure of my work. You have been saying things
lately that indicate a feeling that people can tolerate you
only so long as you don't interfere with anything that involves their own interests. I wonder if you fear you are getting in my way at this point? You said last time that maybe
the only way to prevent being infringed on by a mouse is
simply to keep him away.)

What you put as a statement was really a kind of question, like, "This *isn't* true, is it?" (You have a lot of fear that if you want to make any demands on a person, he or she will be overwhelmed by you. You seem to feel that if you ever let yourself want anything, your wants will be insatiable.) It's better not to depend on people for things you might not get.

(If a man has been starving, he often overeats for a time when food becomes available. To be denied something increases one's hunger for it. You know that if someone puts six identical cakes on a plate and says, "You can have any one except *that* one," *that* one is the one a person will want.) I wanted it before you finished the sentence.

[Pause.] I've heard that the way energy is released in a joke is close to the way it is in genius. I'm thinking of a joke, but I'm not about to tell it. (I know; most jokes are about aggression, hostility, sex, feces, etc.—the kind of things people don't let themselves talk about directly.) This one is about feeling foolish in a humiliating situation. (One can certainly have a lot of anxiety about that. Sometimes to be able to laugh at that kind of thing, one *does* nearly have to be a genius.) Either that or wired for sound.

[Pause.] It certainly must take a lot of rearranging when one first begins to be able to see. At first, the images are reversed and upside down. Why aren't the nerve tracts planned so that the image is right side up from the start? They come in on the lens one way, reverse on the retina, and then reverse again in the brain. It seems too complicated. (Yes. It depends on what stage of the process one is at as to how one sees the image. Mental and emotional impressions are developed in somewhat the same way; at certain stages they seem distorted.)

[Pause.] I've had a feeling that the last four or five times I've been talking differently; on a couple of levels all at once. But it's kind of vague. Sometimes if you stop to think about the process of what you are doing, you can't do it very well. It's like trying to tie your shoelaces; if you think about the complex motions you are making, you become all thumbs. (Sometimes it's more important just to get your shoes on, and not to analyze how you are doing it.)

151. There's been another crisis at home; Mother is sick in bed. (I'm very sorry.) Everything is disorganized.

[Pause.] Four more hours and I fly solo. (I'll bet that makes you feel good.) Yes, but scared. I can't imagine myself with solo responsibility. (I imagine your instructor wouldn't encourage you to fly solo if he didn't think you were ready.) He's been teaching me emergency landings. The main problem is not to get panicky and land in an unsuitable place before you really have to.

[Pause.] I'm wondering why Mother got so very sick. (You were talking last time about people not getting sick unless they "needed" to. Have you some ideas as to why your mother might "need" to incapacitate herself right now?) I know I don't do things like that unless there's a reason. (Tell me what you think might be involved. Apparently you identify your mother's unconscious needs with your own.)

[Pause.] If you pull too much current from a generator, it will kind of whine and stop generating. (I'm trying to pull too much from you on this subject?) I didn't so much feel you were trying to get too much too fast, but that this is a dangerous area. I really think it's impossible for me to think about my feelings for my mother. [Pause.] A car going toward a certain point loses its power. It needs power for braking and steering and accelerating. But as it gets near the point, the steering wheel is pushed in the other direction. (Like a negative magnetic field.) If you bring the strong positive poles of two magnets toward each other, they repel each other.

152. [*He looks very withdrawn again today; has to be prodded to make even short, noncommittal remarks.*] (What's on your mind today?) Nothing. [*Pause.*] (How is your mother?) Back from the hospital, still ill. [*Pause.*] (What now?) I wish something would happen. Everything seems so futile.

[*Long pause.*] (What now?) I'm thinking about a science fiction story. There was a small universe in a capsule. You could make something happen by communicating with it, but you never knew whether you were anticipating it, or it was anticipating you. (You and me.) [*Smile.*]

[*Pause.*] Everything is so useless! Nobody thinks it's important whether you are conscious, or half-conscious, or unconscious, just so long as you do what's expected. There's so much energy wasted in the world. If people would only cooperate, nobody would have to do what they don't want to do. Everyone is busy finding short-cuts through the woods; if they got together, they could build a highway. There needs to be a change in the way people do things. (Do you think there should be some change in the way you and I work together?) No. But it's like filling up a hole on the beach with water.

153. I flew solo today. (How wonderful! How did it feel?) Not so bad. By the time I did it, I wasn't so scared of landing.

[*Pause.*] I was thinking about making a circle around three points. They can't be in a straight line. (Lately you have been talking to me more directly, but the last two times you seem to have gone back to the symbolic talk. This seems to coincide with your mother's illness; can there be a connection?) I wouldn't be surprised. [*He is speaking so softly that I can barely hear.*]

[*Pause.*] (What are you thinking?) Of a line at a tangent to a circle at a point. (Can you translate the image?)

[*Haltingly.*] The point at which they touch is control. [*Pause.*] The circle goes down in fear of losing control. (In what way do you fear loss of control?) Of all the questions that could be asked, you ask the one that makes me hang onto myself. (Like the fable about the sun and the wind. They had a bet about who could make the man take his coat off first. The sun won, but it could have been the other way around if warmth made the man hug his coat tighter around himself.)

[*Pause.*] You will see how panicky I am, because I see another image. (Tell me about it.) The circle and the line again. The problem is to make the circle touch both the point and the line. (Isn't the point a part of the line and also a part of the circle?) I see the circle rolling along the line, but at this point there is a stop. I don't know what the point is. (You don't know what the purpose is, or the place where the point is?) [*Pause.*] It takes a lot of energy for a bunch of electrons *not* to form a pattern.

[*Pause.*] I've got my infra-red tube working. (How does it work?) I don't know, really. Actually, it's a disappointment. The image comes out muddy. I don't know if it can be made better. (Maybe when you have more time to experiment with it, you can improve the image.)

154. [*The first fifteen minutes are composed of long silences, broken by brief, noncommittal replies to questions about what he is thinking. Then there is a sudden change. He makes a remark followed by a long pause, then speaks spontaneously.*]

I was wondering what your response was to what I had said; then I realized that the important thing is that I care at all about your response. (Yes. That *is* important.)

It is often so difficult to communicate my thoughts! When you ask what I've been thinking after a pause, there are usually any number of directions in which I could go, but

I feel ambivalent about going in any direction that seems indicated by the timing of the question. Immediately the particular thought at the time seems more painful than some of the others, although actually there is no particular difference. To verbalize something immediately gives it more reality than it had before; then I have to face my own feelings. I think you must have some intuitive knowledge of just when to "plug in" on my thoughts.

155. [*Smile.*] I'm getting more flying time. It's hard to land when there are other planes around; everything is more complicated when there's a traffic problem. (That's true in life too. One can handle things very differently if nobody else has to be considered.)

Things are very complicated at home; Mother's illness has made her very complaining, and has increased the pressures on everyone else. I'm having to drive her a lot, and keep the house clean. (That's irksome for you. Immobilization must be hard on her too. When a person is used to relieving tension by moving around, immobilization of this kind is particularly painful.) I know. (All these family problems hurt you. You have to feel them, even if you try hard not to.) I try not to show it; but I really don't like insensitive people. (Don't like them, but envy them a little.) [*Smile.*] I guess so. It certainly would be easier to live like that.

[*Pause.*] One might be able to take *some* troubles, but there are just too many. It doesn't hurt if one pebble drops on your head, but if someone empties a whole sackful of them, it may crack your skull.

[*Pause.*] Once when I was a kid, I was swimming; I got caught under a rock that the life guard was sitting on, so he couldn't see me. I finally got loose, but I almost didn't. If you are drowning, you should shout for help, but if you *can* shout, you aren't drowning. (Is that the way you feel right now?) [*No answer.*] (You are telling me that I should see

your need and distress without your having to tell me, and
should pull you out without your having to tell me how. I
will if I can, but I'm not quite sure what you want me to do
to start pulling.) I don't really know. I just know that life
doesn't offer much satisfaction. I can't understand the
tenacity of my desire to live.

We could all go back to living in caves and be just as
happy. Things are too complex. (Unfortunately we can't go
backward. Once we have achieved a certain degree of com-
plexity we have to live with it and learn how to manage it.)
People are trying to live with too much garbage. (True. But
an individual can do away with what seems like garbage to
him, and still live among others who prefer to keep their
garbage.)

It's their world; why don't they make it better? (It's
your world too. What can you try to do to improve things?)
The only positive step I could take would be a token gesture.
(What would that be?) Something like changing the laws of
electricity, or making water run uphill. Make a twenty-five
cent box that could produce anything anybody wanted.

[Pause.] I read a story about some people who discovered that a planet was out of its orbit and would soon hit
the earth. They told everyone. Everyone went about his
immediate business without having to worry about long-
range goals, and everything was running smoothly by the
time the planet hit. (That's the way you feel at the moment.
You expect to be hit by an explosion of piled-up feelings inside you.) It wouldn't take much to annoy me beyond tolerance. Nobody really cares whether I explode or not. (You
underestimate the situation. There really are a few people
who care.) When I said that, I meant 99 per cent; the 1 per
cent is what keeps me from going off on my own somewhere,
away from security. I know you care.

There is a record about a man on a plane who looks
out the window and sees that the wing is on fire. He tells the

stewardess, and she says, "Coffee, tea, or milk?" He says again that the plane is on fire. She says, "Maybe you need a martini." (I know you think I am offering you coffee, tea, or milk while the plane is on fire.) [*Laugh.*] I couldn't say no, because it seems as though that *is* what I'm saying, but I don't think that's quite the way I feel. (A pilot can often land a plane, even if the wing is on fire—that is, unless everyone inside the plane panics.) I dislike people who panic.

1 2

The Therapist and the Fee

A<small>LTHOUGH THERE HAS BEEN SOME DIS-</small>cussion in the psychoanalytic literature about the importance of unconscious conflicts expressed by patients in their handling of payment for treatment,[1] little stress has been placed upon the possible conflicts, conscious and unconscious, which may influence a doctor in determining his fee policy. David's case showed that feelings about elements in the monetary transaction were expressed by the therapist as well as the patient and his parents; attitudes and emotional responses which had important implications in the treatment were brought to focus around problems in collecting payment. Before discussing the problem in this particular case, I should like to consider in a more general way the factors which may influence a therapist in determining his fee policy, and some of the elements which provoke conflict in him when unrealistic attitudes toward money are a significant part of the patient's problem.

The attitude of an individual toward receiving a medical fee is the resultant of many different kinds of forces impinging on him. Both intrapsychic or interpersonal conflicts and more rationally evolved concepts are concerned. Money has important meanings to everyone, on many different levels of psychic functioning. Feelings about it are determined by unconscious connections with basic instinctual life and bodily function;[2] they are also determined on a more conscious level by many factors in the cultural and economic life of our society. During an exchange of money, individuals express conscious and unconscious value systems, and demonstrate their characteristic patterns of interpersonal functioning. The giving and receiving of money becomes symbolic of many important interpersonal transactions.

In evaluating attitudes toward such transactions, the deep-lying, unconscious conflicts have received more attention in the literature than more ego-directed forces in the personality. In the present discussion, emphasis will be placed upon the examination of attitudes which an individual therapist may share with large numbers of people in his culture. Although factors in his own personality play a part in which side he is on in a controversial issue, it is important to distinguish the influence of a position shared by people of many diverse personality structures, from one which is influenced by purely personal unconscious conflicts. It will be assumed here that no gross causes for neurotic distortion are present in the therapist, and that his fee policy, for the most part, expresses a stable, consistent professional attitude.

Certain ideological controversies prevalent in our society have a specific bearing on shaping the feelings aroused in a financial interaction between doctor and patient. As part of a larger philosophical question about the rights of individuals to social security, there is wide disagreement on whether medical care is a "right" or a "privilege." The cost of long-term psychiatric care is well recognized as a major medical expense beyond the means of most people. Political and social identifications of a therapist, and his opinions on the rights of individuals to medical care, may have a part in determining the freedom with which he adapts the cost of psychotherapeutic treatment to the needs of an individual patient.

Conflicting social value systems in our culture may also affect the way a medical fee is viewed by both the patient and the doctor. Some segments of society correlate status with the possession of certain specific material comforts, recognizable educational or training credentials and professional equipment. If the income of an individual is limited, he may have to choose between a costly medical procedure such as psychotherapy, the value of which can be measured only in a rather intangible, subjective gain, or education and material possessions which are universally recognized as valuable. Whether or not a conflict between two different kinds of benefit to the patient influences a doctor to lower his fee may be decided by the degree to which the doctor shares his value system. He may be loath to deprive a patient of education, training, or a standard of living which he himself considers basic, and may be willing to enable some compromise for the patient between conflicting "essentials." The decision will, of course, also be influenced by the doctor's view of his own family's income needs for a standard of living that he considers adequate for himself.

A therapist may likewise share with his patient certain transference attitudes toward the concept of a doctor–patient relationship. A culturally prevalent stereotype which equates "doctor–patient" with "parent–child" is well recognized. Stereotyped images of "the doctor" may thus express concepts of "the good parent" or "the bad parent," depending upon which aspect of ambivalence toward a father figure is activated at any particular moment.

The idealized "good parent" is almost exclusively a self-sacrificing "giver," who asks no return except the satisfaction derived from ability to meet the needs of others. A selfless "old family physician" has entered folklore as representative of this stereotyped image. It is responsible for much of the authority and veneration bestowed upon doctors regardless of their personal attributes; it is also responsible for many negative attitudes expressed for equally unrealistic reasons. Children have mixed feelings toward a totally unselfish parent. Through gratitude for satisfaction of dependency needs they revere him and submit to his authority, but guilt and feelings of relative inferiority breed underlying resentment. If a parent shows any desire for the children to gratify his needs at any sacrifice to themselves, the image of "giver" may rapidly be replaced by that of "heartless exploiter."

These ambivalent transference attitudes have a direct bearing on the well-known reluctance of many people to pay a medical fee even when they are not financially pressed. There seems to be a rather general unconscious resentment of the fact that desire for material compensation enters into a doctor's motivation for giving service. Consciously or unconsciously, many people react as though they felt that the satisfaction derived from relieving pain and obtaining gratitude should preclude a need for high income or social status. Rationally, most people recognize that in the majority of fields in our economy, there is a proportional correlation between income level and degree of advanced training; they may admit consciously that, as a highly trained professional worker, a doctor is entitled to income compatible with that of comparably trained business and professional people in other fields. Nevertheless, there is an almost universal hostility toward a medical practitioner who earns a high income, no matter how competent he may be, or how much good he does. There seems to be a feeling that the emotional and intellectual satisfactions derived from medical practice should be pay enough.

Szasz says, "Our society seems to be so constructed that in professional work there [is] a definite connection between the degree of discomfort to which one puts oneself while performing the work, and the amount of money one can charge for it." [3] When it is recognized that the work of a service profession is emotionally and intellectually satisfying, a reluctance proportionate to the amount of supposed satisfaction develops in the general population toward the idea of giving high monetary rewards. This reluctance is strikingly expressed toward teachers, doctors, and ministers —all members of professions in which parental transference attitudes are strongly evoked. As Dr. Szasz suggests, these attitudes may be the outcome of parent–child interactions in which self-sacrifice is emphasized by the parent as a means of maintaining authority and prestige.

If the doctor accepts an idealized image of himself as "the good parent," he may have difficulty in tolerating the hostility evoked by a fee regarded as high by most members of his community. He may develop the picture of himself as a "heartless exploiter" if he fails to achieve an ideal of absolute self-sacrifice, and feel considerable conscious guilt for maintaining a high standard of living.

Differences in professional traditions and conditions of practice between the branches of physical and psychological medicine, and between groups within the psychiatric profession itself, may become focused on differences in attitude toward treatment charges, and may affect the feelings which both psychotherapists and their patients have about psychiatric fees specifically. The long-standing, well-established medical tradition of charging for service according to the patient's ability to pay is accepted by large segments of the population as standard procedure. Practitioners in other branches of medicine, as well as the majority of people in our society, are extremely resentful that psychotherapists have, by and large, tended to adopt fee practices developed within the special conditions considered most suitable for orthodox psychoanalysis. There seems to be a growing sentiment that in setting psychiatric fees at an hourly rate which makes prolonged psychotherapy inaccessible to the average person, primary emphasis has been shifted from meeting the health needs of patients toward meeting the financial needs of doctors. It is often overlooked that different conditions of practice in other branches of medicine make it possible for a medical doctor to give adequate treatment in relatively little time to many people, reducing the fee in legitimate cases of need without much decrease in his hourly income.

At the present time, it is impossible for the psychiatric profession to serve adequately all the financially needy patients who could profit from long-term psychotherapy. The public understandably resents this. Part of the resentment may be the outcome of the kinds of transference attitudes which have been discussed, but realistic, irreconcilable conflict exists between the rights of psychiatrists to a standard of living compatible with professional status in our society, and the inability of most people to pay for the amount of time required to treat them psychotherapeutically. Patients have widespread sympathy from the public for the genuine hardships imposed by the high cost of psychiatric treatment; they also have strong support for rationalizations developed against any irrational reluctance to pay the doctor. Guilt feelings of individual psychotherapists about this problem may also have sources in both realistic and unrealistic aspects of the problem. Such feelings may be related to unconscious intrapsychic conflicts, but they are also occasioned by legitimate frustration at the inability of the profession to make long-term psychotherapy available to more people who need and want it. The degree of feeling about this may relate in part to whether professional identifications and loyalties of a particular psychotherapist are fashioned by an orientation closer to that of organized physical medicine or to that of the "fifty-minute hour." It may also be a function of whether the therapist gets enough other gratifications from his work to compensate for lower income, and whether he and his family are primarily dependent financially upon income from private practice.

In an analytic type of therapy, reactions of the patient to financial requirements of treatment become an integral part of the material under investigation for therapeutic purposes; the doctor's conflicts may, however, escape notice and create difficulties in the therapy. It is taken for granted that his fee policy is governed by rational processes. Even when this is for the most part true, however, a therapist may be unable to reconcile perfectly conscious but conflicting beliefs and identifications. Such a conflict may occur between his ideas on the rights of patients to receive adequate therapy regardless of ability to pay, and the concepts which govern his own view of adequate compensation. Anxiety may be generated which interferes with the treatment relationship.

If the nature of a therapist's interests and professional gratifications make it necessary for him to treat patients with certain kinds of problems, he is most apt to encounter difficulty from this source. Financial realities, as well as specific unconscious conflicts, make it impossible for many people to adapt to an inflexible standard of meeting fees which may be "current practice" in the community and which tends to guarantee a stable income for the therapist. When scientific interest, or circumstance, inclines a therapist to treat this type of person, he may be subject to conflict in maintaining a fee policy that meets both his own needs and those of the patient. Guilts and rationalizations of attitude toward the fee may complicate his handling of the therapeutic problem.

Among others, the borderline patient falls into this category. His intrapsychic conflicts are regularly expressed in negativism toward socially accepted norms of behavior, conflicts around working at gainful employment, and prolonged dependency upon the family. A major therapeutic goal is that the patient learn to assume more responsibility for his own life, but until his conflicts have been attacked therapeutically, realistic financial attitudes cannot be expected. Initial phases in the private treatment of late adolescent and young adult borderline patients are almost always financed by the parents; after a period of treatment, when it has become possible for the patient to accept more realistic attitudes, it is usually advisable for him to begin paying his own expenses, and to break the ties of at least financial dependence on the family. This creates a problem for the therapist. The kind of job which an insecure, untrained young worker can find, if any, is seldom compatible with independence in living plus a "standard" psychiatric fee. At a point where he considers it therapeutic for the patient to assume his own financial responsibilities, the therapist is faced with a choice of adjusting the fee to the patient's own income or of continuing to require a fee that cannot be met without assistance from the parents. If he takes the latter course, he prolongs the patient's financial dependency, and demands, for his own benefit, continuation of a situation which he considers anti-therapeutic. Some parents use in a controlling and manipulative way the fact that they are contributing to a young person's support; even when they do not, the patient may himself use the threat of losing treatment as a powerful rationalization for prolonging dependent attitudes toward them. The realistic fact of being depend-

ent on parents to pay for treatment may increase the difficulty in breaking through such rationalizations. A therapist
may feel considerable conflict between what he feels he
should do in the interest of the patient's therapeutic progress,
and what he feels he must do to insure reasonable compensation for his own time.

The therapist who accepts young borderline patients
expects that a conflict of this nature will arise sometime in
the course of therapy; unless he is free to make decisions
about the fee according to what he feels is constructive for
the patient, without having to feel excessively penalized
himself, a strain can occur in the relationship between them.
In order to avoid damage to the treatment from this source,
he may find it necessary to limit the number of such patients
in his total practice to a number that he can well afford to
carry if a fee reduction becomes therapeutically advisable.
Even under the most ideal conditions, however, it may not
always be possible to eliminate some negative reactivity in a
working situation which demands a degree of personal sacrifice from the therapist.

At the beginning of David's treatment there was no
problem in setting a fee. He was a minor whose parents
would presumably have legitimate responsibility for his living and medical expenses for some time to come. Conflicts
in the area of taking responsibility, which could be assumed
on his part, did not have to be a consideration in making
practical plans for long-term therapy. The standard rate for
one hour weekly was readily agreed upon by his parents with
the understanding that it might have to continue for a long
time. Both parents were intelligent, educated, and from a
social class and local community group in which psychotherapy is well understood and accepted without stigma.
They had both had some treatment themselves and were
acquainted with the expected routines of monthly payment.

The father had a well-paying semi-professional job. The mother, who had made most of the decisions about family finances, had always been conscientious about health care for the children and had sought psychotherapy for David previously without protest from her husband. Medical bills had always been paid eventually, even when times were hard. There was no reason to anticipate a necessity to reduce the fee so long as the life circumstances of the family remained unchanged.

I nevertheless accepted the case in full knowledge that collections might at times be difficult. I had previously treated a number of cases in which therapy of a child or an adolescent had to continue over a long period of time, and I knew that except in families where money is very plentiful, and sometimes even then, the great expense of prolonged treatment often serves as a realistic focus for resistances from many different sources. Ambivalence which has other origins may be expressed through delays in payment and requests for concessions. Problems of this nature eventually occurred in David's case also.

Neither parent at any time asked for a fee reduction or threatened to withdraw their son from treatment because of the expense. Both professed a desire for therapy to continue as long as I felt it necessary. The mother assumed financial responsibility and paid for treatment out of her own earnings, increasing her working hours in order to do so. At the end of the first two years, payments were up to date although they had often been somewhat irregular. Early in the third year there was a severe financial crisis in the family, and she asked me whether further therapy was necessary; if so, she would get the money somehow, even if payments could not be made on time. I told her I believed continuation of the therapy was important, and agreed that a bill could accumulate until she had herself been repaid on an earlier loan, which she expected to collect before too long.

By the end of the fourth year there was a sizable debt, but during the fifth, sporadic payments roughly kept up with current charges. In the sixth year she made one large payment, leaving only a small residue.

I have mentioned that a state of unresolved transference to her former therapist was focused on me. Assumptions that I would be the "good parent" who trusted her good intentions enabled her to feel that I would not mind waiting until her more pressing bills had been paid. It seemed likely that withholding the last bit, rather than paying in small installments, was a product of the transference, but there was no doubt in my mind that the bill would eventually be cleared, no matter how long it took.

I have described these transactions in some detail in order to show the kinds of factors which may make an inflexible routine of fee collection impractical when dealing with certain types of cases. The parents of disturbed children live under many pressures. As I have mentioned before, unconscious ambivalence toward the child has often been stirred up, creating both a reluctance to make material sacrifices for him and great guilt for such feelings. Parents often need emotional support from the therapist. This was true of David's mother. The knowledge that I trusted her integrity made it more possible for her to bear the many frustrations caused by a necessity to keep David in treatment.

Had the family at any time expressed an intention to withdraw David from treatment purely because of the expense, I would have worked out with them a fee plan that would meet their needs. When I knew that a working relationship had been established with David, I was prepared to make any concessions necessary to keep him in therapy. This attitude was entirely consistent with my usual policy.

Some patients are unable to obtain the treatment of choice for their particular condition unless an individual therapist is willing to make a long-term commitment to them at a reduction of the standard private fee. Those who can best profit from intensive psychoanalytic therapy or psychoanalysis are frequently unable to afford them, and clinics with shifting personnel and community pressure to serve a maximum number of patients are unable to offer forms of treatment which require a durable relationship between the patient and a single therapist. An analyst who wishes to serve patients of relatively low income in a way that is most appropriate to the nature of their problems may do so either by volunteering low-cost time over an extended period for treating them in a clinic or by taking such patients in his private practice at reduced fees. I have preferred the latter course, and reserve a regular percentage of time for treating low-income patients who are well motivated and otherwise suitable for long-term intensive therapies of various sorts. The fee reduction always has a transference meaning to the patient which is dealt with therapeutically as it becomes relevant. In my experience, it has seldom been a major impediment to treatment, either because of its impact upon the patient or upon me. Ordinarily there is no conflict between such a policy and my own needs for compensation.

David fell into the category of patients who would, by my standards, be eligible for a fee concession that could enable him to remain in therapy. So long as he remained a minor, and the financial needs of the family were acute only because of unrealistic attitudes, I continued to charge the regular fee. However, I changed my policy shortly after the boy reached his twenty-first birthday. At that time I told him that since he was legally an adult, I would no longer charge his parents for the treatment. I informed him of my custom in regard to patients unable to pay a fee, and said that since he at present fell into that category, I would carry him at no cost. If and when he was able to pay his own expenses, I would make directly with him a financial arrangement appropriate to his own income. I did not imply that he should go to work specifically to pay for therapy, nor that he should think about paying me before he was financially independent in other ways. This policy seemed therapeutically advisable for a number of reasons.

As David approached chronological maturity concurrently with the increase of tensions in his family focused on money, the mounting bill for his treatment contributed to a build-up of hostility toward him from both parents, particularly his mother. Rising pressure upon him from his family to get a job met with intensification of his negativism toward working. It seemed necessary for me not to add to a source of conflict which allowed the real sources of emotional tension between them all to be obscured.

David knew that the family maintained his brother's allowance for school activities, and paid for his tennis lessons, while the flying lessons allowed to David were obtained without cash outlay through his mother's connection with the aircraft plant. He felt strongly that the therapy was owed to him by his parents, and did not consider this expense in the same class as the others. He therefore held a defiant stand against the responsibility to pay his own expenses. Resistance to the pressure seemed to him a realistic protest against obvious injustice. Under existing conditions, he could rationalize the reluctance to become self-supporting which really stemmed from strong emotional dependency upon his mother, competitiveness with the other men in the family, and unrequited emotional hunger. So long as his family were technically responsible for the bill he could, without guilt, accept my word that their financial dealings with me were not his problem, and remain safe from awareness of his own sensitivity about the situation. He was also able to retain a fantasy that his father was making restitution to him for past deprivations by supporting his therapy, and could justify himself in directing the major part of his hostility toward the mother.

For a long time after the new arrangement was well established, David persisted in "forgetting" that his parents were no longer responsible for paying. When fear of losing treatment was brought up as a clear rationalization of his continued dependence upon them, he could no longer avoid seeing the way he was using the reality problems of others to hide his own conflicts (191).

By endowing me with the idealized "good parent" image previously described, the boy managed to remain unaware of feeling any financial obligation toward me. He made repeated statements of the assumption that although money might be needed to run a practice, desire for financial gain is not important in a doctor's motivation for helping patients; satisfactions come from "doing a good job" and from scientific interest in the problem (62, 132, 147, 156, 192). For me to deny the fact that I did happen to have a scientific interest in his problem would have been clearly perceived as "phony," but his denial of guilt was a problem to be worked through eventually in therapy. Meanwhile I did not feel that it would be useful to demand financial responsibility toward me until he had achieved a much greater capacity for independence in his whole approach to life.

I was fully convinced of the validity of my technical decision, and felt no conflict about it. Although there was no reason to cancel the unpaid residue of his parents' debt, I had no expectation of being paid until every other conceivable need of the family had been met. I maintained a feeling of trust in the basic honesty of David's mother. However, in spite of all this, the only spontaneous outburst of anger that I expressed in the course of this therapy was precipitated in response to an unsupported comment by the boy that his mother was thinking of building a rumpus room. There was no indication that she intended doing so before paying me, if at all, yet I reacted with a violence that indicated a far greater volume of emotion than could be accounted for by the circumstances. The kinds of feelings which I myself had unwittingly displaced onto the fee transaction will be discussed in the section on countertransference and reactivity.

R E F E R E N C E S

(1) Fingert, H., "Comments on the Psychoanalytic Significance of the Fee," *Bulletin of the Menninger Clinic*, Vol. 16, 1952, pp. 98–104.

(2) Freud, S., "Character and Anal Eroticism," in *Collected Papers of Sigmund Freud*, Vol. II. N. Y., Basic Books, 1959.

Freud, S., "History of an Infantile Neurosis," in *Collected Papers*, Vol. III. N. Y., Basic Books, 1959.

(3) Szasz, T., "On the Experiences of the Analyst in the Psychoanalytic Situation," *Journal of the American Psychoanalytic Association*, Vol. IV, 1956, p. 213.

1 3

Beginning the Search

"Now there is only the problem of marriage."

156. [*He stares for a time, and then smiles.*] I feel like a motor slowing down. (Have you been turning over fast today?) Yes. Literally. Doing spins in the plane. It's an exciting sensation. (I'll bet!)

[*Pause.*] I've quit school. Too many details. [*Pause.*] Things are really getting rough at home. Mother is getting wild from being immobilized. There is no money. My brother and I think Dad is gambling. (It must make you feel bad if you think the rest of the family is being deprived for that reason. That sort of thing hurts quite a bit.) I know. I know just how he feels, though—trying to get the things he wants, because he's so unsatisfied. It's too bad he has to do it this way. (It is very too bad.)

[Pause.] (I have been thinking about the financial problem in your family, and have decided that I will no longer charge them for your visits. You are twenty-one now, a legal adult who can make his own contracts. From now on, I will deal with you directly; when you are in a position to pay something, we will discuss terms. I take a certain number of patients at whatever fee they can pay; at the moment, you are without income and can pay nothing, so that's the way we'll leave it for now.) I never let myself think about the fact that this hasn't been paid for; I don't know why. Maybe it doesn't seem important. (This is my problem; at the moment, you have other more important problems to tackle.)

[Pause.] (What are you thinking?) I don't know if you asked me just then by chance or whether it was an educated guess. I was thinking the same thing last time, but I guess I don't want to get into it. Thinking is painful.

[Pause.] I don't want to be left with it. You might go away. If I get into it, I might get stuck with it. (I plan to stay in New Haven for quite a while, so far as I know. I will not be gone, except for vacations.) In the past when we have been working together, I've been able to turn things off. Now I continue to worry between times. (Are you afraid your anxiety will get too high at times?) When you are trying to measure four feet with a one-inch ruler, you are apt to make the line crooked if something doesn't keep bringing you back to the right level. (It is true that from now on it is important for us to work as steadily as we can. In the past, it wasn't as important, for just the reasons you have given. You should keep this in mind in making practical plans for the future.)

Well, I think I've been cheated in sex. The block seems to be unconscious. (We must make it conscious.) [Pause.] It's funny, the mixed emotions one has. If anyone tells me I might be able to get rid of the blocks, it scares me and makes me angry. Too bad one's thoughts get so mixed up. (This has more to do with feelings than thoughts.)

[Pause.] I was thinking of early experience. I used to keep putting my finger in light sockets to see if there was any electricity. (And was there?) Oh yes! Often! [Smile.]

[Pause.] Football can be physically satisfying, but not emotionally. If something has to be missing, one can get along better with the emotional components alone. (But sooner or later, one would like to get the two together.) [Pause.] I was thinking of a sort of fanciful solution. You need two lives, the first to about age thirty, in which you aren't very restricted, but learn to restrict yourself because you know how other people feel; you don't want to hurt anyone because you know how it feels to be hurt. Then you need another fifty years in the regular world. (That isn't so fanciful. It could happen something like that to you, although I hope it won't take quite so long for you to feel able to live in the regular world.

The patient's mother calls for an appointment to talk to me. David has given his permission for her to come and even to use his hour if necessary. I tell her I would prefer to give her the one following his, and this is agreed. We talk about the boy's progress in therapy, and she tells me in some detail about things going on in the family that make life difficult for her. David has been doing much of the family driving for her since her illness, and this is hard on both of them.

157. [David sits down with a slight smile.] (How do you feel?) It looks as though things are beginning to clear a little.

[Pause.] I think I'm going to try to be a commercial pilot. (That would meet both your practical needs and some of your inner needs.) It would be good to meet both. I would be away for long stretches, but home for long stretches. [Pause.] I was wondering about police work. Maybe the other wouldn't work out. (Are you thinking about the work we are doing here? I think we could work intensively, with stretches in between. I don't believe there would be a serious conflict.)

Then there is only the problem of marriage left.

[*Pause.*] I don't understand what goes wrong. I know a couple that seem to have everything I would think of as ideal, but the wife told me it isn't what she expected. (What did she expect?) I don't think what she expected was unreasonable.

[*Pause.*] I was thinking of a jet plane among slow planes. It would have to start later in order not to ram into them, and there would be the problem of landing. (Sounds like a problem of timing.) It could be worked out.

[*Pause.*] I'm wondering how much money I'd need to live and raise a family. (Plenty of pilots raise families on their salaries.) If other things are right, I don't need much, but money can symbolize security. If there isn't security in other ways, one might need more of it.

[*Pause.*] I'm beginning to think in terms of my own needs rather than what my parents want me to be. (I'm glad. If you please others, it's nice, but you are the one who has to live your life.) [*Pause.*] One needs an analogue computer to know about human reactions, so as not to get mixed up in the messes of others. I need more facts before I can make decisions. (You can take it step by step. You don't have to plan your whole life right at this moment.)

158. [*Pause.*] Did I tell you I finally got my diploma? (Well! How wonderful!) [*His face falls.*] (It must be obvious to you that *I* am glad you were able to overcome the feelings that prevented you from getting it, but I wonder if you consider it more of a defeat than a triumph?) I didn't want it. (Why not?) Because I had to ask for it. (How was that so humiliating?)

The requirement was wrong; I had already passed the course in the other school and satisfied the state requirement. It was discrimination to make me take it over; the principal just thought I was trying to get away with something. They compromised and only made me take half, but if I had done half, I had done it all. They were wrong to make me do it. It was the principle of the things that was important to me. I had to give in because I needed the diploma, but I shouldn't have had to.

(I hadn't entirely understood your reasons for holding out. I can well understand your resentment at having to give in to something you believed to be wrong, just because of your need.)

I'm glad I've got the diploma, but ashamed of being glad. I told myself it was O.K. to get it because it meant so much to my mother, but I really wanted it myself. (Your reasons for holding out were good, but it was not worth the cost to you. The principle involved was not quite important enough to you; sometimes it is more realistic to lose even an important fight than to be destroyed.)

[Pause.] I'm thinking of a pattern. The center piece is held in such a way that it can't move without damaging itself. [Pause.] A guy and I are converting a hydromatic into a standard gear. I'm afraid the driving shaft will be pulled out of line by opposing bands that hold it. (I wonder if you are using these symbols to express fears that the penis will be damaged in intercourse?) [Shrug.] I don't know. (How did you feel about my saying that?) Annoyed. It's a hard subject for me to talk about. I don't *want* you to understand me.

(It's easier to talk about, and maybe even think about, painful things in a more indirect way.) I can *think* of them directly, but not talk. (What's the feeling?) Fear that a blow will fall when I don't expect it. Maybe rejection. (I doubt that it is rejection. It's more likely that you fear the intensity of your own feelings.)

Perhaps it's fear that I will express the feelings and

be left. My partner wouldn't think it was important enough
to see it through. (Fear she couldn't tolerate some uncertainty on your part?) Fear she wouldn't want to try again if
I failed once.

159. [*He seems very depressed, and is practically mute ex-*
cept under pressure from me; when he does speak, it is almost
too low to hear. He mutters something about being half man,
half fly; talks of extreme conflict and frustration, again raising
the question about whether there is any value in living.]
     I'm thinking of a story. There was an atomic war in
two upper hemispheres. Radioactive dust was drifting south;
everyone died in the end. (You sound as though you feel
there is an emotional war going on that will kill you.) No
such luck.
     [*Long pause.*] I don't know why I'm alive. (It would
be more comfortable to know the reason.) I know there is
one, but I want to know *what* it is. (Many people think they
know, but people with quite different ideas are all equally
sure they are right. I doubt that we will ever know for sure
which is the right answer.) [*Shrug.*] I don't see why I should
go on living. (There is a strong life force in you; you don't
really want to go against it.) [No answer.] (Do you think this
upset of feelings is all from within you, or is it related to the
turmoil between your parents?) About half and half.
     (Call me if you want to come in before next week,
will you?) [*No visible response.*]

     He calls just at the appointment time, and leaves a
message that he can't make it. He is held up by transportation problems. I call later in the day and make an appointment for three days later.

160. [*During the hour he is sullen and rebellious, making*
several indirect cracks about his mother which could also be

meant for me. They are along the line of complaints about
her demands for conforming behavior from him. Feelings
about my having become slightly frightened by the tone of
his last interview do not come out.

[He talks also about the conflict between his mother
and father, is obviously furious at both of them, and furious
at himself for his dependent needs. He wishes he could be
like the brother who just sneers and ignores everyone but
himself.

[In spite of the turmoil, he refuses to be coerced into
striking out for himself before he feels ready.]

161. [Pause.] I'm thinking about music. There are various
different elements; sound, pattern, vibration, and the part
that's left out. That has to be supplied by the hearer. If one
plays seven notes of an eight-note scale, the hearer automatically supplies the eighth.

(The mind is used to perceiving things as a whole;
if one supplies some of the parts, the mind supplies what's
missing to complete the whole. That's the way it works with
associations; things perceived together make a pattern, even
though some of it may be unconscious. If one supplies part
of it, the rest can be brought to awareness.)

I was wondering how messages are received in music.
Even if the sound is subsonic, there may be a perception of
the pattern. (Through the physical effect of the vibrations.)
The person who receives the message must be the same as
the one who sends it. (Must vibrate to the same wavelength.
But does that always imply being the same?) I assume you
would eventually come out with the same message as I.

[Smile.] I'm thinking, this is a novel way to find a
girl friend. I'm apparently talking about whether I'll ever
find anyone who can love me. (You have grave doubts.) I'm
wondering if I can find anyone who takes it as seriously as
I do. (Love is a very serious business.) So many people have

difficulty staying in love; just the difficulties in living make love die out. (If people vibrate on the same wavelength, they can survive a lot of practical problems in living.)

I wonder if men and women are different? Women seem to feel that when they love, they are giving. Men are taught to feel that when they are loving, they are taking. I want to *give* love more than to be loved, even though being loved gives zest to a relationship. (Many people don't realize that the one who does the loving gets the most out of it. But it is important to receive love as well as to give. Some people are afraid to receive.)

For me, to receive love implies submitting to a demand. I can't let myself be loved for fear that the other person wants something else from me. (Fear of becoming a slave.) Yes. (You doubt that there can be mutuality in a relationship.) The only way one could be sure of such a possibility would be to experience it. If one is afraid, it is difficult to get the experience. (It feels as though you were in a bind, doesn't it?)

Nobody should be allowed to judge a relationship except the people involved in it. (That's right. What is mutually acceptable to two people is their own business, nobody else's. The important thing is that both be satisfied.)

162. There is a job possibility in a quarry; I'd like to be a "powder monkey." They get a lot of money. (Are you fascinated by the danger?) Not particularly. I was just thinking of the money. (I can see how that would be attractive.)

[Pause.] I can't decide whether to do what my parents want or what I want. (What do they want?) Nothing in particular. (But you feel in general that what they want is probably opposite from what you want?) [Smile.] I don't want to do anything, so anything they wanted me to do would be the opposite.

(We have talked before about how sometimes ex-

treme passivity can be activity. One way it is active is in forc-
ing the other person to do something.) If two people want
something done, and neither of them do it, sooner or later
the one who wants it most will do it. (A person might do
nothing just to test how much the other person wants something accomplished. Do you operate like that sometimes?)
Often, I think.

(I think so too. I think sometimes you operate like
that with me. If you sit and say nothing, and I eventually
ask what you are thinking, then you have tested my interest
in finding out what is going on. However, you might also
feel that if I ask you, *I* am more interested in getting something accomplished here than you. I wonder if this is really
true?)

If a person asks what you are thinking, and turns out
not to really want to know, it's *his* responsibility. (Do you
think you have any real fear that I'm not interested in what
you have to say?) It's hard to say, for fear of hurting your
feelings. But it *is* difficult to believe that anyone is really
interested in solving someone else's problems.

[*Pause.*] I'm wondering why my nose is so stuffy. (I
imagine it's stuffy because a person feels sad if he thinks nobody could be interested in him. Also, I think there's a possibility that it's almost as threatening to think it might *not*
be true.) [*He hawks the mucus back into his throat, in spite
of the fact that there is a full box of Kleenex next to him.*]
I was wondering why I can't blow my nose. I guess I just
didn't like showing the need. (If you took a piece of my
Kleenex to give yourself some relief from discomfort, what
might you not want next? Where in the world would it all
end?) [*Smile.*]

It's frustrating to have my parents taking over my
prerogatives. They want to refer everything to you every time
I say anything. They expect you to solve all of everyone's
problems. (They want you to talk to me about things that

should rightfully be worked out with them?) They avoid me. They want to put all the responsibility on you. They don't want to have to worry if something goes wrong. (A parent or spouse of someone in therapy is always ambivalent toward the patient's relationship with the therapist.)

163. [*Long pause.*] I'm reluctant to put energy into thinking. I wonder if anything is worth the energy required to get at it?

[*Long pause.*] There is a treasure hunt on, but if there were a hundred chances, and I bought ninety-nine of them, the hundredth would win. [*Pause.*] I might search, if anyone would do it with me. It would be fun to find it, take the money out, and then re-bury it, to keep people guessing. [*Pause.*] It's something like this situation; I'd like to get what information I can, without letting you know that I'd gotten it. I don't want to be committed to having anyone think I need them.

[*Long pause.*] I wish all the organization in the world would disintegrate. I could travel without having to stick to any particular path. [*Sudden laugh.*] It sounds as though I were saying I wish you were dead. (In what way do you feel restricted by me?) At times any need to communicate seems like a restriction. When I'm having so much difficulty, it is difficult to communicate even the feeling that it's difficult to communicate.

1 4

Countertransference and Reactivity

"**N**O ONE IS, CAN BE, OR SHOULD BE, COM-pletely secure emotionally. . . . Acceptance of a certain amount of anxiety in the lives of the psychiatrist and his patients is one of the constructive forces in the psychothera-peutic process. . . . A therapist must use his own anxieties as they may arise during psychotherapy as a means of spot-ting the patient's anxieties which elicited his own." [1] This statement by Frieda Fromm-Reichmann acknowledges that in psychiatric work with all types of patients, emotional reac-tions on the part of a therapist are inevitable and, if properly controlled, constitute important stimuli for therapeutic progress. In psychotherapy with schizophrenic or borderline patients particularly, reactivity of one kind or another by the therapist plays a major role in determining the quality and direction of a therapeutic relationship. Countertransference reactions are frequent, but are by no means the only type of reactivity that occurs.

The term *countertransference* has been used in the psychoanalytic literature to describe many different varieties of reaction induced in a therapist during the relationship with his patient.[2] Some writers use the term to cover a therapist's every conscious or unconscious feeling about the patient; others confine it to sexual impulses alone. Some use it to embrace all characterological attitudes and eccentricities of the therapist; others say that every anxiety-producing response of the therapist should be called countertransference.[3]

By some definitions, countertransference is responsible for the "benevolent neutrality" which constitutes a successful therapeutic attitude. "Benevolent neutrality [has] roots in identification with a benevolent parent, largely freed from the conflicts of ambivalence," says Weigert.[4] Money-Kryle points out that concern for the welfare of a patient stems from a reparative drive in which the patient stands for the damaged objects in an analyst's own unconscious fantasy, and a parental drive, in which the child stands, at least in part, for an early aspect of the self.[5] When the term countertransference is used to describe these phenomena, it can be held responsible for every attitude of the therapist that is rooted in his early experience. Every therapist has a developmental history from which he derives certain patterns of interpersonal behavior and certain ways of gaining personal satisfaction; some of these are bound to appear in the therapeutic relationship.

By the definition of terms that will be used in this discussion, the above would be called "chronic countertransference attitudes," or what some authors have called "chronic countertransference," [2] or "habitual characterological attitudes" which find expression in almost any situation, and nearly always in the same form, lacking specificity to any given situation.[3] Habitual modes of expression, and chronic defensive patterns of behavior as they appear in therapeutic work, are presumably recognized and understood by the therapist through his own analysis; their effects upon a patient are, or should be, consciously noted by the therapist and dealt with if they seem to create distortions in the therapeutic relationship.

The term countertransference itself will be confined to what has been called "acute countertransference,"[2] or "emergency repsonse."[3] It follows the definition given by Tower, namely, "A transference phenomenon which derives from deep, unconscious conflicts of the therapist, precipitated at a given time, and in response to a given individual, in which are mobilized old, affectively significant experiences in relation to earlier, more important figures."[3] Countertransference, so defined, may be a destructive force in psychotherapy if it interferes with communication by distorting a therapist's view of the patient or the patient's transference; it may be a constructive force, as Dr. Fromm-Reichmann suggests, if it is recognized and utilized for greater understanding of interaction between therapist and patient.

Countertransference, either acute or chronic, must be distinguished from so-called "intuition." The importance of intuitive ability in a therapist who works with schizophrenic patients has been the subject of much discussion in recent years. Szalita-Pemow and other workers from Chestnut Lodge are engaged in studying intuitive processes of therapists in that group; preliminary reports have been made, although there is admittedly much still to be learned.[6, 7] Throughout the psychological literature in general, the term "intuition" is sometimes used synonymously with "empathy," or there is confusion about the distinction between these two terms; it is necessary to define their use in the present discussion.

Intuitive knowledge arises from sensory perceptions made meaningful to a person through his previous experience and combined into new forms under stimulus of emotional factors. The intuitive process differs from other rational thought in that the new forms are created by a series of unusually rapid, complex connections in the unconscious, emerging into consciousness ready to use, with a "flashlike" quality.[6] Intuition is predominantly cognitive, developed in conjunction with the use of affect. Perceptions facilitated by empathy become usable stimuli to direct action via a rapid, unconscious process.

The intuitive capacity useful in work with schizophrenics involves sensitivity to visual cues and the ability to use visual images as a type of shorthand intermingled with organized thinking; this may be a natural endowment of some therapists, which enables them to share to some extent a schizophrenic's type of thinking, and to act upon their ability in the service of therapy. Countertransference may affect such an ability either positively or negatively, but is not synonymous with it. In the present discussion, the term "intuition" will be used to denote the ability of a therapist to perceive non-verbal cues of patients and respond appropriately, or his ability to perceive the realistic nature of a patient's response to non-verbal cues which the therapist has himself unconsciously given.

An example given by Frieda Fromm-Reichmann from her own experience may be used to illustrate the distinction between intuition itself and countertransference. Briefly, Dr. Fromm-Reichmann's patient asked to be released from a pack, and the doctor had started toward the door to get a nurse; something made her turn back and unpack the patient herself. Her intuitive knowledge of the importance of this act to the patient derived from a visual perception of the patient's facial expression which, by empathy, the doctor recognized as indicating despair; awareness of its meaning had been temporarily threatened with repression because of a countertransference-induced anxiety reaction toward the patient's implied demand.* Fortunately, the tendency to repression was counteracted by another momentarily unconscious reaction emanating from the therapist's useful, chronic-countertransference-induced therapeutic attitude. Her ability to perceive the non-verbal cue in the first place was a separate function, related to empathy and perhaps an inborn endowment, unrelated to countertransference.[7]

Empathy, as used here, is an adjunct to intuition and probably cannot exist without it; it comprises the ability to acquire "emotionally felt knowledge" of another person, and is defined as "the inner experience of sharing in and comprehending the momentary psychological state of another person." [8] It plays a large part in the capacity of a therapist to obtain elusive clues to a patient's emotional state through perception of nuances in motility, verbalization, affective expression, and tempo. Schafer suggests that this shared emotional experience is based to a great extent upon the therapist's memory of corresponding affective states of his own, and that it increases with familiarity of the other person's inner psychological processes. The therapist makes a partial identification with the patient via the emotional state which he shares without becoming himself engulfed. He can achieve this by "adaptive use of the primary process" [8] checked by the capacity to maintain reality testing, and is able to fantasy in the same terms as the patient without losing his own ego boundaries.

All other personal reactions of the therapist which may impinge upon a patient during the course of a thera-

* That this was countertransference and not a "normal" reaction to excessive demand from the patient we assume only because Dr. Fromm-Reichmann called it that. The degree to which countertransference influences such "normal" reactions in everyone varies with the individual.

peutic interchange will be called "reactivity." This term includes a therapist's conscious feelings about the patient himself and about other people in the life of patient or therapist who may affect the work they are doing together. The therapist as a person inevitably has reactions toward other people which may be "reasonable and appropriate" by a standard of attitudes prevalent in his culture, as well as by the standards established in his own personal experience. He has relative likes and dislikes of certain personality characteristics, responds positively to some kinds of behavior and negatively to others; he inevitably looks at certain kinds of life experience, and types of relationships, in the light of a value system shared with whatever segment of society he has chosen for his own identifications. An important aspect of the therapeutic problem is that the therapist avoid imposing his own value system on the patient, but he can never totally avoid responses within himself to what he hears or experiences in the relationship between them.

Distortions in communication between therapist and patient may temporarily be caused by reactivity in the therapist. In working with a child or adolescent, feelings about behavior of the patient's parents or other figures in his life may, at times, be momentarily discharged in a reaction of anger displaced upon the patient, or cause an over-compensatory sympathetic response to him. Important communications from the patient may be missed for a while because of distractions due to intercurrent events in the therapist's own life, or his interest in content material and technical problems. Unless a countertransference problem blocks the therapist's ability to become aware of what has happened, the difficulty between them is soon overcome. Such reactions are usually "realistic" responses to behavior or life experience, although, of course, they may also contain varying degrees of chronic countertransference attitude.

All reactivity by the therapist lies somewhere along

a continuum between pure "countertransference" at one end and pure "realistic, appropriate reaction" at the other; even a perfectly appropriate emotional response contains a blend of conscious and unconscious factors related in some degree to earlier experiences of the therapist. Anger may be a "normal" reaction to irritating behavior and still contain elements of frustrated narcissism; an angry response to the patient's passivity may partially represent a defense against the therapist's own passive wishes and still be predominantly a realistic reaction to self-destructive aspects of the patient's behavior which interfere with his therapeutic progress. Negative reactions by a therapist to dirt and body odor contain a component of unresolved anal conflict which exists in most middle-class people, but may be elicited for perfectly realistic reasons. In a truly therapeutic relationship, conscious and unconscious forces, chronic countertransference attitudes and realistic, appropriate responses, are balanced to create minimal distortion in the therapist's view of his patient, and minimal interference in direct communication between them.

Throughout David's case, the relationships between intuition, empathy, chronic countertransference attitude, and realistically determined response are well illustrated; there is also at least one example of the way in which true countertransference obscured the real nature of an important interaction between therapist and patient.

Reasonably appropriate, direct reactivity on the part of the therapist occurs to some extent in all psychotherapy; it creates no serious interruption of communication with the patient if the therapist recognizes and resolves the effects upon himself, or so long as he deals therapeutically with its impact on the patient. A few instances arising in the course of David's therapy may be mentioned in illustration.

Right from the beginning of our relationship, I felt

a positive reaction to the boy as a person, sensing in him a potential capacity for humor and creative imagination, and finding professional interest in his way of talking. Quite soon, however, a puzzling, slightly negative feeling arose. At that period, David's hands and clothing were frequently covered with grease and grime from his work on the sports car, and although dirt on a working man does not usually bother me, I thought I might be reacting with more than the usual degree of feeling about such things. It was therapeutically inadvisable to discuss the problem in treatment because of the boy's autistic condition and the tenuous state of our relationship; in any case, I knew that the need to rebel against maternal demands for cleanliness was important to him at the moment, but was afraid that by some non-verbal cue I might transmit the feeling and thereby damage a growing rapport between us. In any case, I realized almost immediately that my reaction arose mostly from apprehension that the newly reupholstered chair would be soiled by grease; by substituting a chair with wooden arms and dark covering, I could tolerate the dirt comfortably during a period in which he needed to flaunt it. The negative reaction in me was eliminated before he was able to sense it.

Usually, no particular effort was made to inhibit the expression of my spontaneous responses; reality events that affected David throughout the course of therapy often aroused feelings in me that I did not try to hide. I was pleased when constructive actions and participation in activities gave evidence of growth in the boy's capacity for reality testing; even though ambivalent himself, he knew that I was glad when he overcame resistance to getting a high school diploma (158). He likewise knew of my sympathy and concern over unfortunate accidents, repeated disappointments, and the corrosive, long-drawn-out periods of suspense to which he was subjected (120, 134, 138, 183). At a time that he was about to fend for himself in a strange city, I worried about his diet and discussed living arrangements with him (133).

David did not seem to feel such evidences of concern as coercive or seductive; if he had, we would have discussed the problem openly. The only time he voiced resentment of manipulation was when, at the time when my sudden illness coincided with his period of suicidal preoccupation, I wrote a note from the hospital asking him to "take it easy" until we could further discuss his feelings (146); he could protest the idea of having to stay alive to spare my feelings, probably because he had no real doubt that I had a right to assume control in an emergency. For the most part, he did not take it amiss that I cared about his welfare, and did not let his feelings about my concern interrupt the flow of communication.

There were times when a show of my personal feelings was not particularly constructive, but did not cause any serious damage to the progress of therapy. On several occasions, I could not avoid expressing counterhostility, of which I was momentarily unconscious, to hostile acts toward David or me by his parents. When he returned in disgrace from a laboring job to which he had been sent at an extremely inopportune moment in treatment, I asked whether he had ever considered that the emotional problems of others might have had some part in the development of his own (39); although the question was not irrelevant, it was an expression of my anger at the parents for not having consulted me in a decision directly affecting therapy. I was reacting not only to aspects of David's experience that had been hurtful to him, but to the unconscious hostility expressed by his parents toward me. The same kind of reaction was precipitated when the mother told me she "couldn't bear" to go see him in jail "for fear of breaking down." The immediate offer to visit him myself was, I believe, a punitive impulse intended to arouse her guilt, as well as a gesture of genuine concern for the boy (135), but I fortunately recognized this in time to avoid carrying out the suggestion. Neither episode had any effect upon my relationship to David.

There were other times when reactivity on my part did temporarily interrupt ability to understand the boy's communications. Such an episode occurred once after I had obtained historical material from his mother (96). It had seemed necessary to get more information about David's early experiences in order to understand the relevance of his symbolic statements, but I became absorbed in it for a short time, shifting the emphasis in therapy. The boy's expression of resentment at interruption of his own train of thought was missed until the following weeks (97, 98); interest in discussing some of the topics mentioned by the mother blocked my sensitivity to his reaction. On another occasion, distraction by an event in my own life distorted my perception of a whole interview (200). It is noteworthy, however, that when direct reactivity rather than a more deep-seated countertransference reaction interrupted communication, recovery of contact was fairly rapid.

Empathy for David's feeling states must be assumed as an important factor in the intuitive perceptions upon which therapeutic progress was built. Before passing on to a further discussion of intuition, a few illustrations will demonstrate one way in which "adaptive use of primary process" may be expressed in therapy.

Empathic ability to fantasy in the same way as David enabled me to sense meanings in his communications which I then sometimes interpreted through an unconscious play on words; the primary-process mechanism of punning acted as a form of shorthand to express a sharing of the feelings involved. Empathy was, for instance, the basis of my awareness that the boy's theft of a level was a symbolic act. Our interplay around the word "level" in the initial interview has already been mentioned. Use of an unconscious pun by speaking of his need for a "level of economy," indicated this recognition, and was unconsciously confirmed by him in a responsive association to the level. Something similar happened following a series of interviews in which he had been talking about impotence and fear of sexual intercourse. Near the end of an hour, David looked at his watch, commenting that there wasn't time to go on; I replied, "Are you afraid of getting chopped off in the middle of something?" (78). The boy immediately recognized an interpretation of castration anxiety unconsciously made in this way, and commented on it. On another occasion, in discussing his mixed feelings about assuming independence on a job out of town, he said he would "like to have [his] cake and eat it too," meaning simultaneous independence and dependence. I replied, "You haven't had much cake in your life, and I hope you'll get a piece" (128); again he immediately responded to my unconscious interpretation that it was sexual freedom about which he was so ambivalent. The alert reader will find others.

In another empathic expression, I unconsciously adopted the boy's own symbolism to make an analogy which served as interpretation. Responding to discussion of his ability to make contact with the unconscious, I commented, "Something can be a valuable tool in one quantity, and a destructive force in an uncontrolled amount. Like water—it can create power or it can cause a flood" (173); I was unwittingly making an interpretation that fears of losing psychic control were related to his fear of urinary incontinence, and using his own imagery to do so.

Unconscious use of metaphorical terminology, or adoption of similar symbolism, gives evidence of a therapist's identification with the patient's mode of responding to a feeling state which he shares in a controlled way. Such empathy is an important ingredient in the ability to acquire intuitive knowledge of indications for therapeutic intervention.

Treatment of a boy like David is conducted via the therapist's intuition to a greater extent than that of neurotic patients. When dealing with borderline states, a most valuable therapeutic tool is capacity to perceive and make effective use of non-verbal clues to the patient's states of readiness for different kinds of interpretation. Ability to choose "the right moment" for therapeutic activity is a crucial factor in its successful outcome, but this ability is only partially determined by rational processes; intuition may be a very significant factor. Intuition is also important in deciding "the right level" of discussion or interpretation at any particular time.

While the mode of meaningful communication is still predominantly symbolic, a patient's factual statements about daily events may have pertinent meanings on both symbolic and realistic levels; they may be relevant to his preoccupation with early experience, present experience in the therapeutic relationship, or the state of the transference. Whether the therapist picks up on any of these, or on the level of factual reality as presented, depends to a large extent on his intuitive perception of the patient's condition at the time.

In responding to the realistic aspect of a patient's statement, the therapist is guided both by intuitive awareness of its importance and by rational evaluation of the necessity for stressing reality factors at that particular time. If strategically timed, a realistic examination of current events in his life serves important ego-strengthening functions for the patient; if poorly timed, such discussion may interrupt or inhibit the flow of symbolic communication through which he is producing meaningful material. It is necessary for the therapist to be able to trust his intuitive perception of cues from the patient to guide a choice of timing and level of therapeutic intervention, while at the same time he must remain alert to other factors which might be governing his decisions.

A therapist's impulse to discuss reality problems may, at times, be triggered not only by cues relevant to the patient's readiness but by a form of primary-process association in the therapist himself, aroused by empathy with the patient's mode of thinking rather than the content of the communications, and stimulated by a gesture or attitude of the patient. Conversation about reality events may also serve a defensive function for the therapist. He must take care that timing which he attributes to intuitive knowledge of the patient's needs is not dictated primarily by his own.

Along with useful introductions of temporary attention to reality problems, examples of personally triggered and of defensively used reality discussion will be found in David's therapy. On one occasion, the boy, after starting a session with some superficial preliminary remarks, fell silent, settled into his customary stereotyped position, and stared off into space with a suddenly far-off expression on his face. I thought, "We are now on the air," and immediately opened the interview by asking if he had heard from his flying test (179). The question was perfectly appropriate, and was answered briefly and appropriately by David before he switched back to what was obviously of concern to him. My opening question was a response to an unconscious pun upon the concept "on the air," a thought stimulated by a personal association to the bodily posturing with which he had made transition into a serious therapeutic attitude.

On another occasion early in therapy, a discussion of reality was introduced clearly for my own protection. Although we had only been working together for a few months, David was well launched in meaningful symbolic communication. He had responded to the prospect of my vacation with talk about unstable chemical compounds, stirring up regret and some guilt in me over the necessary interruption. When he persisted in further symbolic expressions of hurt and hostility in spite of my acknowledging his feelings, I abruptly cut them off with an unconsciously defensive question about his realistic progress in school chemistry.

Fortunately such lapses were relatively benign, occurring infrequently. For the most part, discussions of reality factors in the boy's life were constructively used to wean him from a need to remain withdrawn in the private world of his own fantasies. Even in the early interviews, some statements which David may have presented for their symbolic significance were picked up realistically because of my "feeling" that important current attitudes needed clarification. For instance, following a series of symbolic expressions about fear of powerful destructive impulses, he mentioned that the police suspected him of cutting down some trees (13). I felt, rather than thought, that he should not proceed symbolically until feelings about being considered "guilty until proven innocent" were explored on a reality level. A little later, enthusiastic response to his comment about being on the winning basketball team was made out of unformulated awareness that he had presented it as evidence of improved ability to participate in normal activities (22). Unconscious perception of cues indicating a decrease of dependent need on David's part was also significant in my forgetting to send him the promised postcard at a moment when he was ready to say, "This is part of my life now; you don't have to send any more cards" (11). His relative lack of hostility about the broken promise seemed to confirm that he sensed the reason and acknowledged the rapport that facilitated my perception of his true need.

Many writers have stressed the importance of intuitive and empathic processes in treatment of schizophrenic and borderline patients. Although this discussion, too, is concerned primarily with the effects of intuition and empathy and their relationship to various types of countertransference and reactivity by a therapist, it must not be forgotten that rational processes also play an important part. In order for effective therapy to take place, intuition must operate within a sound conceptual framework, backed by theoretical knowledge and clinical experience. One often sees a tendency in therapists to mistake impulsive, unconsidered actions for intuitive responses. Intuition is a valuable aid in treatment, but is no substitute for careful planning and rational evaluation of indications for technical maneuvers. Valid psychotherapy of schizophrenic and borderline patients, as well as other types, must proceed within a structure of scientific information about the nature of psychic processes and behavioral patterns.

In working with patients like David, the therapist must conduct a long-term, gradual weaning process, meeting a patient's hitherto-unmet dependent needs until they are reduced to manageable proportions and the patient can relinquish excessively dependent attitudes without developing destructive degrees of anxiety. Intensity of the patient's need must constantly be re-evaluated, and optimal moments sensed for encouraging him to assume the degree of added responsibility that can be tolerated at every step of progress. Unconscious as well as conscious recognition of changes in the patient's attitudes or behavior may determine the outcome of this process. Empathy facilitates it, and countertransference blocks it; success of the treatment will depend largely upon whether the extent of empathy outweighs defensive forces that prevent full use of the therapist's intuition and knowledge.

Because his use of unconscious communication is such an important therapeutic tool, a therapist must give constant attention to the nature of his own reactions as they arise. Necessity to be aware of countertransference has been repeatedly stressed in the literature of psychotherapy, but there may be difficulty in distinguishing it from other types of reactivity. An example from David's therapy will show how my recognition of a countertransference reaction was delayed by focusing on a different source for my emotional response to one of the boy's communications.

One day when he was bored and frustrated, David mentioned that he hoped for summer work on a rumpus room that his mother planned to build. He did not seem to anticipate an adverse reaction from me, although he knew that the family owed me a considerable sum of money, and was shocked when I displayed anger by my tone of voice (166). I was surprised myself. The intensity of feeling seemed excessive, and I spent considerable time after the interview trying to understand my reaction.

As mentioned in a previous section (Chapter 12), I had clearly understood and accepted the problems produced by unrealistic attitudes toward money in David's family, and also had faith in the basic integrity of his mother; I firmly believed that she intended to pay me sooner or later as we had agreed; in any case, I should not have allowed my judgment of her to be so readily shaken by the boy's unsupported statement. It seemed that in spite of intellectual acceptance of the monetary arrangement, I had stored up some unsuspected resentment of the accumulated debt and the need for fee cancellation. Upon thinking it over, I could not see any evidence that anger at the mother was adversely affecting David's treatment, but I focused self-scrutiny upon my attitudes toward her and the financial arrangement between us. I finally concluded that no matter how rational a therapist may be about the need for a fee deferment or cancellation, some feeling about the loss of income might be unavoidable.

David had been frightened by the anger which he insisted was directed at him: "It was straight from your uncon-

scious that you were angry at me" (166). In spite of my
denials and attempts at explaining the feelings, he nevertheless appeared to have taken his observation for granted whenever the subject arose later (171, 199); after quite a long
time, I began to wonder if his assumption might be correct.
From this new perspective I reviewed notes for the whole
period preceding and following the fateful interview, and
found that instead of displacing anger onto David from my
relationship to his mother, I had displaced onto the mother
anger that was really generated in my relationship to the boy
and for an entirely different reason.

David had mentioned his mother's desire for a rumpus room several weeks before the incident under examination without evoking any reaction from me; at the time that
I did react, it had been presented as something that he
wanted, and I realized that it was his irresponsibility to
which I was responding. Why, suddenly, should I have become angry at the boy for an attitude that I considered to be
the major therapeutic problem and which I had accepted
all along? Why had my tolerance for his passivity decreased?

A review brought to light that for several months, the
boy had been giving indication of an increased ability to take
responsibility and an increased awareness of the aggressive
component in his passive attitudes; I had already unconsciously responded to this by telling him that future negotiations for payment of therapy would be made with him as an
adult (156), and by my obvious satisfaction when he got the
diploma (158). We had begun an open discussion of the
aggression in his passivity (162), and had acknowledged together that the law of diminishing returns had set in upon
his doing nothing (165). At the time that I became angry,
I was, in effect, telling him that although small demands
were still acceptable, there were limits to the degree of irresponsibility that I would support, and was also acting as
though I recognized that aggression had been directed at me

in the provocative way by which he brought up the subject of the building.

David became more aware of the aggressive aspect of his behavior toward me than I did. Six weeks later, in discussing the incident, he verbalized a readiness for my reaction, and suggested that he had been unconsciously testing me (171). However, although subsequent interviews were more directly concerned with his passive attitudes, we focused predominantly on effects in the sexual sphere and uses in the transference; hostile, aggressive feelings directed specifically at me were insufficiently explored. In discussion about an incident in which my car blocked his in a traffic jam, it was close to David's consciousness that aggressive feelings were held in check by his indecisiveness, but I did not take this up explicitly with him (180); again we got off the track, directing attention to his fear of sexual aggressiveness. When he himself a little later suggested that we might be overemphasizing the sexual aspect of his conflict in order to avoid something else, I admitted the possibility, but did not pursue it (185). Obviously, there was a block.

After a while, I became aware that I had some conflict over the idea of pushing David toward independence, but considered this possibility to be due to competitiveness with the mother, who was putting great pressure on him to get a job. Quite suddenly it came to me in a flash that my inability to respond to the boy's passivity as aggression toward me as well as others was a countertransference problem which was understandable to me immediately upon recognition.

It is clear that from the time of the "rumpus room incident," the whole course of therapy moved more and more in the direction of working through David's fear of assuming active responsibility for himself in all spheres of his life. The change of direction, and increase of my emphasis on his ability to relinquish excessive dependency, took place long before I became aware of the nature of my own problem. His case, like most cases in the same category, presented so many different sources for reactivity that recognition of countertransference elements may have been unduly delayed. However, intuitive knowledge of the boy's capacity for more adequate functioning tended to offset the effects of countertransference; empathy eventually contributed to my capacity for breaking the block which prevented full understanding of interaction in the therapeutic relationship.

R E F E R E N C E S

(1) Fromm-Reichmann, F., *Psychoanalysis and Psychotherapy: Selected Papers* (ed. by D. M. Bullard), p. 101. Chicago, University of Chicago Press, 1959.

(2) Reich, A., quoted in Orr, D., "Transference and Countertransference: A Historical Survey," *Journal of the American Psychoanalytic Association*, Vol. 2, 1954, pp. 621–670.

(3) Tower, L. E., "Countertransference," *Journal of the American Psychoanalytic Association*, Vol. 4, 1956, pp. 224–265.

(4) Weigert, E., "Countertransference and Self Analysis of the Analyst," *International Journal of Psychoanalysis*, Vol. 35, 1954, pp. 242–246.

(5) Money-Kryle, R. E., "Normal Countertransference and Some of Its Deviations," *International Journal of Psychoanalysis*, Vol. 37, 1956, pp. 360–365.

(6) Szalita-Pemow, A. B., "The 'Intuitive Process' and Its Relationship to Work with Schizophrenics," *Journal of the American Psychoanalytic Association*, Vol. 3, 1955, pp. 7–18.

(7) Fromm-Reichmann, F., "Clinical Significance of Intui-

tive Processes of the Psychoanalyst," *Journal of the American Psychoanalytic Association*, Vol. 3, 1955, pp. 82–88.
(8) Schafer, R., "Generative Empathy in the Treatment Situation," *Psychoanalytic Quarterly*, Vol. 28, 1959, pp. 343–371.

1 5

The Rumpus Room

"He was in the stage just before wanting to...."

164. The family is thinking of moving back to New Haven. Mother uses finances as an excuse, but it's really because she can't have a rumpus room for her entertaining, and she won't stay in the country without one. (How do you feel about it?) O.K. The moving will be something to do. (Have you given up your job?) I was laid off with the other part-time workers.

I'm faced with the need to get a job, but I still don't see any point to it. I don't want to do anything at all. It makes me angry to be forced in that direction. (I think perhaps you equate "doing anything at all" with expressing these angry, aggressive feelings.) [*Pause.*] I don't like to think of it that way; it makes me feel less than I am. (You don't like to

see your inertness as a defense against aggressive impulses?)
No.

[He makes an involuntary movement with his left
hand, opening his fingers, and then closing them in a fist.]
(Who did you want to hit just then—me?) I want to lash out.
The trouble is, there is really nobody to blame; they are all
in the same boat. I don't want to lash out at somebody who
just happens to be in the way; I wouldn't want to be in that
position myself. We are all in the same boat, and I can't
really say who put me there.

(You hate to face the fact that you might have to
jump out and swim ashore if you want to get anywhere.) I
don't want to do anything.

I read a story about a robot. He was constructed to
solve a problem, but the problem was impossible to solve.
He couldn't not want to solve it, and he couldn't want not
to want to. He was in the stage just before wanting to, but
couldn't admit it was impossible. Finally someone came and
adjusted the mechanism, and it came out all right. (How
does this apply to you right now?)

[Pause.] I resent having to answer the question myself. (That would be having to do something, which to you
means aggression. I guess that puts me in the position of
someone trying to seduce you into losing control.) It's like
trying to kidnap a blackmailer. [Pause.] That wasn't a very
good analogy; it's more like being in a tunnel; you want to
come out and join the group, but you want to be bribed to
come out. You could come out a different way, but then you
wouldn't be allowed to join. (You want to be sure they want
you.) I guess so.

[Pause.] I wonder if analysis can be used as a defense
against the need to do something in life. (Sometimes it can.
What have you in mind?) A person who has a tendency to
be too unconscious gets interested in how he got that way,
and escapes into finding out. But the more he escapes, the

less he needs to. How does a person know if he has really solved the problem, and is just hanging onto the rope from habit? (He experiments with letting go and catching on again, but when he really feels ready, he probably knows it.)

165. I'm depressed and bored. I've just been hanging around. Sometimes I go and annoy a friend. (Annoy?) I don't think he's really annoyed. (I know that was supposed to be a joke, but it does express a real feeling that anyone who pays any attention to you is doing so under duress. Anyway, tell me about him.) He's a cynic.

[Pause.] I was just wanting to escape. (From what?) I'm always startled when you say something I don't expect. I expected you to say "Where to?" [Pause.] Everything is so boring. I have nothing to do, but I don't want to get a job. (You had to prove to yourself that you can't be forced to submit to demands. However, at this point the law of diminishing returns has set in. You wish you could give up the battle.) I think I was almost ready to come to such a conclusion myself.

[Pause.] I've met a girl I might be interested in marrying. I think she'd like the same kind of life I would. (Tell me about her.) She's going to marry someone else. But the thing that worries me is that I'd always thought I wouldn't want to marry anyone I didn't love. I don't love her, but I think she'd be a good companion. (It worries you that companionship might be important to you?) Yes. I always thought nothing was important except love.

[Pause.] I'd like to go away somewhere along the beach. I wouldn't even mind fishing, if it was for my supper. I want to get away from people. [Deep sigh.] They all have such big *plans* for me!

166. We're not going to move after all. I'm disappointed. I'm trying to persuade Mother to let me build a rumpus

room as a summer project. (What does she think of that idea?) She thinks it's fine. Now we need to get Dad to think it was *his* idea. I wish I could get started. (How much would it cost?) Over a thousand dollars. (Where would the money come from?) Mother is about to collect an old loan.

(How would you feel if I told you I would take a very dim view of a rumpus room being built when your family owes me so much money?) [*Pause.*] I haven't let myself think how much it has worried me that you haven't been paid. As a matter of fact, mother *did* say she was planning to pay you with whatever cash she got.

[*Pause.*] It upset me that you might be angry. (I *would* be angry if I thought your mother was planning to do building before paying me. I have always trusted her, and I still do, but for a moment I felt I had been taken for a sucker, and that makes a person angry. Anyway, it must have important implications to you that I brought this matter up. I think we should discuss your feelings about my saying that her debt to me should come before a project that is important to you.)

A child's ideas of justice don't last. I think it should be that way. (What one *thinks* is not always the same as what one *feels*. Assuming that you think I have your interests at heart as well as my own, you might very well feel that since I've waited this long, I could wait a little longer.) It would only be a temporary project anyway. (That isn't quite the point. Your feelings are more apt to have something to do with my thinking of my own interests ahead of yours in this case.)

I've tried not to think about how I was getting something for nothing. I felt I needed it. If it was something like the flying, just for pleasure, I could have given it up.

(I told you that the financial dealings were between me and your parents; if I was willing to take a risk, that was my problem. I happen to be interested in you, and I **can** afford to carry a few people who are unable to pay. I've always felt the need in your family was real. No matter how it may look to you, your mother and the rest of them have needs too. They may not always seem rational by your standards but I can understand them. I told you before that under some conditions certain luxuries might be considered essential to a person under a heavy strain. It might even be that a rumpus room could be considered essential to a person who feels deprived. It may look arbitrary to draw the line at one place and not the other. It isn't always true that a debt is more important than a project. You might feel that I shouldn't make value judgments on what is important.)

[Pause.] I've often gone away from here with different kinds of feelings, but I've never felt hurt before. I'm hurt that you think I could ignore you. (It is natural for you to be concerned about your own needs. However, you no longer have to keep your guilty feelings tucked away in the back of your mind. We can talk about these matters, now that you are strong enough to face them.)

I was upset at the way it came out. It was straight from your unconscious that you were angry at me. (I wasn't angry at you, but for a moment I was angry at your mother. I'm a human being, and I get mad sometimes, particularly if I think someone might have taken advantage of my trust. I understand now that this was not the case, but for a moment I thought it was, and I got mad.)

[Pause.] If I were a child, no demands would be made on me. (You sometimes wish you could stay a child. But remember, for you being a child wasn't much fun. Being an adult is for you potentially a much more satisfying prospect, even with its drawbacks.) I'm afraid to trust that idea.

I was wondering if it would be worthwhile to destroy. But I know it wouldn't do any good. (Just the same, you feel like smashing something.) Yes.

This hasn't been a pleasant experience for me today, but I think it was worthwhile. I've gotten some information that I think will be useful to me. (What information did you get that you thought was worthwhile?) I don't know exactly. It's like if you go on a trip—you don't know just what's been important to you, but it was interesting to have made the trip.

167. [*He starts talking spontaneously.*] I'll make a cross-country flight today. It's exciting. But I'd like to be able to fly with a companion. The flight today will be solo. The instructor says I will probably get lost at a certain place, but that it's good experience. I'd like to be able to make my first solo flight without getting lost. (I hope you will. Good luck!)

168. I'm wondering why I don't want to do *anything*. (We've talked about this as defense against aggression, but I imagine there's more to it than that.) If you take a job, it gives people control over you; unless you do what they want, they can take it away. It's better to have nothing than to have something you value, and then lose it.

(I think what you have just said may be at the heart of a lot of your feeling. It ties in with what you've said about aggression being frightening. You know that all small boys go through a period of aggressive feelings toward their fathers when they realize they can't have their mothers to themselves. For these feelings, they expect severe punishment in the form of losing what they highly prize, the penis. I think in your case, these normal feelings were very much intensified by circumstances. You had your mother all to yourself for a few years, and then lost her abruptly. I think you had intense feelings for her, and very intense aggressive feelings. You turned away from seeming to want anything, to protect yourself from losing your penis. Complete passivity was preferable to losing what you prized so highly.) That makes sense. It didn't seem to go far enough when you just said I was afraid of aggressive impulses.

I've just remembered what the impulses were, but it's hard to talk about. (I know. But try, anyway.) I must have been around six. I wanted to rub my mother's breasts, but was tactfully shunted to my father. While I was rubbing his chest, I got a big splinter run deep into my foot. (You felt punished for the desire, and ashamed.) Yes.

(What is so shameful about a little boy having sexual feelings toward his mother?) It beats me. I wish I knew. (You know, the temptation is universal. The drives are biological, but in civilization, it is necessary to inhibit them.) I know. But when I talk about it with you, it's as though I were telling you I have these impulses toward you.

(Talking about it arouses the buried impulses toward your mother and brings them out in relation to me.) Yes. I feel them when I talk about it. (And a good thing too. You may learn eventually to direct them toward someone your own age, but they have to be available.)

169. A friend of Mother's is having a party tonight. (Do you enjoy such parties?) Yes. Why do you ask? (Some people don't feel comfortable in groups.) I was wondering what you thought of my enjoying adult parties. (Maybe you thought I would assume you were talking about wanting to be in on adult affairs in other ways.)

I think I should be with people my own age, but I don't want to. (What is it like with people your own age?) Nothing goes on. Everyone gets drunk as soon as possible. Everyone is trying to escape from being terrified. (That's often true.) It's different at Mother's parties. Everyone is amusing.

[Pause.] Reaction time is sometimes slow. Sometimes it takes a year or more from the time of the stimulus to the

time of the response. [*Pause.*] I'm just skidding on the surface
of my mind. (Perhaps what we talked about last time made
you a little reluctant to get into anything today.) A rest between rounds. But if one starts taking rests, it might get easy
just never to go on. The interesting thing about this process
is that everything is subject for discussion. A problem, or no
problem. It can't help but be rewarding either way.

I wonder how much your being here affects the course
of my thoughts. (You feel my presence influences your
thought, whether you are communicating them or not?) Yes.
I always involuntarily bring the other person into the scope
of my thoughts, even when I'm not necessarily in a position
to talk about them. I can't seem really to shut you out.

170. I've been swimming in the club pool. [*Pause.*] Mother
has found some stocks in one of Dad's safety deposit boxes
that may be worth something. They belonged to his mother
—his wife. (His mother—his wife?) I wondered about my saying that. The way the mind works is fascinating. It's annoying, though, that thinking is really so mechanical. No matter
how original you think you are being, it's always possible for
someone to know just where you are going.

(What about that association between mother and
wife?) People have been making slips like that for hundreds
of years, but since Freud wrote about them, they are called
Freudian slips. (Freud simply systematized the knowledge
that sensitive people have always had intuitively. Many
others have been too afraid of knowing things that they
couldn't have helped knowing if they watched people and
children; they had to make an effort *not* to understand.
Freud himself said that he had disturbed the sleep of the
world, and would never be forgiven for it.) I can forgive him.

If people didn't have to keep so many things repressed, they wouldn't have to drop so many of the blocks
they pick up. (Or they could drop more of the blocks they

pick up.) I meant it like toy blocks—trying to pick up a lot, but not being able to hold them all. Some people give up trying to pick them up, because they know they will only be able to hold a few, and will be wasting their effort. That's not a good example, though. The people themselves are composed of the blocks.

171. I feel twitchy, perhaps because I feel freer to talk today. I don't know if its temporary or permanent. (But it's scary.) Yes.

Maybe part of why I feel twitchy is that I had to hitch-hike to the bus. I planned to go in with Mother, but she went off while I was still asleep. Maybe it's anger. (If she knew you were planning to go with her, it certainly was thoughtless.) I'm not sure she did. But she *is* thoughtless, although she makes great demands on everyone else.

She doesn't *need* another room; she just needs to have her own way. (You feel that when something is important to her, she is apt to forget the needs of others for a moment.) She just doesn't think about anyone else. She gets angry if she has to. (Was she angry about my conversation with you?) I didn't tell her. I feel that in here I can examine my thoughts without fear of blame, but that isn't true outside; I don't take anything out that we talk about. Anyway, I shouldn't have been acting as though she planned to build a room before paying you. As a matter of fact, I'm pretty sure she planned to pay you first. (I didn't mean that I wanted you to talk with her about it; I just wondered if you had, and she had gotten mad at you.) I figured you would take it up with her if you had feelings about it.

(What feelings have you had about our conversation?) I was scared of the anger in your voice. It was like Mother tearing into me. (You felt I was angry at you?) It wouldn't have mattered who. (You reacted to the feeling of anger rather than the content of the issue.) Yes. It scared me that you could depart from the analytic role.

(Everyone gets angry if they are personally threatened. I don't know whether, at the moment, I was angry at your mother or at myself, but I obviously got hit in a sensitive spot. I think, though, that it might have been frightening to you that I could get angry at you if you disappointed my expectations—that I might have demands on you for a certain type of behavior that is personally important to me.) I never felt that.

(On the other hand, I should think that it would be even more frightening to you if you thought I had such feelings but was concealing them from you.) It's a matter of timing. I guess I wouldn't want you to show feelings that would be damaging to me. I think it would be damaging for me to think that you often felt like that, but I don't.

(I wonder, too, whether you have some feelings about the fact that I would really care if I found out I couldn't trust your mother. Perhaps it's a scary thought that I might really care what happens to you.) I suppose it is.

I was just wondering if maybe I didn't have some kind of unconscious readiness to have you react. I certainly didn't consciously present it in such a way as to make you react— I had no plan to test you, but perhaps there was an unconscious plan. (There often is.)

PART III

This section comprises the last year and a half of therapy. It has been presented still largely in quasi-verbatim form, not only to demonstrate the marked changes in the boy's mode of communication, but for the purpose of allowing David to describe in his own words the conflicts and uncertainties confronting not only himself but a large number of other young people in their struggle toward maturity. His expression of feelings, and philosophical view of life's problems, depict the confusion universal among adolescents which is only more accentuated in those who have had severe emotional difficulties.

Occurrence of conflicts at this time of life, relating to assumption of a mature sexual role in both a cultural and a direct physical sense, is by no means limited to neurotic or psychotic young people. The re-emergence of oedipal problems, homosexual temptations, and fears of inability to perform adequately in a physical relationship which David expresses, appear with great frequency among young people in our society. He puts into words the struggle experienced by many between bodily need and romantic concepts of love or stereotyped images of the "ideal" boy or girl. As he describes his feelings of ineptitude in relating to a girl, many others can empathize with the impatience and clumsiness that are inherent components of a growing-up process.

Learning to accept adult responsibility and prepare for making a living is difficult for all adolescents, particularly today when competition for educational opportunity increases and choice of available jobs becomes more complex. In the years just before adulthood, there is always a conflict between "work and play." Most young people are ambivalent about leaving whatever security their families have to offer, and hesitate to take tentative preliminary steps toward any career for fear of being "trapped" in permanent commitments before they know what they want.

Conflicting ideas about the "male (or female) role" in our culture are becoming more prevalent, a reflection of sociological and cultural change as well as psychological problems. Lastly, the fear of loosening control over aggressive impulses combines with other ideological and psychological factors to induce resistance against military service and create conflict for a large number of young men eligible for the draft. Although the therapeutic material as a whole shows the specific elements which contribute to such conflicts in David, he is nevertheless giving voice to general problems that affect many individuals of his age group.

David's language and thinking at this stage show the culmination of a gradual but distinct trend toward direct and realistic communication. Signs of eruptive primary process which were dominant at an early period in therapy are negligible. Occasional momentary recourse to "code" occurs under pressure of anxiety, but the boy is able to recognize and readily reverse the process when it occurs.

Neurotic problems have been brought clearly into focus, ready to be worked out through analysis of transference manifestations. Oedipal conflict emerges in the therapeutic relationship and is explored via open discussion of erotic feeling, conflicts over "closeness" and projection onto me of the possessiveness he felt from his mother. Gradual acceptance of his own part in a mutual clinging process with her takes place through awareness of his desire to act out a similar process with me. His own fears of independence, and ambivalence about assuming responsibility, are tied directly to behavior in therapy; along with freedom to verbalize his resentment toward me for questioning his passivity, signs of increased aggressiveness appear in his general attitudes.

The technical handling of therapy is not greatly changed at this stage, but it is possible now to place greater emphasis on analyzing the underlying dynamic content of his communications, and to move toward realistic discussion of his problems in living. Gross distortions in the nature of our relationship have disappeared, and he is ready to engage in analytically oriented psychotherapy with the same attitudes and conflicts that are present in any well-motivated neurotic patient.

16

Sexual Conflicts

"I don't want to be afraid of fire! I need the warmth!"

172. [Pause.] (What are you thinking?) About a girl. I was wondering if she'd still be around in two or three years. (Any reason to think not?) I don't think so. (What are you worried about?) I'm disappointed that I'm not in love with her.

(What is she like?) Boy Scout phrases—courageous, loyal, and gay. (Nothing the matter with those qualities, even if the Boy Scouts do exploit them. But you don't feel sexually attracted, is that it?) I wouldn't say I'm not; but being in love implies a feeling of "we" rather than "you and I." I haven't got it. (Have you ever had it with someone?) Yes.

[Pause.] I was wondering whether, if I let myself move around and itch and scratch, I'd get more information. I've taught myself to ignore bodily feelings. At first I didn't dare let myself move in here for fear of giving myself away. Now I think the feeling is more to protect you. I don't want to think anything I do will affect you. (It sounds as though you were afraid that if I were aware of your physical sensations, it might be exciting to me—sexually provocative.) I guess so. (What would be the threat to you if it were?) I might think of you like a mother.

(It would scare you to be aware that your mother had such feelings toward you?) Yes. It might make my father very angry. He might beat me up physically. [*Pause.*] Actually, I think it might be more that I would have feelings of attraction toward *him*, and he would push me away. (Homosexual feelings toward your father would be covered up by heterosexual feelings toward your mother.) Yes.

[*Long pause.*] (You know, everyone has homosexual feelings at times without necessarily being homosexual.) I think my fear of becoming an overt homosexual is greater than the actual possibility. I think sex with a woman would really be easier for me, but I might be attracted to men because I'm afraid of women. I'm afraid of damaging women. My getting pleasure from them might make them seem degraded to others.

[*Pause.*] My idea of a relationship with a girl is one in which only the two of us were concerned with what went on. [*Pause.*] Perhaps that's why I'd be afraid of sexual feelings between you and me. This is the kind of situation that would be ideal in a marital relationship; we are responsible only to each other, and nobody outside this room has to know what we do, or say, or think. (You are afraid we might be tempted to act out our feelings?) [*He glances toward the couch.*]

(I think you might be afraid of something else too. There is the whole problem of mixed signals, to which I think you have been subjected in the past. You are afraid I might unconsciously invite you, and then when you responded, would consciously be horrified and slap you down.

But if you *didn't* respond, I'd turn against you.) Yes. I'd be afraid no matter what you did.

[*Pause.*] I see you as a person that should be around children. They could express their desires without panic or blame. You are like a big brown bear that lets the cubs run around the den or chew on her, and it's all the same.

173. [*He is panting.*] I don't think I have very good oxygen storage; I'm breathless. (Maybe you are anxious.) Maybe.

[*Pause.*] I'm wondering why the unconscious doesn't block off bodily stimuli as it does words. There are some things that are hard to talk about, but you are aware of them bodily. (Feelings that want expression come out in unconscious body movements and reactions.) I resent that I don't have the choice of expressing them directly or not at all.

(There might be certain feelings that are both welcome and unwelcome at the same time; welcome to the conscious but not the unconscious, or vice versa.) [*Nod.*] But why should the unconscious perceive and express more than the conscious? (Because its mechanisms are more primitive, and have developed earlier in life. An infant at first reacts to all emotions with a total body reaction, and can only later channel expression.) [*Nods again.*]

(I think you probably have a more direct pipeline into your own unconscious and that of others than most people. This is an advantage in some ways, but it is also good that you have worked so hard and brought about more conscious control. Some people have no contact at all with their unconscious, and others have too little contact with the world of consciousness and reality. A reasonable balance is necessary.)

At first that sounded rather hopeless. (Something can be a valuable tool in one quantity and a destructive force in an uncontrolled amount. Like water—it can create power and run machines, or it can cause a flood.)

[*Pause.*] I think I might be talking about something that's interesting to me, and still using it to avoid something that's hard to talk about. [*While he is saying this, he brings his hands up from his lap and clasps them under his chin.*] I was wondering whether you would start talking again if I moved my hands. (Were you hoping I would?) Yes. (Wanting me to talk might be part of the same resistance you just mentioned; even a meaningful conversation can be used to avoid things.) I know.

I was wondering if you would think I moved my hands to make a barrier between you and me. (Did you feel the need for a barrier just then?) I wasn't aware of it, but maybe.

I wonder if it's true that people can tell what kind of personality a person has by the color of his eyes? On TV, the leader's eyes are always blue or steely gray. The brown-eyed guy is always the bartender, or something. (You think people might be able to know what you are thinking or feeling from some bodily characteristic like that?) Maybe.

[*Pause.*] (What are you thinking?) Nothing; just relaxing. I feel as though everything I've said today is sort of mechanical. Like if you touch the "A" key on a typewriter, "A" appears on the paper, without anything intermediate.

(There are two more weeks now before my vacation.) I know.

174. Mother went off and left me again today. Something always happens on Thursday. (I imagine that's true; I'm sure she has very mixed feelings about your appointments.) I think she has feelings about my loving anyone.

(I think it's quite likely that you yourself have mixed feelings about forming any other relationships with women.)

[*Pause.*] I'm wondering whether two straight edges can ever meet on an exact point. I can see the point where they meet as made up of microscopic particles of graphite, so it's more of a curve. (If the two lines are straight by definition, how does a curve come in?) I can't see them as meeting directly. (I wonder if you are saying something like that two lines of relationship can't meet without getting muddied up?) I guess so. People can't get close to each other.

[Pause.] I'm thinking of a way to drive a space ship. If the stuff that gets thrown out of the rocket could be packed so that there wouldn't be any space between the atoms, more could be gotten into a smaller space. (Are you concerned with packing more into the little time left before vacation? Maybe you have some feelings about the fact that there isn't much time left.) Have I had reactions like that when you took vacations before? All I'm aware of is that it's a rather welcome resting space.

(Often when you revert to that kind of indirect, symbolic talk, it means you are disturbed by something. You have been communicating very directly in the last few months; I wonder if this is your way of withdrawing gradually.) That might be. I've been feeling terrible fatigue. I think that might be a shield against having any feelings.

It's ridiculous for people to think all their little problems are so world-shaking. The things they get all shook up about aren't really that bad. (Things people get "all shook up" about often represent things that have been very devastating.) I've never found that the things I've talked about were nearly as devastating as I feared they would be.

(It's a matter of timing and dosage. If things hit a person at an age when he's most vulnerable, they may be overwhelming even if, in retrospect, they don't seem so terrible.) I suppose that's so.

[Pause.] I don't have any way to judge whether I'm overly afraid of dying. (What do you mean?) So afraid that it interferes with my living. (Perhaps you are using fear of dying to express other kinds of fears, like fears of sexual functioning.) Yes. Perhaps I'm so afraid of failing that it keeps me from trying.

[*Pause.*] One reason I have trouble talking about this is that when I have a problem, you help me to solve it. I'm afraid you might want to help me solve it directly. (Like "Tea and Sympathy"?) Yes. (Acting out a sexual role with you is not the way I can be of most help to you. My function is to help you understand your feelings and get at them. Perhaps these fears about functioning prevent you from finding a young girl who would be a suitable love object for you.) I can't find any young girls I think are very interesting. (If you did, it might arouse those fears.) I don't want to have intercourse with "just anyone." I want someone I can love. I want someone that when she looks at you, she sees you.

[*Pause.*] I wonder if it would be possible to find someone to share unconsciousness. (Unconsciousness is always personal and lonely. When it is shared, it already has consciousness in it. Real communication combines conscious and unconscious factors.) I suppose it is possible for a person to learn the code. (I think you know it is. However, the code is used defensively. When people are not afraid to communicate, codes aren't necessary.) Yes. I suppose the only connection between two unconsciousnesses is by way of two consciousnesses.

175. [*He looks withdrawn. Long pause.*] (I get the feeling you are somewhat disturbed today.) It annoys me to give clues I don't know I'm giving. I'm not conscious of anything to be disturbed about. (Perhaps you have some feelings about the fact that this is our last hour together for two months.) I hadn't let myself be aware of it. (You quite often turn off your feelings about things that might be expected to be upsetting.) I like to think I don't show any emotion. (In view of the fact that you have been moving along well here

lately, one might expect you to feel some annoyance and frustration at being interrupted.) Yes; I guess I do. I don't like to break up a chain of events.

Time is like laying down a row of blocks. If you come to the end of a row, there's an empty space. You can start another row, but the first row ends. Perhaps I should learn to think of the empty spaces as part of the pattern. (But that isn't easy when you don't know what the pattern is.) That's right. [Pause.] I think of the work we are doing as a rebuilding. You have to be careful to keep the part that's being rebuilt away from the part that's already rebuilt.

[Pause.] I wish I could control the energy of the sun. [Smile.] I was wondering if that should be spelled "sun" or "son." (I was wondering too.) I meant "sun" when I said it. The trouble with releasing energy—like from a gun—is that there's a kickback. One should be able to release it in a forward direction without losing energy in kickback.

I was wondering how I was holding my hands. I noticed I had both thumbs pointing up, and had the feeling of annoyance again that I might be making a communication. Sometimes, though, interpretations of things like that are more of a distraction than they are worth.

[Pause.] The people who teach Communications have a lot of screwy ideas. I asked the teacher why they didn't pay more attention to meaningful communication. We got into an argument; he said that inanimate objects can't communicate; I said they could. This led to a change in his definition of communication. There has to be an intent to communicate on the one hand, and an ability to receive on the other. This would rule out accidental things, like someone leaving on a tape recorder that was heard by someone else. (Sometimes such things aren't purely accidental; one has to consider unconscious intent. There is also projection and wishful thinking; sometimes, if a person has a feeling himself, he may perceive it as a communication from someone else. Or if he wants very much to be told something, he may interpret someone else's action as a communication to fill his need.) I know.

(Well, our time is up for now. We will have to continue when I come back.)

It is the end of the fifth year of treatment.

176. [*He walks in smiling.*] (You look well; how do you feel?) Fine. I took my exam for commercial pilot, but haven't heard the results yet. I'm back at college, taking an advanced course in math; things are O.K. At home it's status quo.

(Your mother just called and asked you to do an errand for her. Are you taking part in her activities?) No, but I'd like to. I've thought of trying to pick up a skating dance I used to do when I was about nine. (How come you gave it up?) [*Laugh.*] I outgrew the costume. (I wondered if that wasn't about the time you began to feel you needed to restrict bodily movements.) Maybe so.

(I've noticed that lately you seem to be freer in moving around here; you move your hands and your head.) Well, I guess I finally decided you weren't going to beat me. Maybe it wasn't so important to keep from expressing things unconsciously with gestures and movements. (That might be it.)

177. [*He nods in a friendly way, then stares into space.*] I'm wondering why I can't fall in love. (Tell me about it.) She's a perfect girl for me, but I can't seem to fall in love with her. We are exactly alike in the way we look at things. (But you can't feel love?) No. (Perhaps you have been too much hurt in the past. "A burnt child fears the fire.") I don't want to be afraid of fire! I need the warmth! I should be able to get close enough to get warm without getting burned.

(What is it about a person that *does* stimulate erotic

feelings?) The kind of person I like to be with is what one might call childlike—enjoys life positively—perhaps more like an animal, that lives with all its instincts alive. A person who moves freely, laughs loud, enjoys eating—you know what I mean. (The free movement is important?) That's just part of it. I guess youngness is important.

(There's often a difference between liking to be with a person and being emotionally and erotically aroused by them. One's conscious image of an ideal mate is sometimes quite different from the unconscious image that is linked by associations to the arousal of erotic feelings. Perhaps we could get a clue to your unconscious image by examining what kind of fantasies arouse erotic feelings, in masturbation, for instance.)

[Pause.] I think what is important to me is youth combined with large size. It occurs to me suddenly that this is connected with that woman I knew as a child. *I* was the young small one. (And you felt a mixture of pleasure and fear of being overpowered.) Now I want to be the adult in that situation, and at the same time, the small body. [Pause.] Maybe one reason I've been afraid of marriage is that I've been afraid that a big girl wouldn't be enough. (Perhaps.)

178. [*He enters with some talk about the weather; ends with the comment, "When it finally does rain, it will probably flood."*]

[Pause.] I was thinking of a story of a computer in the form of a human. He was created to solve the problem of how to end war, but the problem had no solution. He couldn't solve it, and he couldn't stop trying. He couldn't even say he wanted to. Finally someone guessed, and fixed it so he could stop. (But what if his whole mechanism was geared to finding a solution?) He just sat in a corner and did nothing.

(You?) I guess so. (Is the war internal, external, or

both?) Both, I guess. I just don't think I can ever find a way to live and be happy. (Often you get discouraged just when you have hit on something that frightens you a bit.)

[*Pause.*] I was thinking about sleeping with a woman. I need to know that I can, but I don't want to find out by trying it. (What's the feeling?) I don't know whether it's fear of failure or a feeling that one shouldn't unless one is married. (I doubt that the latter is a major part of it for you. I think the feeling "I mustn't do it" has meanings other than the conventional one.) [*Smile.*] I imagine so. But whose idea is it? (You have incorporated a strong prohibition, but what it's all about isn't entirely clear.)

[*Pause.*] I think I'm afraid that in a sexual situation the woman might be the male member. (It sounds as though you were afraid she might literally steal your penis—that it would be bitten off.) I might be in the same situation I was in that time as a child. (Except that you are no longer small, weak, and helpless.)

She might be the aggressor, and I the passive one. (You might enjoy being in the passive position, as you did then. But I suppose you believe a man isn't supposed to enjoy passivity. Actually, of course, lots of men do, but people talk as though it shouldn't be that way. You seem to be afraid that if you enjoyed having a woman be the aggressor, you would be laughed at and thought unmasculine.) That sounds logical.

(I wonder if this feeling enters into a situation we've discussed a little when it occurs between us. You seem to want me to be the aggressor, asking each time what you are thinking—taking your thoughts from you instead of having you offer them. You want me to do it, but still fear I'll look down on you for wanting it.) That sounds possible.

[*Pause.*] However, I certainly didn't get anywhere with a male therapist. (Perhaps to be in the passive position with a man has homosexual implications to you. You seem to feel an analogy between the therapeutic relationship and a sexual relationship.) What you say sounds true, but I'm without a reaction, as though forces pulling in opposite directions had brought me to a neutral position.

179. [*He offers a few preliminary remarks about the unusual heat, then becomes silent and stares into space. I have the thought, "Now we are on the air."*] (Have you heard from your flying test?) I didn't get enough points to pass, but I can take the test again. Now I know how to prepare for it.

[*Pause.*] (What is the feeling?) I don't like what we were saying last time about my passivity, but that seems to be the way it is. I want to be active about sleeping with a woman, but I don't seem to be able to. (I know it is uncomfortable to feel like that.)

[*Pause.*] I felt then that you were just using a formula to draw me out. (You were afraid I had no feeling about it, and was just being mechanically conciliatory? That must have made you mad.) No; I wasn't aware of that—just scared of being "drawn out." (Do you think some of the reaction was just plain scared of what might come out?) I guess so.

[*Pause.*] The trouble is, some days I feel a need to hang back. I feel as though I'm being pulled along too fast. (As a matter of fact, I was just wondering myself whether I was trying too hard to pull you along. I guess we both have mixed feelings about it. I want you to work all this out as soon as you can, yet I know how difficult it is for you. I imagine I do sometimes prod you more than necessary.)

[*Pause.*] It made me feel good to have you say you want me to work it out as soon as I can. I guess I was afraid you might lose interest. I also like to be let in on what you are thinking sometimes; it's interesting to get an idea of what the doctor's role is in a process like this—trying to make decisions about when to push and when not to. It makes it seem more like we are *both* working on it.

(I'm sure it is sometimes frustrating to us both to have relatively little time to work on the problem each week.) Actually, I think it's probably O.K. that there is a week in between times. Sometimes, if I hit something painful, it takes that long to build myself up so I can talk about it. The time isn't lost, because I need it to work at keeping down the feelings that want me to push it out of consciousness again.

180. [*He is wearing a bright red shirt, looking scrubbed and dapper.*] (That's a mighty red shirt!) I picked it out myself. (It looks nice.) It doesn't go with anything except these slacks. (So what?) I guess that was just conversation; I really don't care if it's practical. (I didn't think you did.) One is supposed to spread one's money as far as possible. (Sometimes one just buys something because one likes it.) [*Smile.*] Yes.

[*Pause.*] I was thinking about a traffic problem. As I was coming down the street, you were coming across the street in front of me. At first I didn't recognize it was you, and I was mad because there was a traffic jam. (Did recognizing me make a big difference in the way you felt?) I'm always more tolerant of someone I know. (In a traffic jam one gets irritated at the blocking, no matter who is involved. It just isn't so easy to express the feelings if one knows the person.)

Sometimes when I'm in traffic, I'm mainly interested in jockeying for an advantageous position to go ahead, but people get the idea that I'm going to ram into them. I'm just trying to get into a good position myself. (But you are afraid people will think you are being aggressive toward *them*.) Yes.

[*Pause.*] I'm thinking about Hallowe'en; the kids out our way really cut loose. (More trick than treat?) There was no pretense at trick-or-treat—they wanted to throw things! [*Smile.*] The adults were standing in front of their houses with baseball bats. But the kids didn't want to fight—they wanted to release tension and laugh. (That was the original point of Hallowe'en pranks. People need something like that, but there is always the fear that destructiveness will get out of control and bring disaster not only to the recipient of the prank, but to the prankster himself.)

If *I* were in charge, I'd offer a prize for pranks that showed real thought and originality. That would divert some of the aggression into creative channels. There would be real group spirit between kids and adults. (That sounds like a good idea.) [*Pause.*] The police made threats, but couldn't carry them out and just made themselves foolish. However, kids need a target for their aggression. Maybe adults ought to pay police double for allowing themselves to take the brunt of the hostility. Kids need to do a little damage sometimes, but they have to have enough control to keep the damage from being too final. (That's right.)

[*Pause.*] I was thinking of a pattern. It looks something like two eye-droppers facing each other. (What does that image suggest?) Homosexuality.

(Are you concerned about that?) Perhaps. Sometimes I think I have more of the feminine in me than masculine. (What do you mean?) Well, I seem to see things from the female point of view, but I don't think that's entirely bad. I think sometimes that homosexuality is a more desirable state than heterosexuality, and I resent anyone who says I haven't the right to feel that way, so long as I don't *do* anything about it. (You have a right to feel any way at all. Let's talk about it.)

I used to think homosexuals were terrible, but I don't any more. (People have a tendency to condemn violently in others the things they can't face in themselves. You can face these impulses in yourself, and don't have to fight to keep them out of consciousness.)

I used to think that was the worst thing possible.

Now I think the worst thing is rape. (The thought of a sexual experience being forced upon a person before he is ready is certainly frightening.) Yes. (I think you have some fears of being forced into a sexual act before you are ready.) Maybe.

181. It would be good if one could just live off the land and be free of commitments—if you could work just enough to be able to play the rest of the time! (Some people *do* live like that; there are many different ways of life.) I would like to choose a life of play, but that wouldn't be acceptable. (That depends on how one sees play. You apparently see it as freedom from specific commitment. I think maybe this ties in with what we were discussing last time—fear of being committed to a specific sexual role before you have really made up your mind.)

Work is masculine; play is feminine. If you choose play, you run the risk of being alone. (Not always. Many men choose to play a feminine role, and work out a way of life with someone who takes a masculine role.) I feel that the worst thing in life would be inability to love a woman. I feel my only alternative is to work out my conflicts about that. If I can't do it, I would rather have nothing.

[*Pause.*] I've got the feeling that if I wanted to be a homosexual, you wouldn't stop me. I was counting on you to protect me from that. (I could only do so by helping you to work out your fear of women. I would certainly *hope* to keep you from taking steps that would establish a homosexual pattern of response before you knew what you did want; on the other hand, I don't condemn homosexual feelings. Most young people have them in one degree or another, and even sometimes act upon them without permanent harm.)

The thing is, it's necessary to be both male and female. I would like to be sexually a male, but in other ways closer to female. Most things that are thought of as male are so dull! (Maybe you are talking about pseudo-masculinity—big muscle stuff, which is really often a mask for feelings of insecurity.)

It's hard to know what the male role is. (Even harder in your family, where the roles have to some extent been reversed. Even that isn't clear cut, because you feel that in your father, a lot of aggression is masquerading as passivity, and in your mother there is also ambivalence about sexual role. It must have been impossible to know which to identify with as a male.) Yes.

(However, I think a lot of your conflict is related to more basic unconscious fears about bodily harm. I think you see the vagina as having big teeth that will bite off your penis.) Not consciously. (No, but your fears of sexual activity have more to them than feelings about aggression and passivity.)

182. My heart is beating too hard. (Have you been more anxious lately when you come in here?) Yes.

I had the idea last time that you were warning me against homosexual activity. I wondered if you saw something I wasn't aware of. (Last time you said just the opposite. You were afraid I wouldn't *protect* you against an impulse in that direction. You had said the time before that you maintained the right to consider homosexuality as the most desirable state, and I had agreed that you had this right. However, I was pointing out some of the factors involved in choosing homosexuality as a way of life, separate from having homosexual feelings which are universal.)

I don't think I said what I meant, or meant what I said. I feel it is desirable to have a big dose of femininity, but I wouldn't want to be homosexual. (You mean you want to have certain qualities which are often considered to be feminine. What are they?)

Calmness; the ability to withstand shock. Perhaps I

feel that way because you are a woman, and that's the way you are. (You want to identify with certain qualities that you feel are in me, and assume these qualities are feminine.) Yes. (You know, some people would say that the qualities you have named are masculine, and that if a woman possesses them, she isn't entirely feminine. The prevalent cultural attitude is that men are more stable, women more flighty.)

It isn't stability I mean so much, but a kind of stable reactivity. (An ability to make emotional contact?) Yes; exactly. (Well, I agree with you that that is a good quality to develop, but I don't believe it is found exclusively in either sex. Although it is inhibited in many people of both sexes, it nevertheless exists widely among members of each sex. In American culture, men often feel they have to conceal their emotional responses more than women do.)

People in American society are hypocrites; they say one thing about sex, but do something else. (There *is* a lot of hypocrisy about it, but it is also true that a lot of people push off onto "society" their own conflicts. I think to some extent that is what you are doing. It isn't the prohibitions of "society" that are stopping you, but your own conflicting feelings. For instance, things like fear of impotence related to masturbation guilts and fantasies, and your experiences with Jane.)

[*Pause.*] It shocked me to hear you call her by name; I scarcely mention it to myself. (Why not?) I don't know, but I don't think of her by name.

[*Pause.*] I'm thinking of a book I read about Zen. (What aspect of it?) The position they take for meditation. They sit cross-legged, with their feet on their thighs and hands in lap with palms upward. [*Pause.*] That seems vulnerable to physical damage. (Specifically genital damage, with the thighs spread like that.) I guess so.

[*Pause.*] That reminds me of an unhappy dream I had. I was trying to break in somewhere—into some kind of dark passage—and things came at me from all sides to destroy me. (Fear that if your penis tries to enter the vagina, it will be destroyed, as we said last time.)

[Pause.] I was thinking about Jane. She used to read me things out of the paper about people being cut up in little pieces. She said she was the one who had done it. (Did you believe her?) Not exactly, but maybe I made associations between her and getting castrated. (Maybe so.)

[Pause.] I think I could work through my fear of impotence if I could find someone who was willing to take it with me slowly, step by step, and not demand too much at first. But I'm afraid I'd get thinking too much about what I was doing, and not be able to lose myself in feeling. (It's like what you once said about tying your shoes—if you have to stop and think about all the complicated movements you are making, you become all thumbs and can't do anything.)

Imagine your remembering that! It's almost unbelievable! (Often the way you say things is very colorful, and I am apt to remember the words. However, I imagine what you feel so amazing is that anyone could think anything you say is interesting or worthwhile.) That's true.

[Pause.] I was looking at the fold in the curtain and imagining it cut straight across. I suppose that's an image about castration. (I imagine so.) [Pause.] I was wondering what you were thinking. (Reversing roles for a minute? All right—I was thinking that there must be a close tie-in between your feelings of worthlessness and fantasies about castration.)

183. [He sits down in an even stiffer position than usual.] (How scared are you?) I'm just trying to get prepared. (You look as though you feel whatever is going to hit you is going to come from an unexpected direction.) [Smile.] I'm trying to relax.

[Pause. Smile.] There isn't much oxygen up here on

the second floor. (A girl told me the other day that I must scatter pollen in here, because she always starts to sneeze when she comes in.) I hope if she's been coming for any length of time, she meant it as a joke. (I'm sure she did.) Doesn't anyone come here and feel more relaxed instead of more anxious? (Yes. Often the same people at different times feel different ways.) [He smiles directly at me.]

[Pause.] I'm thinking about a book—the Confessions of St. Augustine. The only part I've read is his logical argument on why one shouldn't have a wife. (Did you agree?) I could only agree if I believed God was a person. He says if you are single, you dedicate your life to pleasing God, otherwise to pleasing a wife. (You feel you would have to have a physically satisfying relationship with a higher being before you'd be willing to give up the satisfaction of a relationship with someone who was equal in human terms.) Yes.

[Pause.] I have an image of a trick jar. (Whatever you have to say is trying to come out in an indirect communication.) [Pause.] I'm thinking about the sound of a clap with one hand. I'm wondering what part of a piece of paper is cut with one side of a scissors. (Both seem to be paradoxical ideas.) [Pause.] I think maybe I'm wondering what is my part in a physical relationship with a woman.

[Pause.] I wish whatever is bothering me would come to the surface. It's something about sex, but I can't think what. I'm trying too hard. It's like giving a guy a pill and saying, "This will cure you if you won't think of the word 'monkey' when you take it." [We both laugh.]

[Pause.] I wish Mother was more enthusiastic about my taking a trip. (Why isn't she?) She thinks it's dangerous. She thinks I'll lose control if I so much as leave the house. She's afraid the guys will get drunk and whoop it up in some town and we'll all land in jail. (Will they?) Not if enough of us keep our heads. They will only do what is acceptable in the group. They are guys who hurt inside, and sometimes need to let loose their aggressions, but I think we can find ways to let off energy without getting into trouble. (You have had some experience with what happens when things get rolling in a group. Are you sure enough of your inner controls to hold yourself in check?) I'm pretty sure, but anyway, I'm going. I think that for myself, I'll have a certain amount of happy energy to release.

184. Again I'm conscious of my heart beating hard. (I suppose it doesn't always have to be fear; there could be feelings like excitement or pleasurable anticipation.)

[Pause.] I was thinking of what we are doing here. I bring up problems and we discuss them; one by one, they drop off. Sooner or later one finds there aren't many problems, or that there is one real problem. (What have you in mind?)

I guess the problem is physical love between me and a girl. Until I've solved that one, we've gone as far as we can. (What are the barriers?) I think difficulty in communication. (You've solved that to a large degree in one area; I see no reason to assume it can't be solved in that area too.)

[Pause.] I don't want to find myself on a tilting slope, unable to check the momentum. (You are afraid of losing control.) One can walk among a lot of clay pots on the level, but one doesn't want to go charging into them without being able to stop. I suppose I mean—well, just losing control. But of course, that's the kind of situation in which one is supposed to be able to let go and be spontaneous. (Yes. That's the whole point.)

[Pause.] I want to find a girl who understands the conflicts, so that we can work them out together slowly. (I'm sure that when you feel ready, you can find such a girl.)

[Pause.] I wonder if sometimes you have a hard time keeping ahead of me. (I don't try to keep ahead of you; I try to keep with you as much as possible. What do you mean?)

Like you're the teacher—asking a question, or making a comment at just the moment that keeps me going forward.

[Pause.] I'm afraid of not being able to satisfy a girl. (You are apt to assume that if anything goes wrong between you and another person, you are a failure. Satisfying sex between a boy and a girl is a learning process—something they both have to achieve together. Each person has to teach the other how to satisfy. It doesn't happen all at once.)

[Pause.] Everyone is against my having sexual relations with a girl. (Everyone?) I guess I mean Mother. I don't think she wants to share me with another woman. (That might be true. Lots of mothers consciously or unconsciously want to keep their sons for themselves. But I suspect that there is also some reluctance on your own part to share *yourself* with another woman.)

Maybe I'm afraid to give up one mother until I'm sure I've got another. (You expect a girl friend to be a mother?) Isn't mothering a part of it? (There is always some mothering and fathering in a close relationship, but it is possible for two mature people to support each other without having one taking care of the other. It is also possible to have a close emotional and physical relationship with a girl and still maintain a relationship with a mother. Even when mothers feel some jealousy, they can usually manage to handle it if the son is able to handle his own ambivalence.)

185. I'm afraid the trip won't come off. (I'm sorry. There have been so many promising plans that had to be deferred.) Oh well, I don't really mind, so long as I don't have to feel that anyone has worked against me.

[Pause.] I was trying to balance the folds in the curtain. I'm aware of a need to get things in balance. It has something to do with sex. [Pause.] I'm feeling annoyed that so many things end up on that subject. (You remember the story about the psychology professor with the white handkerchief, and the boy who said it reminded him of sex because *everything* reminded him of sex?) [*He laughs, getting quite red in the face.*]

[*Pause.*] It seems as though there is something wrong with just accepting what I say as though I were an oracle. I say something, and we assume what I said was right. I just hope that when I think of something, it's valid, and that when sex comes to mind, I'm not ignoring something else. (Things that come to mind may mean a number of things. What you think of first is nearest the surface. If other things are important, they will come out sooner or later.)

Maybe fear of sex isn't the whole answer. I think I might be afraid that if I sleep with a girl, I have to assume adult responsibility in other ways too. (Maybe.) [*Pause.*] (I wonder if there isn't more to what you were saying last time —fear that if you make a relationship with a girl, your mother will cast you out.) I thought you didn't want me to talk about that. (How come?) I've brought it up several times in different ways, but you didn't pick it up. I didn't think you were interested.

(It may be that at times I don't get what you say, or pick it up only on the second or third bounce, but if you feel something is important, what's to prevent you from pursuing it? Why so much emphasis on my interest?) I assume you have a better idea of what's important at any particular moment. (I think that idea is an excuse for avoiding things about which you are ambivalent yourself. Sometimes you bring things up in a way that is intended to make your meaning obscure, you know.) I brought this up fairly directly. (Yes, and as a matter of fact, I picked it up fairly directly. We discussed it quite a bit last time. I told you that although I think it is possible that your mother has an unconscious need to keep you to herself, it is still a problem of your own to discover how this attitude plays in with your own needs toward *her*. I wonder if you had some need to forget our discussion?) I guess there are some things I can let myself talk about, so long as I don't let them penetrate.

(You have said in several different ways at different times that your mother and I are in conflict over you—over who is to "own" you. Maybe your mother does have some unwillingness to share you with me, and for all I know, I may have an unconscious desire to be a better mother to you than she. However, assuming *she* has a problem, *your* problem is your *own* ambivalence.) I see. If *I* didn't have feelings of my own, hers wouldn't be a problem to me. (Exactly.)

[*Pause.*] I think I've felt cheated out of my childhood. Maybe I don't want to give it up. I think when I was born, my mother got from me what she needed from my father. I think I owe her something now, because she loved me when I needed it. (You were a baby. A baby is supposed to get unconditional love from its mother. If she wants him to meet her erotic needs, she is making an unreasonable demand. If he meets it, the situation is distorted. If an adult child and his mother need to meet each other's erotic needs, there is also a distortion in the relationship.) I think that is beginning to get straightened out.

186. I've been driving a big Ford truck. It's fun. [*Pause.*] I'm thinking of having a lot of power to use, and using it. (What kind?) Destructive power. The only kind of constructive power is the power to leave things alone. (That's protective, not necessarily constructive. It's a little bit like being suspended in space, isn't it?) It's like being unborn.

(Being unborn is being well protected. The uterus is safe, but a baby can't move around much on his own in there.) [*Smile.*] I saw a sign in a lab—"Don't throw cigarette butts in the urine; it makes them soggy and hard to smoke." [*Pause.*] "Don't keep a baby in the uterus; he can't breathe in there." (The uterus is necessary to a foetus at certain developmental stages, but once it has developed to a certain point, it isn't good for either the baby or the mother to keep it unborn.) My trouble is, I've gone too far into consciousness to be able to go back. I'm stuck with being committed to wanting life. (Very few people would want to crawl back once they had learned to breathe on their own.)

[*Pause.*] (Of course you recognize that we are continuing our discussion of last time—your need to distinguish yourself from your mother.)

[*Pause.*] I'm thinking about the need to live forever. (You don't have to live forever to get a good many of the satisfactions that you want from life.)

[*Pause.*] I'm thinking of myself as married and having some children. I'm afraid it will be difficult. (Nobody ever said it was easy, but many people think it's worth the effort.) It's the last resort of an inadequate male to have a lot of children. (The sense of adequacy as a male should come before the having of children. There's a step between having children and where you are now.) I think I want to skip that. (You are afraid to think of yourself as an independent, sexual male, so you see yourself as still part of a family, but parent instead of child. You really would like to keep the satisfactions of both states at the same time, but you have to give up one gradually as you take on the other.) I'm afraid to try. I'm afraid of getting into what I see at home. (Afraid you can't satisfy a woman.) Satisfying a woman must be quite difficult.

It might be like Atlas, who agreed to hold the world for a little while, and got stuck with it on his shoulders for eternity. (If you have a responsibility to your mother, it is as a son, not as a husband.)

[*Pause.*] I resent terribly having feelings that aren't in control of my conscious thinking. Ideas like that are like a dog in the manger, keeping life away from me. (The dog in the manger of your unconscious can't be forced to give up what he needs to hoard. He must be persuaded he doesn't need those ideas any more. A while back, you couldn't even tolerate the thought that you *had* such feelings. The best way to destroy their power is to make them conscious.)

The next week he neither comes in nor calls to cancel. Two hours *after* the appointment, his mother calls to say that he is out of town.

17

Transference

TRANSFERENCE IS A UNIVERSAL PHENOM-
enon in psychotherapy. It has been the subject of much discussion in the psychoanalytic literature and, like countertransference, is variably defined. Most analysts accept the
general concept of transference as a displacement by the
patient onto his therapist of attitudes and affects which have
characterized his relationships with significant figures in the
past. As described by Fenichel, "The patient misunderstands
the present in terms of the past; and then, instead of remembering the past, he strives, without recognizing the nature of
his action, to relive the past and to live it more satisfactorily
than he did in childhood." [1] The dynamic psychotherapists
are in essential agreement. According to Frieda Fromm-

Reichmann's description, "the patient repeats consciously and/or unconsciously with the therapist the vicissitudes of his early relationships, and he endows the doctor with the personality trends and other characteristics which he first encountered in the significant people of his past life." [2] Divergent opinions have to do with the question of just what is transferred in the transference. [3]

Often only those reactions are considered to be transference phenomena which are inappropriate to the current interaction with the therapist. However, even when a reaction by the patient happens to be appropriate to some aspect of the present reality situation, it may be termed a transference manifestation if it is overdetermined, or if it derives its major affect from recapitulation of significant earlier experience.

Appropriate reactions which are nevertheless overdetermined by transference are characteristic of borderline patients. It has been mentioned that such a person has usually been highly sensitized to certain types of ambiguous interaction with others. He quickly detects subtle insincerities and attempts by others to hide their real attitudes through overt expression of the opposite. When such "hidden attitudes" are uncovered, the patient reacts with intense hostility and distrust. If and when he encounters them in his therapist, he displays anger and resentment which is perfectly appropriate to the fact that he has been deceived, but is still of a degree that is out of proportion to the quality of feeling existing in the therapeutic relationship as a whole. The intensity of reaction results from transference elements.

It is almost impossible for any therapist to avoid all conceivable ambiguity, even if he is conscious of the need to do so and tries sincerely to act honestly. He is almost sure to give the patient occasional cause for complaint. When the patient has a "realistic" reason to be angry, he often finds it more difficult to perceive the nature of transference involved.

Ability to perceive when the attitudes of a therapist are, on the whole, different from those in his earlier experience may be delayed for a long time in patients of this type, not only because their perceptions of reality are often distorted, but also because they over-react so greatly to actual realities in the therapeutic relationship.

Transference must be distinguished from other responses by a patient toward his therapist. As Frieda Fromm-Reichmann has repeatedly stressed, one must separate transference from realistic reactions to the therapist as a person.[2] Even when patients are in a grossly regressed state, they are often able to separate their irrational responses, which are the product of transference, from their rational perception of the therapist's reality characteristics and attitudes toward them. As David phrased it, "Human beings often don't realize that animals understand as much as they do understand" (193). To repeat what has already been discussed in the section on countertransference, a therapist must keep in mind the possibility that a patient may be reacting to some realistic aspect of the relationship between them, and that not all hostility, nor yet all feelings of affection on the part of the patient, are transference.

A particular source for affectional reaction lies in the nature of the therapeutic process itself. Human beings have a strong basic need to be accepted and understood. One who has withdrawn into deep emotional isolation will acquire very intense feelings for anyone who is able at last to penetrate his lonely world and introduce the understanding he had hitherto despaired of finding. When someone meets the fundamental needs of another, he assumes in the life of that person a realistic importance proportionate to the intensity of pain previously induced by deprivation and frustration. One who has never felt able to trust develops powerful positive feelings for one who lifts from him the burden of constant suspicion.

The affection felt by a patient for the therapist who has helped him to emerge from isolation is a realistic love, appropriate to the nature of their relationship. The quality of this feeling is unique. Although it may attenuate as the patient acquires distance from his period of hopelessness, it seldom disappears altogether. To use David's words, the person who shares a feeling of "we" rather than "you and I" (172) retains a special corner of the patient's emotional life forever, regardless of the number and quality of satisfactory relationships subsequently developed by him. Transference plays a relatively insignificant part in the evolution of such a feeling.

Identification, too, must be distinguished from transference. In all psychotherapy, there is some modification of the patient's superego, and a strengthening of certain ego functions. In the psychotherapy of an adolescent with basically weak ego structure and an unformed sense of personal identity, the therapist functions as an important model. He may be vitally instrumental in helping the patient incorporate an image from which he can derive a measure of self-esteem. The borderline patient, particularly, has originally incorporated extremely ambivalent, inconsistent objects, and has achieved a very unstable sense of self-differentiation. Identification with the therapist may become the basis of his first sense of a "good" self. Upon this identification the patient may have to build almost his entire ability to test reality, to trust people, and to assume responsibility for himself and others. Acceptance of himself as an adequate person may depend upon the sense of self-value derived from his relationship with the therapist.

A patient's attempts to incorporate those qualities in the therapist upon which he can build self-esteem may become increasingly manifest in the course of treatment, as the original transference distortions in his perception of the therapist gradually diminish. This tendency toward identi-

fication is not a transference phenomenon, but is closely related to resolution of certain transference elements.

It is beyond the scope of this discussion to study intensively the influence of transference phenomena upon
David's therapy. I will merely give a few illustrations from
throughout the material to show the way in which both positive and negative feelings toward me were influenced by
transference, and to distinguish transference reactions from
those more directly generated by realistic aspects of our
interaction.

Feelings derived from David's relationship with his
mother were often expressed inappropriately in the therapeutic relationship. Important attitudes toward her colored
his perceptions of me, regardless of the actual interaction between us, and were expressed in various forms at different
stages of treatment.

It may be recalled that from the boy's earliest life, a
high degree of ambivalence was shown to both parents, particularly toward the mother who was seen as the dominant
family figure, possessing both masculine and feminine attributes. Admiration and dependence upon her strength and
power were combined in David with strong unconscious
erotic wishes toward her. He also reacted with intense hostility toward her in response to attitudes on her part which
he felt to be seductive and manipulative. He felt unconsciously that their relationship, and even literally the mother
herself, would be destroyed by the force of his anger. Fear
of being possessed conflicted with fear of being abandoned
or of himself destroying the person upon whom he was
dependent.

All these feelings were carried over into the relationship with me. Dependence and erotic attachment fluctuated
with expectations of desertion and seduction. I was seen as
strong and aggressive like the mother, but equally unable to

tolerate the impact of his rage. The conflict between dependent needs and fear of instability in the relationship was expressed frequently in the early part of treatment through symbolic communications. For instance, a pellet was attracted to a star, and the "force of attraction was very great." David feared not only absorption of the pellet, but destruction of the star (24). Four years later, after extensive experience with treatment, David was still quick to interpret that my illness indicated inability to bear his hostility (150). From the beginning the boy was convinced that he "might need armor" against Cupid's arrows (12). In the sixth year of treatment, when able to talk openly about erotic feelings toward me, he still expressed fear that I might also be sexually stimulated and act upon erotic feelings toward him. "I might think of you like a mother" (172); threat to him lay in the risk of encountering a double bind in our interaction.[4] I might unconsciously give him an invitation to make sexual advances, but react consciously with horrified rejection if he should accept the invitation. David thought I might respond to discussion of his sexual problems by directly seducing him (174), just as he himself reacted to such discussion with open sexual feelings toward me (168). Terror of erotic impulses from the mother paralleled his own toward her; the conflict was transferred unmodified into our relationship.

Reactions related entirely to transference may be distinguished from those which have a slightly realistic base but are nevertheless almost entirely inappropriate in the present relationship. It has been mentioned in an earlier section that David exhibited extreme sensitivity to stereotyped expressions and small subtle insincerities in others. The intensity with which he feared hidden attitudes was a direct product of transference, consistent with past experience and appropriate to situations in which he had previously encountered deception, but out of proportion to the danger that might be anticipated in a relationship with any reasonably trustworthy person. He had a right to hope for honesty from his therapist and to feel some annoyance at ambiguities in communication. However, even in the early days, when he did not know me, the degree of his suspiciousness was far greater than would be warranted by a mild transgression against utter clarity. Expressions like "That's all I can say" occur so frequently, and with so little intent to misrepresent the real attitude, that a negative reaction is highly overdetermined by traumatic interactions in the past. My stringent attempts to avoid even such small misunderstandings have been described elsewhere, and the subject is repeated here only in the context of distinguishing a transference reaction from an appropriate reaction to realistic errors committed by the therapist.

Whenever David had a realistic cause for complaint against me, I tried to admit it promptly and to comment upon the justifiability of his anger. Transference affected such situations only through his tendency to assume that no matter what went wrong in a relationship, he would be blamed.

David had other feelings toward me which could clearly be separated, even by him, from erotic or dependent transference. Affectionate feelings toward me, as the person who had broken his sense of isolation and taught him to trust, developed steadily throughout our contact. This growth of an emotional attachment based on the quality of our work together has been discussed earlier. By the fifth year of treatment, David could admit that while in the past he had been able to "turn things off" at will, he was now deeply involved (156). In spite of fears, emanating from the transference, that real mutuality in a relationship was impossible, he had convinced himself that at least he and I would "eventually come out with the same message" (161). He had perceived the true nature of our interaction, and he responded to it realistically. "I am operating on the basis that we have a common rate of exchange. Both of us are fair" (193). "There is trust between us" (188).

A gradual process of identification with me had also taken place. David recognized this, and stated directly a feeling that qualities which he considered admirable in himself were derived from his experience in therapy. "I've had some experience with consistency . . . I'm using with other people some of the methods I've learned from you" (188). For a time, awareness of this identification added to his confusion in sexual identity. "I feel it desirable to have a big dose of femininity . . . it isn't stability I mean so much as a kind of stable reactivity . . . perhaps I feel that way because you are a woman, and that's the way you are" (182). A boy like David finds it difficult to distinguish incorporation of single attributes from total identification with all aspects of the other person. Several times he had implied that two people who see things in the same way must be identical in all respects (161, 214). Here the feeling was expressed that in order to identify with me in any quality or method of operating, he would have to assume feminine identification totally. Transference was, of course, responsible for the confusion in sexual identity, but not significantly involved in the boy's tendency to use his therapist as a realistic model for attitudes and behavior, and to incorporate qualities seen as important in the constructive progress of his own development.

R E F E R E N C E S

(1) Fenichel, O., *Psychoanalytic Theory of Neuroses*. N. Y., W. W. Norton, 1945.

(2) Fromm-Reichmann, F., *Principles of Intensive Psychotherapy*. Chicago, University of Chicago Press, 1959.

(3) Orr, D., "Transference and Countertransference: A His-

torical Survey," *Journal of the American Psychoanalytic Association*, Vol. 2, 1954, pp. 621–670.

(4) Jackson, D., "Toward a Theory of Schizophrenia," *Behavioral Science*, Vol. 1, October 1956.

18

Transition

"I can't let any one person understand the whole of me."

187. I had fun in the vacation. (Good.) [Pause.] (What are you doing these days?) Fancy skating lessons; otherwise nothing. (What kind of nothing?) Visiting mostly. (Whom do you visit? Can you give me a picture of what you do outside of here?) You seem to be starting into a new area—changing the emphasis. [Pause.] (You seem reluctant to talk about day-to-day activities. What's the feeling about my asking?) Resentment, I guess. I don't seem to want to let anyone know what I'm doing.

[Pause.] (There's a kind of paradox here. You seem willing to share your inner life with me, but resent sharing your outer life. If you don't feel completely free with me, I should think it would be the other way 'round.) I have to have some area of my life that's completely my own. If nobody knows what you are doing, they can't interfere. (You are afraid I will try to manipulate your activities?) I don't know, but I want to separate my inner life from my outer life. I can't let any one person really understand the whole of me. (I know. Again the fear of being "taken over." But mind and body, inner and outer life, all work together. You can't understand one separate from all the others. Their functioning has to be integrated.)

You can't let yourself be known if it is going to hurt other people. (You mean if anyone really knew how bad and destructive you were, they couldn't stand it?) [*Smile.*] Maybe. (There may be other factors in your reluctance. For instance, when you told me you were taking fancy skating lessons, there was an expression on your face that looked as though you hated to mention it.) [*He flinches.*] You sure do hit the jackpot questions.

I think it has the implications to me of homosexuality. (Are you afraid that if I thought you had leanings in that direction I would be ashamed of you, or hurt?) Perhaps. (No matter what I say, you are sure I have another goal for you.) All doctors have goals for their patients.

(I wonder if it is possible for you to believe that I really have no prejudice about this? Although I do have for you a goal of the maximum self-realization possible for you, it really would not hurt my feelings if you made a homosexual adjustment, provided that it was satisfactory to *you*.) I suppose that is possible. (The important thing is that we be able to discuss the various conflicts involved, so that we can both see clearly what really *is* best for you.)

I know I have felt some tendencies in that direction, but I think I might be on the way to working them out. (Let's find out what's going on.) It's like you have the possibility of two kinds of dinner—a real good dinner, and a plain dinner. You want the good one, but you're afraid you can't get it. You are tempted by the plain dinner because you are hungry, but you don't want to fill up in case you can get the good one. It's hard to decide, but it's probably better to wait for what you want.

188. [*Pause.*] I've been to see the Navy Air Corps recruiter. I've taken some aptitude tests. (How would you feel about going into the Navy at this time?) I'd hate to go away, but it seemed too good an opportunity to turn down. (You think the advantages of going into such a training program would outweigh the disadvantages of stopping our work here for a while?) I think so, although as I said, I'd hate to go away. (I think you are probably right. One sometimes has to make a choice as to which of two desirable alternatives is most important at any given time. I don't feel you have any need to run away from here at this point.) Quite the contrary. I'm anxious to continue here, but this might be worth leaving for.

They asked me if I knew any foreign languages. [*Smile.*] (Do you—besides your own?) [*Smile.*] I know a little Spanish too.

(You have been talking English for quite a while now. I have the feeling that you only revert to your own code language under stress.) Yes. But since I've been talking English, it doesn't seem as important. When a person has to penetrate the code, they are bound to pick up the feelings behind it. (And if you communicate directly, they may not bother to try any more.) Yes. (That reminds me of something you said when we first started. You indicated that you had to set up conditions which would prove that a person was willing to bear some discomfort in getting close to you, so that you would be sure they really wanted to.) I suppose that's so.

(What we were talking about last time may also have something to do with it. You seem to have removed your feelings from one area, but may now be hiding them in another. You feel you have to have some private area in which to keep your feelings.) Yes. I've got my day-to-day activities set up to compensate for the shake-up in my inner life. I don't want anyone to come along and rearrange my re-arrangements.

(What kinds of projects have you got going?) Flying; guitar; skating. Flying is the most important. I really enjoy that. (Don't you enjoy skating?) Well, I'm not sure I'm much involved with the dancing itself, but I'm interested in being in the class and hearing the women talk. I learn a lot about women. (Anything that helps you to understand people will stand you in good stead.)

Trouble is, it's subject to change without notice. (In your experience, you haven't had much chance to come in contact with consistency. Not many of the people you have known have been very stable or consistent in their behavior and attitudes.) Not in quantity. I haven't known so many people like that, but I've had some experience with consistency.

[Pause.] I think I'm using with other people some of the methods I've learned from you. In making relationships, neither to push nor to pull. Not trying to get something in particular to come out, but just something. Like spreading icing on a cake—not pounding it on with a sledge hammer, but just pushing it around gently.

I think, too, I've drawn some conclusions from the work we've done here. You have to sit back to see what makes people tick. Someone will say he doesn't like something, and I ask myself "What could make a person feel like that?" Then I wait, and pretty soon some other little bit of evidence comes along, and after a while I get a better idea of the whole picture. I think I have some talent for understanding people. (I think so too. You have an unusual ability to make contact with your own unconscious, and when a person understands his own, it is easier to understand the unconsciouses of others. Unconsciouses by and large are more similar than consciouses. All the instinctual impulses in the unconscious are common to human beings in general, but there are innumerable different ways in which people learn to manage them.)

I was thinking of the "Jet Propelled Couch." Wouldn't it be fascinating to have tape recordings of the fantasies, so people could see how that is! (That suggests something I've been thinking about for a while. When you first started using the code, I took fairly detailed notes on what we said to each other, mostly so that I could understand better what was going on between us. I have wanted for some time to write a book for doctors about it. You have a colorful way of expressing the problems that trouble a great many people, and I should like to use your own words and mine, to show how it all developed. How would you feel about that?) I think it would be wonderful!

[Pause.] It makes me feel good that you think what I have said is worth telling about. I'd like to read the book. (Of course I would let you read it, and take out anything you didn't want published. I imagine, though, that my telling you this will have lots of different meanings to you. In addition to the positive feelings, you may have some negative ones. You may come to feel that I've been more interested in your language than I am in you.) If you understand and appreciate my language, you must understand and appreciate me. My language *is* me.

(Not quite. There is a lot more to you than your language. If I didn't know you knew I felt that way, I wouldn't have suggested this. You have a pretty good idea of the kind of basic feeling that exists between us.) Yes. There is trust between us. We can work together without having to hold

too much back. (Your capacity for trust was what has made
it possible for you to do what you did. In spite of all your
distrust, there was always hope that it wasn't so.) All I needed
was to find someone that was trustworthy.

189. I passed the first test; now I have to take the qualifying
test. Maybe I'll really get to work on jets. (That would be
right down your alley.) Yes. But it would be making a living.
I don't *want* to make a living! (But you might have to in
order to get in on something that you *do* want to do.) I
guess so. (What does all this mean?)
    [*Pause.*] We don't seem to be communicating very
well. I'm halfway trying to think what it means, but really
just listening to the rain. One can't very often just relax and
be comfortable listening to the rain. But I feel guilty about
wasting time. (It's not a waste of time to relax and feel comfortable. Just feeling is important too.) I feel part of the
world when it's crying. (Sometimes people cry from relief.)
Mother Nature wetting her bed.
    (Apparently "letting go" in any way, even from relief,
is associated in your mind with "letting go" from the bladder. This may enter into your sexual fears too.) I was just
thinking that. But it should be just the opposite; I got from
bed-wetting the kind of comfort and relaxation one should
get from a woman. [*Pause.*] Maybe I associate relaxation
with my experience with Jane. I can remember a great feeling of relaxation when she took me in bed with her. (Orgas-
tic?) No, just general. (Like a baby feels when it is cuddled
by its mother. You must have had a great longing to be held.)
    You wind a string around a stick; when you turn the
stick, it moves along the string. (What was so frightening
that it had to come in code?) [*Slight smile.*] When there are
two strings, the stick doesn't bend. (Several times you have
used images in which a penis symbol seems to be bound and

immovable. Can you understand that?) The code seems to say that if the penis tries to enter only one woman, it will be pushed aside and bent.

[*Pause.*] I have an image of trisecting an angle. Something about three people. My first thought is Mother, Father and myself. (Or your mother, Jane, and yourself. I think one reason she became so important to you is that Jane became the focus for fantasies you had about your mother. Your mother was the person you really wanted to be cuddled by, and about whom you had unconscious sexual fantasies. This was complicated by the fact that the most nurturant figure in your early life was your father. He gave you the physical care that a child usually gets from a woman, and got your ideas of feminine and masculine all mixed up. You saw your father as passive and feminine, your mother as aggressive and masculine. But it wasn't that simple, because you also saw your mother as sexually seductive and your father as unconsciously hostile and aggressive.)

I think I also see you as strong and aggressive. (With your tendency to think symbolically, I believe you see your mother as a vagina that at the same time wants to gobble you up and to push you away. If you don't see me as either closed against you, or wanting to eat you, you can't believe I'm feminine.) I'm beginning to realize that.

I see my hands are in my security position. (Yes. You are well barricaded at the moment.) I'm trying to get out. I'm just not sure enough of the material outside.

190. I took the second test, but I'm not sure I passed it. (Would you be interested in any of the other programs they offer if you didn't make this one?) No. (You would risk being drafted?) That would be one year instead of four. Even one would be a terrible waste. (Unfortunately the draft is something you might have to submit to, no matter how you feel about it.)

I wouldn't want to be forced to fight anyone. I think if I ever got into a physical fight, it would be the death of one of us.

I'm thinking again of the story about the astronomer who discovered that the world was about to be hit by a planet. He told people it was going to happen. At first everyone went into a panic and ran around aimlessly; after a while, they went back to what they'd been doing, and tried to get as much satisfaction as they could before the end. It finally turned out that the planet was going to miss the world, and the astronomer knew it all the time. He just wanted people to see that they could handle things better by doing their regular jobs. There was nothing else they could do anyway.

(For a while you were running around in a panic because you thought you were going to blow up. Now you want to handle your anxiety by doing something more constructive and satisfying. Could you get training in something that you *would* enjoy doing?) The trouble is, when I'm doing it, I feel so completely alone. I don't feel much communion with anyone. (The number of people in anyone's life with whom he can feel communion is limited, but if he finds one or two, the others aren't important.) I know.

How I wish I were stupid! (That's one avenue of escape that is forever closed to you. But it isn't a good one anyway.)

191. I seem to be panting again. [*Pause.*] I qualified for the Navy cadet program, but I find you can't be sure you will get to fly. I don't want to do anything else. I want to be the one to handle the controls. (In any case, it must make you feel good to have the choice.) Yes! This is the first time it's been *my* choice whether to go or not!

I may be able to get training for work on a computer. Then I wouldn't have to go away. (Would you be more interested in the Naval air training if it weren't for therapy?)

I would be more interested in suicide if it weren't for therapy. The world is a grubby place. Unfortunately, I can't quite wish not to be experiencing. (No. In spite of your temptation to feel like a nothing, you can't quite do it.)

[*Pause.*] I have moments of happiness with the family, but I feel I'm expected to get out and make a living. If I do, they will abandon me. [*Pause.*] Maybe I feel that being independent of them would mean having to give up therapy. I see this as a "gift" from them that would be taken away if I were on my own.

(You need to have something with which to rationalize your reluctance to be independent. I told you a long time ago that I was no longer charging your family for these visits, and that I would make a deal with you when you were able to pay something. You are confusing financial needs with other kinds of needs.) I get it from the family. They are always fighting about money when the real trouble is something else. (I know it. That's why I decided the way I did. I didn't want to be involved in *their* conflicts.)

[*Pause.*] Giving can be used as a defense against having demands made on you. (You seem to feel I might be threatened by your demands.) It is more satisfactory to give to someone who isn't reaching for something, but will enjoy it if he gets it. (I don't know about that. It can also be satisfying to give to a person who wants something enough to reach out actively for it.)

192. [*As he sits down, he pulls up his socks, while making some general comments.*] (The thing that strikes me today is that you seem to feel free enough to pull up your socks.) [*Laugh.*] I noticed that, but I'll be damned if I'm going to worry about what it means. (It might only mean that they were uncomfortable, but the thing that's important is the feeling that you *could* pull them up.)

[*Pause.*] I enjoy playing the guitar. I'm learning to fit

the right chords to the right moods, and the right strums to go with them. It would be interesting, though, to work out a way to tune it by computer. Once you have the first note, the rest is all by a specific relationship between the strings. (Another way of doing things from a distance?) One could have a motor tighten the strings by a formula that would bring them into the correct relationship. Theoretically, all sorts of chords are possible that can't be played because the span of a hand's reach isn't long enough. If the strings could be held down mechanically, one could play all the chords that are outside human range. (There are lots of nice chords within human range.)

[Pause.] I might be able to get the job on the computer, but there are practical problems, like transportation. I don't want to be dependent on anyone else. When I'm making a plan, I want to be in control of all the variables; then I don't have to worry about other people's problems.

I've also thought of a wonderful variation on the chain letter idea. One could make a lot of money, but I've heard it's illegal, and I don't want that black and white car driving up to my door. You sell the letters instead of just sending them to people. In that way, only the ones that want to participate are in on it.

When anyone makes a big profit, someone else is paying for it, but at least nobody buys who isn't willing to gamble on making a profit. A person might not do better than break even. Of course, not many people want to make an investment unless they are sure of making a profit. (Unless they enjoy the enterprise, and are not dependent on the outcome for their living.) People who gamble do it either because they want to make a large profit or because they enjoy the excitement of the risk. Sometimes they are tempting fate and really want to be shown that they can't win. (Sometimes it's because they believe in the goals of an enterprise and can afford to make an investment that might not pay off. They think it is worthwhile to try to keep certain kinds of projects operating.) Nobody should gamble more than he can afford to lose without getting hurt. (I agree. Then they have no reason to resent it if things don't come out as they hope.)

It would be a challenge to try to set this up, but if I can't do it illegally, I guess it isn't worth it. (Did you notice the slip you just made?) [*Laugh.*] I guess it shows I really don't want to do things legally. I think I can't stand the idea of doing something wrong and not getting caught.

193. [*Slight frown.*] (What's the feeling?) I feel good today. (Is that bad?) [*Laugh.*] I hate to let anyone know. As soon as you feel a little better, they will find more work for you.

I wish I could enjoy things like a lovely day without feeling I have to watch out for danger. (Do you think the fear of danger is tied up with the concept of enjoyment itself?) I don't know, but I feel that way around my family. (You feel it's dangerous to be with them, but also have fears of being away from them. It's like the story you once told about the man who fought his way out of a hostile city and then died on the desert.)

[*Pause.*] I feel a lump in my throat. I don't like it! (You don't like to show that you are touched emotionally by an idea like that.) I don't like anyone to sneak up on me without being seen. The only way to prevent it is to keep a wall around myself. (And not let me know that there are chinks in your armor.)

I'm afraid of closeness. Closeness means demands. I don't like being ordered around just for the sake of being ordered around. Sometimes parents just get satisfaction out of having someone that's working for them; they like to touch a button and have a machine start up.

(I wonder if you sometimes feel that's what I do when I start you off with a question—touch a button and expect you to whir into action just to satisfy myself that I can get you going.) [Laugh.] I can remember the times when I couldn't get started at all without prodding. I wish I could remember how you put your questions—the most noncommittal way possible. No, I don't think so.

What I mean is—like a person holding a door open for someone. You want to hold it open because it's the kind of person for whom you want to hold it open, not just because the person demands it in order to feel like that kind. (I think you are talking about my holding open the offer of therapy for you. You want to feel it's because I value you as a person, not that I'm submitting to a demand from you to make you feel important.) I have to be very careful not to sound as though I'm making a demand. (What's so bad about making a demand?) I guess I expect you to feel as I do about them.

(I suspect that you feel there is a demand from me implicit in the offer—a demand for you to meet some goal that I have in mind. Even if it were something you wanted yourself, the help I give might be for my satisfaction.) I feel I need this. I don't see why I should begrudge you any satisfactions you might get out of it.

[Pause. Clasps hands in front of his chin.] (I see you have gone behind the barricade.) I think love is an important demand of mine. (And you are afraid of what my response might be.) [Nod.]

I'm thinking of a faster-than-light space ship. I don't know if that's important, though. When you change a thought, you change its importance when you change its direction.

As far as I can see, there are three possible attitudes for you. One is to be interested in what I say, which implies a demand on me to produce material. Two, to be disinterested in keeping the material coming, which implies a rejection. Three, to be as interested in the silences as in the words.

(To be interested in all aspects of you. I think, though, that you aren't quite sure of the motives of anyone who is interested in you. As we said when we discussed my writing about your code, if I'm interested in your words, I might not be interested in you as a whole. You might be flattered by my interest, but still consider it a rejection.)

I'm operating on the basis that we have a common rate of exchange, even though we don't quite know what it is. Both of us are fair. [*Pause.*] Human beings don't always realize that animals understand as much as they *do* understand.

1 9

Indecision

"...Design a house with automatic disposal of everything."

THROUGHOUT HIS LIFE DAVID ENJOYED CER-
tain kinds of work or play in which he acquired useful, pleasurable skills. He learned to manipulate tools and machines
according to his interests and special abilities, deriving from
control over the objects a satisfying sense of accomplishment.
The activities had realistic purposes, and he enjoyed them in
their own right.

Nevertheless, the boy's choice of activity at each
phase of his development was dominated by the symbolic
meanings of these tools and skills. For a long time, as we have
seen, he spoke of a machine or instrument as though he were
at least partially aware that it also represented to him his
penis or his mind, his total personality or his life in a more

general sense. Motorcycle, car and gun, airplane, guitar, and computer—each had multiple meanings for David. The penis symbolism of guns and tools was quite obvious to him at all times. Even early in treatment, he recognized that "Any tool can represent a penis" (130). Later, "To a man, a gun is something . . . concrete and knowable, over which he can achieve mastery. . . . Women should let men keep their symbols of masculinity" (216). Use of the machine symbolized personal functioning. Driving a sports car or flying a plane was recognizable to him as symbolic of sexual activity, and when he spoke of eagerness to "fly with a companion" (167), there could be no doubt about the double meaning. He knew that in learning to play the guitar he was also trying to learn about forming sexual relationships (192). In his own words, "I think playing the guitar is a kind of sex play . . . playing any instrument is sexual" (197).

David seemed to choose working with objects which are classically known as sexual symbols, in activities that are universally associated with sexual activity in symbolic form. Preconscious and conscious awareness of the symbolism did not, however, detract from his ability to operate on a realistic level. To him objects were sufficiently differentiated from symbols to permit their use without interference from affect attached to the body parts and functions represented. The level of symbolic function upon which he operated may be contrasted with that of the deeply regressed schizophrenic described by Segal, who was unable to play the violin in public because he directly equated his musical activity with the act of masturbation.[1] By learning to master tools and instruments, David gained mastery over his own body and achieved a sense of capacity for successful sublimation of instinctual drives. Although he attempted to work out inner conflict symbolically through activities, he also enjoyed realistically the fun of driving or flying, and derived aesthetic pleasure from making music. Much mechanical ability and intellectual capacity found expression through his construction of a workable machine gun in the school metal shop. Both the symbolic and realistic aspects of his work and play contributed to a therapeutic effect upon David.

The boy was also able to be aware of the unconscious symbolism expressed through one of his major bodily symptoms. A generally acknowledged connection between bedwetting and fire-setting was readily accessible to his conscious thinking. Early in therapy he expressed the idea that "the only way to put out a fire is to pee on it" (94). Later, there was an instinctive recognition of the association between the penis and a fireman's hose (210). He understood that aggression was being expressed in the same way by both "instruments." Nevertheless, the realistic aspect of a fireman's job held considerable interest for David; his awareness of symbolism would not have interfered with ability to function in the fire department had an opportunity presented itself, even though the symbolic meaning was a determinant in his interest.

Symbolic meanings of activities were, in fact, important determinants in David's choice of jobs at various stages of development. While still strongly identified with machines and trying to handle personal conflicts through mastery of symbolic objects, he made serious attempts to find work in machine shops (121ff.) and later as a computer operator (191). At another phase, preoccupied with desire for successful sexual functioning, he made realistic preparations to be a commercial flyer (157). Still later, in partial awareness of the link between fire-fighting, bed-wetting, and aggression, he thought of subduing destructive impulses in himself through assuming a realistic role in the community (197). The struggle for internal mastery of delinquent impulses undoubtedly played some part in the choice of work on a police force, and feelings about the development of self-knowledge in therapy contributed to the boy's ambition to be a teacher of children

(217). Although there was at each stage a quite realistic basis for decisions to work in the particular field chosen at that time, the choice was also directly influenced by unconscious aspects of the work under consideration.

---

194. [*He enters with a slight smile.*] You mentioned that you might write a book; I've had the idea that maybe you've already written a book. (What gives you that idea?) I don't know. I just think you might have. (No. I haven't written one yet. As I told you, though, I've kept some rather extensive notes.) I don't mean about me. (What have you in mind?) The *Fifty Minute Hour*; I think you might have written that. (I wish I had!)

[*Pause.*] (What makes you think I might have written that?) The architect in it. Once, when we were talking about my not wanting to finish my course, you told me about an architect you knew who wanted to build something the way he wanted it, but wouldn't conform to requirements. I know an architect who might be the one you told about, and the one in the book. (Tell me about him.) He's doing some work for my mother.

[*Pause.*] I'm thinking about aluminum sliding doors. The architect says the problem is to find a type of lock that's effective. The locks they usually use are easy to force, and the place is vulnerable. I'm trying to see if I could devise an effective one. [*Pause.*] I would like to have a job that involves the solving of problems. For instance, this problem of locks shouldn't be too difficult. They want something secure enough so that the average person can't break it, but not so complicated as a bank vault system.

[*Pause.*] I'd like to rig up a door that would open electrically to the sound of only one person's voice. (An electric ear like the electric eye?) Yes. But it would have to be sensitive to such fine gradations of tone that it would be complicated to make.

As a matter of fact, I'd like to build a house. But everything about it would be so complicated that nobody else would be able to live in it. Every door would open a different way, so that any person that wanted to come into any room would have to know the specific code word or combination. One could have something like a telephone dial system, with a dial for each door; you could come in if you knew the right number. But there would always be someone like me who set up a system where, if you figured it out, you would have access to the whole house. (That sounds like what you would like to do in your mind. You'd like to give a person the key to one or two rooms, maybe, but not the whole house. If you think someone might have access to all of them, it makes you anxious.)

[Pause.] I'm thinking about playing the guitar. I'm learning some very complicated kind of music. It's what the idle rich have thought up to see how difficult they could make guitar playing and still play. (That's along with your general theory that it's the problem that makes something interesting.) Sometimes my teacher lets go and just plays for hours. I love to listen to the music and get lost in it.

195. [As he comes in, I am receiving a call from his mother about where he is to pick her up. I relay the message to him. He makes no response, stares, and looks depressed.] (What's the feeling?) I'm tired and cold. [Pause.] (What are you thinking?) I was wondering why the tail of the horse on your desk isn't more tapering. (What else?) I've been doing research on thumb nails. When you break a nail playing the guitar—to be able to have something to replace it.

[Long pause.] (You are using the code today.) I thought of that, but it didn't seem worthwhile to think

about it. (Why not?) [*No answer. Pause.*] (You have suggested that the horse's tail might be broken off at the end,
and mentioned a thumb nail that's broken off at the end.
What do you think you might be concerned with?) [*Pause.*]
I start to think about things, but I get a half-thought, and
then forget it. (The thoughts are broken off too.)

[*Long pause.*] (If I were to guess which of all the possible ideas connected with something being broken off is
most central to you right now, I would say it was the idea of
being broken off from your family. Being cut off from them
seems almost like having a part of your body cut off from
you.) I thought of that.

[*Long pause.*] I'm listening to music. It's funny how
some music you hear immediately becomes a part of you, and
some just goes right by. [*Pause.*] People assume that creativity arises out of happiness, yet almost everything worthwhile
that has been produced in art has come from unhappiness.
(Unhappiness can find a creative outlet. So can happiness—
maybe in different ways. Anyway, maybe happiness isn't so
much the goal as self-realization.)

[*Pause.*] I'm wondering about the length of the universe. It is thought of as a sphere; if one traveled along it,
eventually one would get back to where one started. But as
it moves through time, the radius constantly changes.

196. [*Sits staring.*] (What's the feeling?) Kind of miserable.
I'm fed up with people who reject my solution, but have no
solution of their own, and expect me to have one.

I don't know what the problem is, but everything is
in a muddle at home. Mother is trying to work out a project
that will save money, and Dad isn't any help. They are fighting again. I have no money, and they won't let me use the
car. It's three miles to the nearest town, and seven miles to
the nearest bus. They are trying to force *me* to take a job, but
they can't handle their own affairs.

(I can appreciate your dilemma. To become independent of them is to submit to force, and your pride won't let you do it, even though it's what you want yourself. I'm in a dilemma too. If I add my voice to those who are urging you to extricate yourself from this situation, it will be just another angry buzzing in your ears. However, I feel strongly that you would be much happier if you were in a position to choose the degree to which you wish to remain involved in the home situation.) If I take a job, I lose my freedom. (Are you free now?) I'm in a trap either way. (You see it as black or white.)

Mother complains about the demands made on her, but she is constantly making demands on everyone else. How many demands do I have to meet to pay for my keep? (That depends on the kind of demand. What do you think is fair?) It doesn't cost much to feed me. They waste all kinds of money, but I don't even have a few dollars. (I can see you feel you are being coerced by the withholding of money and use of the car, and that you resent it very much. That is understandable.)

Dad doesn't coerce me, nor I him. It's Mother. (You don't coerce each other, but I think you should face the kind of pressure your mother is under, too. It is as hard for her as it is for you.) I know.

(I believe that by withholding money from you, your mother intends to create a stimulus that will force you to make a move that will save you. I know there are other factors too, but in any case, the effect on you has been the opposite. It's like an electric shock—if it's just strong enough, it will make a person jump, but if it's too strong, it paralyzes.) Yes. It's like passing a current through a metal solution; a little keeps it circulating, but too much causes it to break apart. (I'm sure you feel that's what's happening to you right now.) Yes.

I don't want to take a part-time job and live at home.

I'd like to be able to use a job to climb all the way out of the hole, but I guess I'll have to start that way. It isn't fair, though. My brother is doing what's expected of him, so they give him what he needs. I'm being penalized by not doing what's expected of me. (I know that's hard to bear, but if you want to go your own way, you will have to be the one who makes it possible for yourself.)

197. It's not my fault I'm late. (I know.) [*Pause.*] If I got a job as fireman here in town, I could move in. (Are you considering that?) Yes. I've decided it would be a good kind of job; on twenty-four hours, and then off twenty-four. (How did you arrive at a decision that you wanted a job?) I would like to think I made the decision because it's the right time. I'm tired of listening to the hot air at home. (You would like to put *out* fires instead of staying right in the middle of one.) I guess it *is* getting pretty hot at home.

[*Pause.*] I feel relieved that I've finally decided to move out of the house if and when it seems convenient. I don't think I'd mind working steadily for an average wage if I could have some free time to pursue my hobbies. (You would be buying freedom with labor.)

[*Smile.*] I was just thinking of a TV program. An old farmer is getting on a plane. The stewardess says, "Good evening. I'm your hostess, and I hope you will have a comfortable flight." He answers, "Well, Ma'am, I'm not much on dancing, but I'll sure buy a couple of tickets." (Yes. I know that freedom also means freedom to pursue your sexual life.)

I'm reading a book called *The Many Faces of Love*. He says there are three kinds of love—appetite love, benevolent love, and adoration. (It isn't always easy to separate them so clearly. Love can involve any combination, or all of these aspects. Of course, there are some people who have to keep them separate.) It would be very sad if you couldn't love the person you were sleeping with. (Yes. The people who have to separate these aspects of love are often so guilty about their sexual feelings that they think anyone who would sleep with them must be as bad and worthless as they feel themselves to be.)

[*Pause.*] I think playing the guitar is a kind of sex play. I hate to tell it. (What is it about that idea that seems dangerous to share?) To share with someone who is intelligent and sensitive enough to be able to understand more of what it means than I do myself; I don't like to have anyone know more about me than I do. (What are your own feelings about it?) [*Bitter smile.*] I could just say I feel the moon is made of green cheese. (You mean that wouldn't be any more meaningless than an attempt to describe your feelings?) Yes.

I think playing any instrument is sexual. (Of course it is, to some extent. So is any creative expression—music, art, dancing, or anything performed with feeling. Some sexual feelings may be released in any kind of satisfying activity.)

198. [*He looks withdrawn; stares into space.*] (What's the feeling?) I'm in love. I don't know if I want to talk about it; I might have to give too much information. I'm afraid if I talk about it, the feelings will be damaged. (I can see why you are reluctant then; it's a very important feeling. Has it happened in the past that when you talked about a feeling it was destroyed?) I don't know.

In this case, it's frustrating, because she's already married. (Even if you don't feel you can act on the feeling, it's a good one to have.) I guess one good thing is that I haven't been afraid to let myself have it. (I think sometimes the knowledge that one *can* fall in love is the best thing that can happen to a person, no matter what comes of it.)

[*Pause.*] (Tell me something about the girl.) Well,

you remember when we talked about the kind of girl that would attract me—she's like that. Reacting sort of like a child or an animal. (Instinctually free.) Yes. Unself-conscious.

[*Pause.*] I was thinking about people with realistic values and people with unrealistic values. I think in some ways she has unrealistic values, but in a way that isn't damaging to others. (How do you mean?) About raising children. I think she takes over too much of the raising. [*Pause.*] I think she isn't getting enough from her husband—he's too analytical. I don't think that's the way love works.

[*Pause. He raises his clasped hands to cup his chin.*] (I see you are behind the barricade now.) Yes. I guess in this area I think my views might be unacceptable. In the first place, I don't believe in marriage, as things stand today. I think it's fantastic to have to have laws to protect people from each other who are supposed to love each other. A lot of men get a wife as they would get a new car or a refrigerator —just an appliance to run the other appliances. (Yes. Many marriages are built on stereotypes and fantasies rather than on real relationships. In some cases, the people involved hardly see each other at all.) They haven't time to; they are too busy keeping up repairs on the house and paying the taxes. The house takes over. (And swallows up the relationship. There are people, however, who don't allow themselves to be owned by their possessions. So long as their basic needs are met, they don't make material things as important to them as relationships.) Houses make demands. [*Pause.*] Maybe one should have two houses. Let someone live in one of them and assume all obligations for both, and you live in the other, not tied down to it. (Why own a house at all?) You have to have some place to come home to.

199. [*He is in fairly good spirits today. Early in the interview, something comes up about the time I lost my temper. David talks realistically most of the hour about his ambiva-*

lent feelings in this connection. Although we discuss it from various angles, it is not clear what really bothers him about it. One important aspect is that it is the only time I have expressed anger. "The therapy is like a steel ball with just one dent in it. One almost wants to make another."

[He also seems to feel it as an attack on him, in spite of my denials; he expresses a need to be more careful in the future to avoid mentioning something from his outside life which might bring blame upon him for something in which he had no part.

[At the end of the hour, I tell him I have to go away unexpectedly. There is no evidence of reaction from him.]

200. [He seems withdrawn. An upsetting event has occurred in my own family which I thought he might have heard about, but since he lives out in the country I am not sure that he has. I wish to bring it up if it seems relevant, but not without evidence that it is. I am aware of a tendency to attribute his mood to the ambivalence which would be anticipated if he had heard it, and to assume a sensitivity on his part to my own depressed mood. Every topic he raises is searched for meanings within this framework. My perception of the entire session is, therefore, distorted, and I find it difficult to reconstruct. Certain interchanges stand out with great clarity in my memory, and others are hazy.

[He is silent for some time, fastening his gaze on the row of books which face him from the front of the desk.]

(What are you thinking?) I was looking at the journals. I noticed for the first time that they are in order. (It isn't always easy to keep things in order.) [He glances at me quickly, and then away.] The things least used are the easiest to keep in order. (That's very true.)

[Pause.] I have been thinking about designing a house. There would be automatic disposal of everything— ashes from the fireplace, garbage, any kind of mess. (A house without any evidence that anyone had lived there? Wouldn't that have a rather sterile atmosphere?) I suppose so. I guess any house has a certain amount of muddle. (I'm afraid so. Muddle is a part of life sometimes.) I used to think life wouldn't be worth living unless one could eliminate it, but I guess one has to learn to live with it. (Yes. Even with all the muddle, there are a lot of good parts.)

I haven't had much experience with the good parts; it's hard to believe they really exist. (I know. You may have to take that on faith for a while to tide you over the moments of doubt. Fortunately, one of your great strengths has been the ability to have faith. If you hadn't had, you couldn't have done the difficult job you have been doing here.) This has been the *one* thing that has been worthwhile. (There will be others.) If there isn't at least *one* other, I'll be pretty griped. [*Wry smile.*]

[*Pause.*] (What about the woman you love?) No change. Trouble is, just about the time I would be wanting to raise a family, she would be all through and wanting to retire. (People of all ages can love each other, but for the purpose of marriage, youth is for youth. People sometimes try it another way, but they usually get into difficulties if they do.)

[*Pause.*] I was seeing your horse raised up on little stools—rocking back and forth, putting up first one foot and then another. (He seems to have his feet firmly planted on the desk. Why do you want to raise him?) To get him out of the way of something dangerous sweeping across the desk. But the only thing that crosses this desk is conversation.

(You apparently feel our conversation is dangerous to the horse. We must talk more about that, but for now the time is up.)

201. I may go to work in a few weeks as a computer operator. (How do you feel about that?) It sounds interesting, but it's

really very routine. I'll have to have transportation. I'm thinking of getting a surplus armored car. It still has racks inside for guns and flares. I would like to restore it to its original use. The turret is missing, though. I don't think I really need a turret, but I don't like to think anything is missing.

(Last time you were talking about the fear of being destructive to my horse. Now you are talking about riding around in a fortified armored car. Is this idea protective or aggressive?) When I was thinking about protecting the horse, it was more from dirt than danger. (Oh? It's *dirty* talk flowing across the desk that you think might be destructive to him? What have you in mind?) I don't know, but I feel it's dangerous only to living things.

(What kind of dirt do you feel might pass between us?) What comes to mind is semen. (You feel it would be dirty for us to have intercourse.) Yes. (It wouldn't be dirty, but it would be inappropriate. As we said last week, people of all ages can love each other, but physical intimacies and marriage are best confined to one's own age group. Even if this were not so, it would be inappropriate to the nature of the work we are doing together.)

[*Smile.*] I'm tickled at the idea of my being so protective of the horse. (I wonder if you have in mind any living creature that might have been damaged by the relationship between us.) Maybe my mother. (Have you ever had any thoughts that some member of my family might be threatened by you—that our relationship might be destructive to anyone in my private life?) I never thought about it. I feel completely anonymous as far as anyone in your life is concerned. I think of the person in here and the person you are outside of here as different people. I'm afraid if I were to enter into your world, I would become interested in learning about you, not about me.

[*Pause.*] I feel I need to be completely unapproachable. (You want to avoid being exploited. But it's good to be approachable when you think it's safe.) Like falling in love —you would have to be somewhat approachable in that situation. If there were no dangers coming from any other direction, one might be able to turn one's attention to that. Actually, there *does* come a time when one can say with assurance, "This person won't damage me."

202. [*He starts talking spontaneously as soon as he sits down.*] I've been interviewed for the job. I think I convinced them I'm not a juvenile delinquent, but I still have to be passed by Security. (I do hope you will be allowed to live in the present, and not have the past hold you back.) I hope so too.
    [*Pause.*] (What are you thinking?) Of a geometry problem. (When you talk about geometry problems in here, you are often also referring to another kind of problem. What might it be this time?) [*Pause.*] Well, I feel I'm committed to this job; a lot of people have gone out of their way to help me get it. (You aren't committing yourself for life. All anyone could ask of you is that you give it a fair trial for long enough so that you can find out what possibilities it has for you.) I need to feel free to get out of it if I want. (A girl was telling me the other day that when she first got married, she couldn't bear to see cabinets being nailed into her new house because she had to know that at a moment's notice she could pick up everything and move out. Once she knew what it was all about, the panic passed. You are in the same frame of mind now.)
    [*Pause.*] Maybe I can start on my plan to set up a fund for retirement. I need to save a hundred thousand dollars in eight years so that I can retire at thirty. (When you find out how to accomplish that, I hope you'll tell *me!*) [*Smile.*]
    [*Pause.*] I was looking at your horse. One leg is twice as thick as the other; the design is disturbing. If he is going

to hold down that piece of paper, he should have all four of his feet on it. (He seems to be quite able to hold it down with one foot. Maybe he needs to have his other feet free in case he feels like kicking up his heels. It might be the same with you—that you could hold down a job and still have freedom to kick up your heels if you want to.)

If I have a family, I want to be able to move around and go interesting places. You don't need much money for that, but you need to know that it's coming in regularly.

[Pause.] I would want to be with my family all the time and not have to go to work, but, of course, I might wear out my welcome. (At present you are hungry for a family of your own, and feel that if you had one, you could never get enough of being with them. Once the hunger has a possibility of being satisfied, the intensity of it may decrease to manageable proportions.) A starving man may overeat at first, and then he may become actually revolted at the sight of food, but I suppose eventually he might be satisfied with a normal diet. (Yes.)

203. [He looks very withdrawn and starey all hour, talking so softly that I have to keep asking him to repeat. The interview starts with a long silence.] (What are you thinking?) That has a fateful sound. (How do you mean?) As though I have to talk now. (No; I was just wondering what you were thinking.) I don't know.

[Long pause.] (Has the job come through yet?) Not yet. (So it's another long waiting period?) Yes. (You must feel like a rubber band that's been pulled and pulled until it's about lost its elasticity.) Yes, but not about the job; that's not important in my life. It's about love.

Unfortunately I'm in love. (Unfortunately?) There's nothing to do about it. The trouble is that the feeling of wanting is so intense that it prevents me from looking for someone more eligible. (I know how that can be. It's like an acute physical pain.) Not exactly a pain, but I've had a rock in my stomach all week. (Anything particular happened to make it so acute?) I was exposed to a story. A woman who adopted four children found that the eight-year-old boy had been raping the four-year-old girl. It's terribly upsetting. For two days I've felt I wanted to kill.

I've thought of large destructive forces around me—not hurting me, but destroying everything around me that I don't like. I think of an explosion outside me that I can see as myself exploding. (You feel threatened by terribly explosive impulses from within, that you would like to think of as outside yourself. I think maybe you have combined the idea of rape with ideas about your own hungry feelings of wanting, into a fear that you also might be tempted to grab what you want.) Rape would destroy the only thing that could give me any reason for living. (The possibility that someone would voluntarily have intercourse with you.)

A person who would want to rape fills me with terror, like snakes and spiders affect some people. (Many times you have expressed the feeling that you are a dangerous, destructive person, and that you see the sex act as one that will destroy the other person.) Like a giant grabs at a house made of sticks and paper. He gets what he wants, but all he's got is a lot of broken sticks and crumpled paper.

[Pause.] As two magnets come closer together, the strength of the pull increases. Perhaps I'm afraid to come close to anyone because I'm afraid I'll be pulled in two. (Into her?) Pulled in two. (But perhaps it *is* fear that your intense need will cause you to be sucked in—literally and figuratively.) The pull might be so strong that after a certain point I wouldn't be able to stop even if it was wanted. (You are afraid someone might induce you to get to a certain point of closeness and then want to push you away. You feel a sexual situation would be like so many situations in your life

—a build-up of tension and anticipation that never comes to any real climax.) Maybe.

(You used to express fears of impotence. I wonder if you fear there would be a build-up, but at the last moment you couldn't perform?) [*He stretches his arms stiffly.*] I'm not afraid of that any more.

[*Pause.*] I don't see how the electromagnet can maintain an exact balance of forces. An electron is held in the center between two magnets with exactly equal pulls. If it got slightly off center, it would be pulled irresistibly one way or the other. (You feel balanced between desires and controls, and are afraid any shift would mean that desire pulled you away from all control.)

I guess I'm afraid to go anywhere near a woman. But I *must* find someone to fall in love with that's eligible. If I do, I think I wouldn't feel it was too dangerous. (I think too that it's from the older women, the mother figures, that you feel the danger—and the pull.) I was just going to add that myself.

204. [*Pause.*] I always seem to fall in love with people who are separated from me by some obstacle. I wonder if I'm only drawn to that kind. (Why might you be?) Perhaps to protect myself from finding out that what I wanted wasn't there. (Or from something else, like physical intimacy.) I can't imagine *that*.

[*Pause.*] I was wondering how much of a burden my problems would be to you. (To me?) Yes. Whether hearing about my problems is upsetting to you. (I wonder if you are displacing onto me the feelings you have expressed about your mother—fears that she will be hurt and jealous if you show interest in another girl.) There was something about my mother in the thought, but I'm not sure what it was.

I don't think my mother is fair. Since it is obviously

impossible for her to have physical relations with me, she shouldn't expect me to be the man around the house—doing chores, being at her beck and call every time she wants anything. (Do you feel she looks to you for the companionship and emotional satisfaction that she feels deprived of?) *That* part is O.K.—that falls within the mother-son relationship. (But chores don't?) Maybe I don't see it right, but chores are what she demands from Dad—they fall more in the husband-wife relationship.

(I think you are so very reluctant to become aware of any physical impulses you might have toward your mother that you might not connect your resentment at having to be near her all the time with a threat that lies in the proximity itself.) I'm wary of saying it isn't so, because it often turns out later that what you've said is true, but I haven't any feelings I can recognize as that.

(You do have a tendency to feel that any close relationship with a woman has a sexual component. You remember the fantasy about semen flowing across the table between us? To see either your mother or me as jealous of your girl friend might be both horrifying and pleasant to you.)

[*Smile.*] There's something funny about your saying "horrifying." (It suggests to you w-h-o-r-i-f-y-i-n-g?) [*Laugh.*] I guess it does. How funny! (Many people make an analogy between a man coming to see a woman psychiatrist and his coming to see a whore. They feel that talking about sexual material is practically the same as performing sexual intercourse.) I think the unconscious comes closest to being undistorted, direct communication.

[*Pause.*] I'm disappointed that I didn't fall in love with a girl I've known all my life. (What were you looking for that you didn't find?) I don't know; I never got close enough to look. (Perhaps you never really got acquainted. One doesn't have to fall in love first off—sometimes when people get acquainted, it just happens after a while. Maybe you ought to think first about getting to know a girl, and see what comes of it.)

205. I'm thinking of building a wooden box. The design I have won't work, and I need a better one. (Why the code today? Usually when you revert to it these days, you are talking about something that might be disturbing.) [*Smile.*] I wonder what there would be to talk about that we haven't already mentioned.

[*Pause.*] (The image of a box is sometimes the unconscious way of talking about female genitals.) I wish the box could be made stronger. (Anything tough and flexible enough to let a baby out will let a penis in without being damaged.) Emotional damage can be worse than physical.

[*Pause.*] Intercourse certainly isn't very esthetic. To the observer there's nothing beautiful about it—only to the participants. (How does beauty enter into the situation?) I don't know. But there's nothing beautiful about dogs copulating. (Some people find it sexually exciting to see, and therefore anxiety-provoking.) I don't want to be aroused sexually by sexual activity that isn't *mine*. (You want to be in on it.) Yes.

(Have you had any experience with seeing a couple make love?) I don't think so. (Did you sleep in your parents' bedroom as a small child?) No. (Children often have pretty active fantasies about parental intercourse anyway. One might have such fantasies, and have strong feelings about wanting to be in on the activity.) I guess so.

With fantasies you are more nearly in on things, although not enough. (Can you tell me something about the fantasies that arouse you?) I don't know that I can. They are so close to me that I would feel too vulnerable. They are too real. (It would be like having me watch you having intercourse, and you are afraid I would find it unbeautiful, or be aroused myself. You think it would be too real for *both* of us.) Yes.

About the dogs—they always look as though they were doing something they don't want to do, but they are forced by their bodies to do it. (You're afraid it might be like that with people.) I'm afraid I might be tempted to take the passive position. (That you might not want to, but couldn't resist responding physically to someone who was aggressive sexually? I wonder if maybe you see my wanting you to talk about fantasies as an attempt on my part to arouse you here?) I was looking at the letters on a book title and building them up to a pyramid. (Having an erection.) [*Smile.*] Yes.

(You think talking about fantasies might be so real that you would have an erection here, and be embarrassed?) I hate to say it, but it would be like having sex forced upon you. (A form of rape by me.) It could be seen like that. (You apparently do see it like that. On the other hand, of course, talking about fantasies is a good way to understand the kinds of feelings that are interfering with your ability to enjoy an active sexual life more directly.)

206. [*He is breathing heavily. Slight smile.*] Our talk last week about fantasies has scared me out of having any during the week. (Is it that easy to stop?) It seems to be easier than to talk about it.

(What have been the feelings?) I'm trying to think how to put them into words. I'm afraid it will be too clear. [*Laugh.*] A fine attitude toward therapy! (I suspect you feel that my urging you to talk about them was a very seductive gesture on my part. The whole idea is very frightening.) The ones I'm most afraid of are those that involve something like rape.

(One thing seems encouraging to me. This subject, frightening as it is, hasn't caused you to plunge back into the code.) This is too starkly realistic to code! [*Laugh.*] I suppose I could try. (You don't need to.)

[*He begins to speculate about the correlation in his mind between sexual activity and destructive aggression; sexual excitement and anger; sexual freedom and loss of both emotional and bodily control. We have an active discussion about the origins of such feelings in his early experience, when uncontrolled urination was an expression of both anxiety and aggression. Talking about sexual fantasies threatens him with wetting in front of me "like a little puppy." Ejaculation in intercourse is equated with urinating into the body of a woman. "I don't see how I could ever do that to someone I loved." A little later, "I don't see how I ever grew genitals."*] (They must have been very frightening, if you saw them as weapons of aggression.)

[*Long pause.*] Now I'm thinking in code. A triangle with three rollers at the corners. (Always three in your designs.) Five people make six combinations of three. It would be nice if a design could be made to include five. (Which five?) I forgot you. I was thinking of the four in my family and Jane.

R E F E R E N C E

(1) Segal, H., "Notes on Symbol Formation," *International Journal of Psychoanalysis*, Vol. 38, 1957, pp. 391–397.

2 0

Responsibility

"I guess I'm beginning to think more directly."

207. (What are you thinking?) About getting some kind of work this summer. Oh, did I tell you I passed my flying test? (Wonderful! Now you can take a passenger.) Not quite; there's a little more to do, but the rest won't be difficult. (Good. Have you heard about the job too?) I didn't get it; they wanted someone with a college degree. (Were you disappointed?) Slightly disappointed to be turned down, but not about that particular job. There's a machine shop in Hartford where I can get one if I want.

    (Have your feelings about working changed?) I've never known what my feelings really were. (I know they were mixed. You really have wanted to do something for a long time, but didn't want to be forced into it.) I don't like to

have to get up in the morning and work eight hours. (I sympathize. It's often very hard to get up in the morning.)
[Smile.] I now say "difficult," because of the joke about "Is
it hard when you get up in the morning?" (Is it, in the way
that the joke means?) Both hard and difficult.

[Pause.] The trouble is, I'm afraid I'm stuck with living. (I know. For you it is impossible not to value awareness.) That's it. I don't want to get a degree in science, but
I'm wild to know about myself and others.

[Pause.] I was counting again. (Counting what?) How
many times six makes a pyramid. (Six or sex?) [Smile.] Not
only because of the similarity in the words, but because of
the six journals I'm looking at. (In other words, how much
work will you have to do before you can successfully have
intercourse?) Yes.

(That's one of the areas where "practical experience
has to go into the computer." We have talked quite a bit
about the kinds of reactions you might have, but we don't
know much about the kind of reactions you do have, because
you don't let yourself get close enough to a girl to find out.)
[Smile.] I think one thing that might stop me is the idea of
having to come and talk to you about it. (Maybe it's like talking about fantasies—it would be too real.) Yes. (I wonder if
you would be afraid of my reaction in some way?) I can't
imagine you having a reaction.

[Pause.] I'm wondering—if I got married, would I get
restless and want to get out of it? (One doesn't get tired of a
relationship if it's a good one.) I guess not. I don't get tired of
coming here. There's always something new, or if there isn't,
I manufacture something, and it eventually turns out to be
worth something.

[Pause.] My jaw and sinuses feel under pressure from
allergy. [Pause.] Why can't one grow new teeth after the second set has come in? [Pause.] Now I'm thinking about a
new kind of strum for the guitar. [Pause.] It seems silly to

keep mentioning these seemingly meaningless images, but I don't suppose it is. (No. I think you know from experience that these images may add up to something you are trying to express.)

I never realized until recently that I was even coding things for myself. The other day I had a thought; I felt there was something strange about it, and suddenly realized it wasn't in code. I guess I'm beginning to *think* more directly. But I hate to lose the ability to code. I hate to lose anything.

(I don't think one ever loses the tendency to think symbolically at times, or metaphorically. All creative people have an ability to move with a kind of flexibility in and out of the unconscious. It's a good idea, though, to have one's unconscious under control.) Not to have it under control, but to take the pressure off so that it doesn't *need* to be under control. (Yes. That's a better way of putting it.)

208. [*Pause.*] Why do people live? (Are you having qualms again right now about living?) Not that I know of. I was looking at the horse—thinking about how to lift him. It's like doing this kind of work; you might have to empty one leg so that he could lift it and shift his weight to another; then empty that so he could lift it, etc. (Yes. There are a number of different areas to explore.)

[*Pause.*] I'm thinking of a song on the guitar. (You are talking code today, and you are also talking so low that I can hardly hear you. Those are both fright signals. When it's like that, it's usually that the external pressures have increased in some way, or the material you are talking about is frightening. What do you think it might be this time?) Probably the material.

I think I've found the girl I'm going to try to sleep with. She's the one I told you about before—that I said I wished I could fall in love with. Now maybe I'll sleep with her for a different reason—to see what my reactions are. (Did you feel I commissioned you to do something like that when we talked about it last time?) You couldn't push me in a direction that I didn't want to go in, but a nudge is sometimes a good idea. I think the feeling that I had to be in love was a defense against the desire to sleep with her, when I'm so afraid of it. Now I think that if she was interested, we could see if something mutually satisfying could be worked out.

We are very much alike; same age, living at home, and both being pushed to work. (I think you feel I am trying to push you into a sexual relationship.) No, although after we talked about it, and I realized that at least one person didn't think it was too horrible, I was more willing to think of doing something that I want to do anyway. (I hope that whatever you do, whenever you do it, you act according to the way you really feel, at a pace in which you feel comfortable.)

[Pause.] Your journals are not in order. (You seem to be concerned with the sequence of events—afraid of taking a step that might be premature.)

[Pause.] I wasn't going to say this, because it would put you in the position of a co-conspirator, but I was mad at myself for not knowing what I was talking about in code. I thought this was a nice dangerous subject, so I might as well talk about it. (But you think it might have been something else that was concerning you?) Maybe. (Maybe. If so, it will come out sooner or later.)

209. I will know next week whether I've got a job as fireman in my town. (Do you like the idea?) It's not all that I want, but I can get experience. Part of the pay is a room. (How do you feel about living away from home?)

[Pause.] Someone was telling me that the only way some people can leave home is to get mad and stomp out.

(To cover up other feelings. What do you think you will miss?) My freedom. (That's interesting. Most people think that when they leave home they *gain* freedom.) It's a different kind of freedom; I don't like to have to be bound by ordinary working hours. The part of living I like best is when most people are asleep; then I can play the guitar and talk philosophy. (I'm sure you can find time to work in some of that too.)

[*Pause.*] I was talking to the girl I told you about. We had a long conversation about marriage and things like that.

[*Long pause.*] I realized as a thought that bodies have different characteristics. Just as it is difficult for Americans to tell one Oriental from another because they aren't used to knowing what kind of differences to look for, I don't think I could see that one body was different from another. (You didn't let your senses be aware of bodies.) It's not so much so with smells. I wonder why a little girl smells so different from a woman? (There are lots of differences between the bodies of little girls and women.) I guess it's like baby deer; at first there is no smell at all—it's for protection. (Later they don't need protection so much, and develop a positive drive to attract the other sex.)

[*Pause.*] I've noticed that when a woman is unhappy it makes me unhappy. (And when she's excited does it make you excited?) Perhaps.

I've been thinking—one thing that's been lacking in my life has been conversation. I decided to talk more, and a few days later, I realized I'd been doing it. It's nice to know that you can decide something consciously, and act on it unconsciously. (Perhaps by the time a desire has formulated itself consciously, you have already been working on it unconsciously, and are pretty ready to act.)

210. [*Long pause.*] I was wondering whether it's a good idea to be childlike. (What do you mean by that term?) Irrespon-

sible. I suppose it's easier. (Easier, maybe, but it has its price. For you, I think, the price is loss of self-esteem.) That's certainly true.

[Long pause.] (You don't feel much like communicating today?) There doesn't seem to be much to say. [Long pause.] I feel guilty for wasting time. (I guess it is sometimes hard to put what you are feeling into words.)

[Pause.] I went to a fire the other day. One of the firemen was more interested in knocking down a fence with the stream from his hose than in putting out the fire. I think I felt the man was too much identified with his hose. I guess if he'd realized I was thinking that, he'd have thought I was crazy. (Not if he knew anything about unconscious symbolism.)

(That is an important factor in some people's desire to be a fireman—having that big penis to help deny fears that his own penis is inadequate. Often, too, the fire that's being put out represents the fire of some impulse that he is unconsciously trying to control in that way.) I hope that isn't all that's in my desire to fight fires, because I hope to change my feelings about dangerous impulses.

(Even if some basic infantile conflict is involved in one's choice of an activity, the activity may also have value on a conscious, rational level. Some say that the desire to be a psychiatrist comes from unresolved infantile sexual curiosity; it does in part, although later, more adult motivations also enter in. Actually, you yourself used the symbolism of peeing on a fire to put it out when you were talking about your bed-wetting. I imagine your interest in fire-fighting is in part a constructive way of trying to sublimate certain impulses.)

The thing that annoyed me was that the man's destructive impulse was greater than his desire to put out the fire. It was frightening that he seemed to be just playing at a time when the fire was getting out of control. (I guess his destructive impulse was too strong to be handled by that kind of unconscious mechanism *alone*. He probably needed an opportunity to deal with the impulse in other ways as well.)

[*Long pause.*] I was wondering about the difference between therapy and analysis—wondering whether analysis would be better for me. (I don't think so. The technical difference in procedure meets different kinds of needs. Being on the couch is better for some people, but not for you. It's better for people who are not close enough to their unconscious. You have been too close to yours at times, and need to integrate it more with the world of reality.)

I'm disappointed. I like to think that my goal is to listen to my unconscious. (I hope you will continue to listen to it. You have a capacity to move in and out of it, and that's a gift which can have great value. For a while, though, you weren't able to move out of it.) I know. I think I thought it was my only friend. I suppose I still have a little of that feeling. (Even a good friend may not be good for you if he's your *only* friend, and if you are forced into his company by fear of the rest of the world.)

211. [*Before this hour, I had decided to avoid my usual questions about what he was thinking, in order to bring the problem of taking responsibility into the treatment.*]

[*Soon after sitting down, he smiles and gives a little laugh.*] I was thinking of an expression that the kids use for going around to different used car lots pretending you are going to buy a car. "Masturbating the car lots." (What's the association right now?) I don't know. (Do you think there is some feeling that coming in here is a form of sexual gratification?) Could be. [*Pause.*] I'm wondering if self-awareness is connected with that; I'm listening to myself breathe. (Aware of body sensations?) Yes.

[*Long pause.*] I've got another trip to Florida planned. Some guys are driving down and I can go along. (I hope it works out this time.) I think it has a better chance than last time; these guys are all level-headed.

[Long pause.] It must be interesting to sit where you do. People come in here, and you never know what they are going to say. (It is interesting, but what brings it to your mind right now?) Like the way I started out—it must be interesting to figure out what that means. (Isn't it interesting to you too?) Yes.

[Long pause.] I'm a little disappointed. A fireman is going on vacation, but I didn't get the job because the chief needed someone with experience. He said the best thing for me to do to prepare myself is just what I'm doing—hanging around and learning how to operate the equipment. Maybe I'll get a chance later. I hope, though, that it isn't at just the moment I'm taking off on the trip. Maybe I'd better let him know my plans so he won't think I'm not serious about wanting a job. (That's a good idea. If you had the choice of the trip or the job, which would you take?) The work. I've waited this long for the trip—I could wait a little longer.

[Long pause.] I was thinking about how to get the center of gravity of an irregular plane. (What are you trying to say in that image?) Oh! That is code, isn't it? Well, I don't know. I was looking at the horse and seeing several planes, some of them in the solid material, and some in the spaces between. It's like a Rorschach. [Pause.] One of them is straight up. [Pause.] I think of an erect penis. That one is in the space. The one in the solid material is hanging down. [Pause.] The space is like female, and the solid male. The erect plane is in the female portion.

(You do seem to reverse what is usually considered masculine and feminine. You see the phallic, aggressive element as female, and the passive, dependent one as male.) That is certainly what the images indicate. (You see it that way in your family. What you identify with in your father, you see as female, and vice versa.) I can understand that. The question is what to do about it. (The first step is to recognize the distortions.)

[*Pause.*] I realize there isn't anything I can do about my parents' problems. (That's right; you have enough to do in handling your own. You can feel sympathy for them without letting yourself be destroyed by the situation.) The trouble is, I don't understand it well enough to be sure it won't happen to me. I wouldn't want to perpetuate the problems by transmitting them to my children. (By the time you have children, I hope you will have things worked out so that you haven't got those kinds of problems. People who are trying to be aware of themselves are more apt to be able to avoid the kinds of difficulties your parents have had.)

212. [*He comes in rather jauntily and plops down in the chair, but then assumes his stare and pauses for a long time. Finally, he gives a little laugh.*] Coming up the stairs I sort of forgot I was coming to a session. It took me a few minutes to think where I am; now I feel as though I were scrambling through my desk, looking for my notes. (But at first you felt more casual.) Yes.

[*Long pause, ending with another laugh.*] On trips to New York from school, the teacher used to pass out "tightening pills." [*Long pause.*] It seems strange in here; outside it's summer. (You feel as though someone had given you a tightening pill; you felt looser before you started.) Yes.

[*Long pause.*] I'm wondering how to tell my parents I'm going to Florida. They are afraid I will get into trouble, and they think I should get a job. (Are you worried about getting into trouble?) No. I think I've developed automatic controls. (That's important.)

[*Long pause.*] I noticed I was waiting for you to ask me what I'm thinking. I don't want to take the responsibility for saying. In order to have the privilege of not taking that responsibility, I'm willing to take a chance on whatever I

happen to be thinking at the time you ask. (I think at this
point you can take the responsibility yourself. I'm not going
to ask you any more.)

[*Long pause. Smile.*] I wonder what would happen if
I looked at you as long as you look at me. (What's the feeling when I'm looking at you?) It doesn't bother me, but I'm
aware of it.

[*Pause.*] I was thinking about horse-race betting in
Florida. [*We proceed with a discussion of gambling. He
makes the points that all odds are in favor of the house; that
most successful gamblers don't bet when the odds are too
much against them, and that the best games involve skill
rather than pure chance. At the end, I suggest that the kind
of gambling he is really interested in may not be what we are
talking about, and that the odds he really wants to know
about are in regard to success in his own life ventures.*]

Could be. I would like to be able to influence physical
phenomena, like the guys at Duke who can "will" the way
the dice will fall. (Sometimes what seems to be control of
the dice is a matter of knowing the odds on how they will
fall, and "willing" accordingly.) That's what I'm trying to
test—whether things are really what they seem to be.

After this interview I talk with both parents at their
request. They have decided to get a divorce, and both are
very upset and angry. Each wants to be sure that I understand the whole picture from his or her point of view. Both
want reassurance and sympathy for their positions from me,
and hope in some magical way I can help them.

213. [*Even though he does not speak for a while, he does not
look depressed.*] (Well, I hear that all hell is breaking loose
at your house. How do you feel about it?) It should have happened five years ago. [*Smile.*] I don't know why you think
it's any worse now than any other time. (Perhaps I hadn't

sufficiently appreciated how it's been all along. This week I felt a little of the tension directed at me. However, when an actual break-up is in the wind, I thought you might have some feelings about it.) I can't let myself have feelings. There is nothing I can do. (That's true, but one can't always control one's feelings so easily.) I have learned.

If I have to, I can always make a living. A friend has already offered me a job in a store, but I don't want that unless it's necessary. (What about the job your father says he is trying to get you?) I don't want a job my father gets me; something always turns out to be wrong with it. I want to get one myself, no matter what it is. (That's a good idea.)

(Your mother tells me she hasn't been giving you any money. What have you been getting along on?) I've been doing without. What I've earned, I'm saving for the Florida trip. I have $10. (That doesn't sound like much to go to Florida on.) My friends and I have it planned. We are going to camp out and fish. We did it before on less. (I hope you make out all right.) We will.

[Long pause.] That horse makes me think of a science fiction story about a computer. Everyone fed their problems into it and got the answers back, but pretty soon the computer committed suicide. (Is that what you think is going to happen to me?) [Smile.] Maybe. (Although I really like both your parents, and feel terribly sorry for them both, I am not personally threatened by their troubles. It isn't so hard on an outsider as on someone who is living there.) I know.

[Pause.] There was a news story on TV about a whole group of people who went to live on an island, but they are having trouble because they can't organize a society. Nobody knows what to do. I would like to volunteer for the job of getting them organized. I've had to learn to become self-sufficient myself, and I think I could teach others how to organize for self-sufficiency. (When you complete the job on yourself, I imagine you will be able to do anything you want.

I don't think the job is quite finished yet, and perhaps you had better concentrate on finishing it before you take on the problems of others.)

I was reading a comment on analysis. The article said it was like water. Water doesn't care whether you bathe in it or drown in it; it can wash away your fields or irrigate them. If you have a desire to use it, you can profit from it. The analyst may have personal feelings about what he hears, but he serves his function best by staying outside the conflicts of others. [Pause.] The next thing I thought of was the suicidal computer again. I wonder why. (I wonder if you are afraid that I will be devastated if you really become self-sufficient, and I find that my function has been served.) I don't know. [Pause.] If the computer is a composite of the personalities fed into it—maybe if it was deciding to commit suicide, it was because the race was getting ready to die out. (Let's say that in English.) If I thought you couldn't take it, maybe it's because I don't think I can take it. But I don't think that's true. (Neither do I.)

214. [He sits silent for five minutes.] I'm thinking about the problem of a guy that's rather similar to me. The fellows he works with are interested in partying and coming to work drunk. He believes in doing his job, but he's sort of ostracized socially. (That's a hard spot to be in.) He doesn't like to be ostracized, but he hasn't much choice. (People can often be accepted as "different" and not disliked for it. It's the way they say No that matters.) A lot of the time I either get along very well with people or antagonize them completely by going in exactly the opposite direction from them. (One can often maintain one's own position without rebelling against the other guy's.)

[Pause.] I told Mother I'd been invited on a skin-diving trip, and she didn't blow up. (That must have been a surprise to you.) I don't know whether she's under less stress herself, or under such a great strain that she doesn't care *what* I do. I think she was somewhat impressed by the guy who's going; he has good manners, although actually that doesn't mean a thing. (Good manners sometimes "grease the wheels" of social relationships.) Well, actually I think so too.

The reason Mother is interested in having me go back to school is that she wants to be able to deduct me as a dependent on her income tax. (Do you think that's her main reason?) It's one of them, but I think she also wants me to get an education. (I think so too. Whatever troubles there are between you, I think she wants for you what she thinks will be best for you. Her ideas of what will be best may not be the same as yours, and they may not always be the best for you, but I am pretty sure she wants what she thinks will be best for you.) Her methods of pushing me are wrong. (Maybe. But there's a difference between method and motive.) I know.

It is getting harder and harder to be an individual in this society. One wants a way of life that is consistent with one's own values, but also wants to find a wife who can accept those values, even when they will not bring middle-class status. Although I want to assume a masculine role, many of my values are not consistent with a stereotype of masculinity. (You want to function successfully in a masculine sexual role. Other aspects of a masculine role in our culture can be worked out according to their merits for you. There are plenty of girls who do not necessarily want to live a middle-class life according to the stereotypes.)

[*A long pause, close to five minutes.*] I wonder whether, if one cut off one's five senses, one would lose the relative sense of time.

[*An equally long pause.*] I heard a Zen lecturer. He had been hospitalized once—found it very difficult to adjust to this society. (Many people do. But those who are able to live with themselves manage to work out a way of living in whatever society they are in.)

[Pause.] Another Indian once said, "Reincarnation is a fact, but what good does that do?"

[Long pause.] I was thinking about your asking me what I'm thinking—whether knowing something of what it means to me has made you change your method. (You told me the other day that you wanted to become more responsible, and also that having me ask you is a way of disclaiming responsibility. I told you I didn't think you needed to do that any more.) I know, but it's important for me to know that something I've said has meaning. (You just said a minute ago that you wanted to be able to go by your own value system. Now you seem to be saying that something you say takes on value to you only if I respond in a certain way.) I think I'm more interested in why you ask me at a particular moment than I am in the thought itself.

(You seem to think I "plug in" on your thoughts by some kind of ESP. Actually, what usually prompts me to ask at a particular moment is some change in your facial expression.) I like to think it's like two identical computers that have the same information fed into them, and come out with the same answers.

215. [Long pause.] I'm worried about what to do with the things I want to keep. (Are there many?) Some guns and tools. The kinds of things Mother wouldn't think it necessary to keep. (Have you told her they are important to you?) No. (There seems to be a failure of communication.) There is difficulty in communicating, all right, but even if I do tell her, it usually ends up that we keep only what *she* considers important.

(I think that again we are talking about something else. You might be telling me how you feel about my having said that it is no longer necessary for us to keep up the routine of my asking what you are thinking before you speak. You have told me it is important to you, and are angry that I am not respecting your wishes.)

It's difficult for me to start. It seems like an intrusion for me to break the silence. (You need an invitation?) Maybe I fear rejection. (I doubt it.) Maybe I need someone to tell me it's worthwhile to go on. (Can't you trust your own judgment?)

Has anything really been accomplished in therapy? (How do you feel about that yourself?) Therapy was a haven where I only had to cope with one person at a time. All I know is that I'd do it over again, but I don't see that I'm any more capable of doing anything now than I was at the beginning. (You are angry at the moment, and resent the implication that I made a demand for you to give up a way of operating that has become comfortable for you.) [*Sarcastic tone.*] "Do anything you like, so long as you do it my way."

[*Long pause.*] I'm afraid if I'm just left on my own, the information will stop coming. If I were left to choose for myself, I might lose direction and go all over the place. (My asking a question is like playing roulette. I gamble by stopping the wheel and seeing where the ball falls. You seem to have more faith in my chance choice to give you direction than in your own.)

[*Pause.*] Once you have put things into words, you are irrevocably committed to what you have said. Adults judge you by what you say. They don't reckon on the possibility that you might change your mind. (A mind that can't be changed is pretty inflexible. I think the first of the four freedoms is the right to be wrong.) [*Smile.*] Most people don't look at it that way.

[*Pause.*] If I say just what comes to my mind, I can't censor. I want to have control over the situation. (But in what you have been doing, you surrender all control to me.)

See! I haven't been thinking too much what I've been say-ing today, and now I'm trapped in an inconsistency! (What's so terrible about that? How can you ever reach valid con-clusions if you don't play around with ideas until they make sense to you?) Well, I don't know.

216. [*He has about a two-week growth of beard, which was not conspicuous last week. He has to push rather hard to shut my door, which has swelled with damp weather. Pause. Opens his mouth to say something, but closes it again. Pause.*] The door is getting harder and harder to close. Pretty soon I will have to make a noise closing it, and draw atten-tion to myself. (That would certainly be dangerous.) [*Smile.*] I wouldn't like that.

(When you were somewhat angry at me last time, you were saying, "What progress have I made anyway?" I think it might be important for me to point out the progress I think you have made. You have learned to talk. You are now in the position that a child is in when he is able to get all the new satisfactions that come to a creature who can communicate, but is reluctant to give up the pleasure of having things done for him without his having to ask for any-thing.) I hate to give up anything. (But you wouldn't go back to being the "child who can't talk" either.) No. I don't want to give up any acquired skill. (That's good.)

[*Pause.*] I think I feel there is more mutuality if you ask. I feel your part of this process is to ask; my part is to give the information. That way we are both working at it. (But you don't feel I am participating if I just listen and try to help you understand the information you offer?) It isn't quite the same.

[*Pause.*] I think I feel the same way about a sexual situation. (You feel that if the girl asks for it, you can give it to her, but that if you take the initiative, you are being too aggressive. You aren't sure she will value what you offer unless she has openly expressed a wish for it.) Yes. I'm wondering whether my wanting you to ask is elevating you or making you more of an equal. (How do you mean?) Making this something we do as equals, or having you in charge—kind of like in the mother position—or both. (You do seem to have ambivalence about the role of a mother figure in relationship to you. You sexualize your relationship with me and with your mother too.)

[*Pause.*] I don't think I have as good an idea of female psychology as I do of male psychology. What do guns mean to men and women that make their attitudes so different? Most women are afraid of guns and don't want a man to have anything to do with them. (Of course you are not talking about a woman's realistic fear that a gun will go off and hurt the man. You know as well as I do that guns are sexual symbols to both men and women, and you are talking about a woman's fear of the man's penis. It is true that many women fear it; it is also true that all women wish they had one. Some women do express their envy by unconsciously trying to castrate men. Others solve their wish by taking pride in the penises of the men they make their own. They can achieve a mutuality in enjoyment.)

To a man, a gun is something he can understand completely. He can fix it up and make it perfect. It is something concrete and knowable, over which he can achieve mastery. It is different from life, which is so unpredictable and has so many variables.

[*Pause.*] I suppose it is possible to make one's life orderly too, leaving only certain areas of disorder. One wouldn't want to be *too* orderly, or there wouldn't be any chance for spontaneity. (Yes. One certainly wouldn't want to eliminate the possibility of surprises.)

We're off next week for the trip. They say that where we are going, you can skin-dive and pick up as many conchs as you can eat. I suppose if people have had fun, they concretize their memory of pleasure by remembering things like conchs instead of just a feeling of fun. It would be nice to eat fresh conch on the beach, but I think it will be fun just to get out in the sun and sea. (It sounds wonderful! I imagine you will come back with a full-grown beard.) I will have to come home on a Friday so that you can see it before I shave it off. (You aren't planning to keep it?) Mother hates what she thinks it stands for. Anyway, she thinks mine looks scraggly. (All beards look scraggly when partially grown. Maybe she'll like it better if it is fully developed.)

Women should let men keep their symbols of masculinity. If little boys are allowed to become accustomed to guns when they are small, they develop the unconscious feeling of being at ease with them that isn't so easily acquired later in life. (That's true. But it can be acquired, even after a late start.) Men should also try to be more conscious. Lots of times they overdo being masculine, and act just plain mean. I think on the whole, though, if I had the choice of whether to start over again as either a man or a woman, I'd let well enough alone and stay a male.

This is the end of the sixth year.

2 1

The Turning Point

"There can be meaning in just living."

THE FLORIDA TRIP SEEMED TO BE A DRA-
matic turning point in David's life. During the succeeding
six months of our work together, he showed in therapy, as
well as in his approach to living, marked changes of attitude.
He took great strides toward active assumption of responsibility and toward independence, apparently well on the way
to a transition from boy to man.

He and the other boys had had a wonderful time, fully
enjoying life in a little beach town. They did not go in for
promiscuous sexual activity, but participated in beer parties
with young people of both sexes. There was no trouble of
any kind, and David returned with a feeling of warmth for
his experiences and the people he had met in the beach town.

Now at home again, however, he took an active, realistic approach to job seeking. He relinquished the controversial beard without regret, and followed leads given by employment agencies. He made efforts to inform himself of jobs available to someone with his present educational background and experience, but also looked into training requirements for more suitable kinds of work. He hoped eventually to return to college and prepare for a career in high school teaching.

David had begun to see that reluctance to get a job was at least partly motivated by a need to protect himself from participation in social life. If he had no money, he could not take a girl out, and could rationalize his timidity about making relationships. Now he no longer felt threatened to the same extent, and was tired of being so limited in all his activities by lack of funds. It was necessary to become active in changing the picture, and David was doing so. His efforts met with some success.

After a few weeks, his application was accepted for an opening on the police force. He withstood the competition through several sets of preliminary tests, and remained one of several serious contenders for the position. David did not have great desire to be a policeman, but he stated simply that the pay was good for an untrained worker, and it might be a job that he could actually *get*. During a period of relative unemployment in the community, he could not afford to overlook an opportunity for work that might offer some sources for at least temporary satisfaction. Although he "might be tempted to let everyone go," he really felt from his own experience that it is not necessarily damaging to an individual to be arrested for crimes. "It all depends on the way it's done. I think a few cops like me wouldn't hurt this town." He believed he could be objective if doing a clearly defined job without personal need to pass judgment, and that in any case, it was worth a try. I agreed with him. While waiting for the job to materialize, he and another couple of young men hired some power machinery and a truck. They were well on the way to success in a small business venture, selling a manufactured article on commission.

One of them violated the rental contract by taking the truck out for personal use. The owner found out, but did not know which boy had done so and threatened to penalize all three. David was in a dilemma. Again he felt himself to be caught in a situation with divided loyalties, but at this stage of his development, no longer got vicarious gratification from the other boy's delinquency, and did not feel obligated to suffer for it. Although he refused to make any public statement fixing the blame on his friend, he privately cleared his own name with the owner of the truck. Later a new work team was set up, eliminating the irresponsible boy.

David also moved toward establishing independence, both in his daily life and in the treatment relationship with me. For a short time, he moved out of his mother's house into the apartment of a boy who invited him to stay in town while job-hunting. He took a share in responsibility for their mutual living by doing all the housework and marketing to pay for his keep. However, a strain soon developed in the relationship. David recognized that the other boy and he were both having conflict about latent homosexual feelings which contributed to rising ambivalence between them, but disliked his friend's way of handling them by "Nazi attitudes" and pretentiousness. David protested against the sloppy state of the apartment. "At home my room was always a mess, but away from home I like things to be clean." The other boy finally withdrew his invitation suddenly, and although David resented the "ultimatum," he was greatly relieved. A transitional period of keeping shared "bachelor quarters" had been good for his sense of differentiation from the family. Upon return home, he was able to live more independently and also more companionably with his mother.

Perceptible signs of motion toward a more independent role in the therapeutic relationship appeared in an early interview following his return. I had telephoned to change an appointment hour and found him out. Instead of calling again, I left a message which the mother "forgot" to give him. The next time we met, he almost immediately took the opportunity to reproach me for encouraging him to be responsible and then not taking the trouble to deal with him directly. I apologized and acknowledged the justifiability of his complaint. From this point on, he was able to bring ambivalence about aggressive feelings toward me directly into focus for discussion.

On one occasion, I interpreted a statement which he had presented in the form of an image. He accepted the interpretation, but immediately pointed out that there might be many other meanings. I said, "Yes, and when I interpret it, my association gets followed up and not yours. I'm glad you recognized that." This was, I believe, the last time he spoke symbolically without making a spontaneous attempt to follow up with an interpretation of his own.

During this period, David gave quite a bit of thought to his experiences in treatment, trying to evaluate the respective roles of patient and therapist. He obviously wanted to see himself as an active agent in what had gone on between us. He placed stress on the "do-it-yourself" aspect of therapy, and couldn't "quite figure out just what the analyst really does." The boy felt a need to see therapy as a "logical process between two people rather than one in which the patient is manipulated by irrational forces of emotion within himself," and developed increasing interest in understanding my techniques. At this point I entered into occasional theoretical discussions with him, explaining psychic structure and psychological processes. He converted my words into concrete images of his own. "Superego says what's good or bad, ego says what's real or unreal. Id just says 'Zoom!' " "Id is a car, ego the driver, and superego the stop lights. If a car hasn't got a driver, it can be a lethal weapon. On the other hand, if the driver runs it along the highway with its brakes on, it's bad for the engine. If the driver is color blind, he may have to go more carefully at intersections until he develops other ways of telling when the light is green." David wanted to have intellectual mastery of the elements involved in psychotherapy, and to feel the significance of his own part in the process.

He did not deny the value of emotional release as a by-product of the work, but wanted to participate in a decision to use time for this purpose. "If a person sits gibbering in a corner, he might be involved in a perfectly valid process of relieving tension, but he shouldn't mistake meaningless gibbering for great intellectual truth. He might want to go right on doing it, but he should know what he's doing." He expressed no wish to terminate therapy, but established an intention to get on a paying basis as soon as he was working, and continue as a responsible member of a team, with major responsibility for getting work done.

David began to see that he did not have to deny the value of my activity in therapy in order to recognize his own. At one point, expressing disappointment that I had not reacted with enthusiasm to what he had described as "a successful sublimation of sexual power," he wished I could become "a more ordinary type of person who just accepts a story without having to look for meanings behind it." He could, however, readily respond to my interpretation that the wish was a defense against his own fear that successful sublimations might have to serve as *substitutes* for direct sexual gratification. After we had discussed how pleasurable uses of the body do not necessarily detract from sexual ability even though they may derive some energy from sexual drive, he commented, "Analysts really *do* help in the best way. It's like if you have a field to plow—they don't plow it for you, but they put the plow in your hand and show you *how* to do it for yourself."

He knew that his sexual conflicts still needed to be worked upon in therapy, and that in moving toward a girl friend "on the same level, neither a mother nor a daughter," he was "going into unknown territory" with some feeling of panic. However, he admitted that in the unknown territories he had crossed before, "nothing too terrible had come out of the shadows." He was determined to go on trying.

Suddenly David received a notice to appear for pre-induction physical examination. He was on the verge of being drafted. The boy had long been aware that such a call might be imminent, and had adjusted realistically to the fact that he would some day face a choice between taking a shorter span of service under the draft, or risking a longer span, with better opportunities for choice of a training program, in some other branch of the armed forces. Now he had to make up his mind, and he wasted no time. On the same day he talked with a recruiting officer who had previously accepted him for a Naval cadet training program, and was allowed to enlist immediately. He telephoned me to say goodbye, and was off the next morning. Among the last things he said in therapy had been the statement, "I'm still looking for meanings in life, but there can be meaning in just living." He was about to prove it.

INDEX